RUSSIAN LAW BOOKS

1999

Published in collaboration with
The Vinogradoff Institute
University College London

"Russian Law Books" a wood engraving
by A.I. Kalashnikov, RE(Hon), SWE(Hon)

The Vinogradoff Institute
University College London

RUSSIAN LAW BOOKS 1999

Books Published on Russian Law and Private and Public International Law in Russia during 1999

Compiled by

William E. Butler
and
Jolanta Murjas

SIMMONDS & HILL PUBLISHING LTD

KLUWER LAW INTERNATIONAL
The Hague • London • Boston

Published by Kluwer Law International,
P.O. Box 85889, 2508 CN The Hague, The Netherlands.

Sold and distributed in the U.S.A. and Canada
by Kluwer Law International,
675 Massachusetts Avenue, Cambridge, MA 02139, U.S.A.
tel: (617) 354-0140; fax: (617) 354-8595

In all other countries, sold and distributed
by Kluwer Law International,
P.O. Box 85889, 2508 CN The Hague, The Netherlands
tel: 31 70 308 1562; fax: 31 70 308 1555

Russian Law Books 1999

British Library Cataloguing-in-Publication Data:
A catalogue record for this book is available from The British Library

I. Butler, W.E.

ISBN 1-898029 55 5 (Simmonds & Hill)
ISBN 9041188541 (Kluwer Law International)

First published in 2000 by

Simmonds & Hill Publishing Ltd

and

Kluwer Law International

CONTENTS

Russian Law

Reference Works

Treatises and Legislation

Private International Law

Public International Law

Foreign and Comparative Law

INTRODUCTION

The present Bibliography contains books published during 1999 principally in the Russian Federation, together with some titles on Russian Law published abroad. It makes no claim to completeness, but it has drawn extensively upon available Russian indexing and reporting sources for information.

The subject classification is based on that used in my earlier bibliographies.[1] It adapts the classification long in use at the Harvard Law School Library (and since superseded there by another), but for Russian Law that system of classification contains virtues not to be found in the later models. It also is a system which has much in common with contemporary Russian approaches to classifying legislation and books.

The subject classification is followed by a Section in which all titles are gathered in alphabetical order by author, and in the absence of such, by title. This section is ordered, as are all titles within each subject classification, according to the Latin alphabet, which means in the case of cyrillic language titles that they are placed as though they had been transliterated according to the Library of Congress system of transliteration (short form), omitting diacritical markings. For the most part Russian cataloguing practices are followed: entries appear under author, followed by the title in the original language, a translation thereof in square brackets into English, principal editor and/or compiler, associated or sponsoring institution, place of publication, publisher, year of publication, print-run where specified, and ISBN number. On very rare occasions a supplementary annotation may be provided.

In the case of multiple editions of codes, they are grouped under a single title, followed by an indication of the publishers of the various versions.

---

[1] See W. E. Butler, *Writings on Soviet Law and Soviet International Law* (1966); V. Mostecky and W. E. Butler (ed.), *Soviet Legal Bibliography: A Classified and Annotated Listing of Books and Serials Published in the Soviet Union since 1917 as Represented in the Collection of the Harvard Law School Library as of January 1, 1965* (1965); Butler, *Russian and Soviet Law: An Annotated Catalogue of Reference Works, Legislation, Court Reports, Serials, and Monographs on Russian and Soviet Law (Including International Law)* (1976).

The "market" for law books remains traditional – advocates, jurisconsults, judicial and procuracy personnel, arbitrators, investigators, policemen (the majority have law degrees), military lawyers, tax and customs personnel, law students and legal scholars – with some interesting and important additions: business people themselves, entrepreneurs, accountants and auditors (whose ranks are increasing exponentially), foreign law firms and lawyers, and the law libraries of the remarkable number of new law schools and faculties throughout Russia (up from 30-40 in the late 1980s to more than 500 today).

The so-called "August Crisis", referring to the stock market crash in Russia on 17 August 1998, had a minor impact on Russian legal publishing for 1998. The great majority of titles had appeared or were in progress. Notwithstanding the drop in the value of the ruble, law publishers followed general publishers and did not change their prices. One beneficial effect was that back stock moved quickly and generated cash flow. By the end of 1998 some new titles reflected price adjustments required where imported paper or equipment was used. In general, however, price stability was the rule.

In 1999 the market for law books remained surprisingly robust. The number of titles published seems not to have decreased substantially. Prices for books newly published, however, went up considerably (although not for the foreign purchaser because exchange rates kept pace with price increases and even produced some bargains).

One example of an increase in price is a major treatise on the law of contract. Volume one, which appeared in a revised edition in 1999, was priced at 46 rubles. Volume two, published in March 2000, cost 205 rubles. Both volumes were approximately the same size and print run. At the relevant moment in 1999 the exchange rate was about 24.5 rubles to the U.S. dollar, while in March 2000, it was 28.5 rubles to the U.S. dollar.

Russian law publishers, on the whole, may well believe that in the aftermath of the crisis, things could have been much worse, all things considered.

Russian Law

Reference Works

Dictionaries and Encyclopedias

Безопасность России: Правовые, социально-экономические и научно-технические аспекты. Словарь терминов и определений. [Russia's Security: Legal, Socio-Economic and Scientific-Technical Aspects. Dictionary of Terms and Definitions]. 2d. rev. ed. M.: MGF "Znanie", 1999. 368 p. 1000 ptd. ISBN 5-87633-039-6.

Домашняя юридическая энциклопедия: Женщинам. Ответы на все вопросы. [Domestic Legal Dictionary: For Women. Answers to All Questions]. M.: AST, Olimp, 1999. 576 p. 4000 ptd. ISBN 5-7390-0363-X, ISBN 5-7390-0485-3, ISBN 5-237-03950-2.

Энциклопедия судебной экспертизы. [Encyclopedia of Forensic Expert Examination]. Eds. T. V. Averianovaia, E. R. Rossinskaia. M.: Iurist', 1999. 551 p. 5000 ptd. ISBN 5-7975-0262-3.

Энциклопедический юридический словарь. [Encyclopedic Legal Dictionary]. V. N. Dodonov et al. Ed. V. E. Krutskikh. 2nd. ed. M.: INFRA-M, 1999. 368 p. 5000 ptd. ISBN 5-86225-708-X.

Краткий словарь терминов по уголовному праву: Учебное пособие. [A Short Dictionary of Terms on Criminal Law: Instructional Manual]. Eds. B. V. Iatselenko, V. B. Borovikov. M.: MIUI MVD Rossii, Izd-vo "Shchyt-M", 1999. 128 p. 1000 ptd. ISBN 5-13004-032-X.

Luneev, V. V. *Юридическая статистика: Учебник.* [Legal Statistics: Textbook]. M.: Iurist', 1999. 399 p. 10000 ptd. ISBN 5-7975-0156-2.

Мир права в афоризмах, мудрых мыслях, эпиграммах. [The World of Law in Aphorisms, Wise Thoughts, Epigrams]. Nizhegorod. pravovaia akad. Comps. V. M. Baranov, Z. Sh. Idrisov. N. Novgorod, 1999. 152 p. 5000 ptd.

Новый юридический словарь-справочник. [New Legal Dictionary/ Manual]. Iu. N. Adonka et al. Ed. E. V. Butenko. Smolensk: Rusich, 1999. 512 p. 11000 ptd. ISBN 5-8138-0042-5.

Российская юридическая энциклопедия. [Russian Legal Encyclopedia]. Ed. A. Ia. Sukharev. M.: INFRA-M, 1999. 1110 p. 100000 ptd. ISBN 5-86225-925-2.

Saviuk, L. K. *Правовая статистика: Для вузов.* [Legal Statistics: For Institutes of Higher Education]. M.: Iurist', 1999. 587 p. 10000 ptd. ISBN 5-7975-0135-X.

Shutak, I. D. *Теория и практика оговорок в праве: система понятий: Терминологический словарь.* [Theory and Practice of Clauses in Law: Terminological Dictionary]. Spb.: Aleteia, 1999. 203 p. 2200 ptd. ISBN 5-89329-187-5.

Словарь административного права. [Dictionary of Administrative Law]. I. L. Bachilo et al. M.: Pravovaia kultura, 1999. 328 p. 5000 ptd. ISBN 5-87759-033-2.

Treatises and Legislation

General Studies

Alekseev, S. S. *Частное право.* [Private Law]. M.: Statut, 1999. 159 p. 5000 ptd. ISBN 5-8354-0007-1.

Law Reform

Alekseev, S. S. *Право - надежда наша.* [The Law - Our Hope]. Ekaterinburg: Sred.-Ural. kn. izd-vo, 1999. 319 p. 10000 ptd. ISBN 5-7529-0728-4.

Petrov, V. *Россия. Кризис федерации: Прошлое, настоящее, будущее.* [Russia. Crisis of the Federation: Past, Present, Future]. M., 1999. 281 p.

Rulan, N. *Юридическая антропология: Учебник для вузов.* [Legal

Anthropology: Textbook for Institutes of Higher Education]. Trans. from French. Eds. V. S. Nersesiants. M.: NORMA, 1999. 301 p. 3000 ptd. ISBN 5-89123-303-7.

Теоретические проблемы формирования правовой России. [Theoretical Problems of the Formation of a Legal Russia]. Ed. A. K. Chernenko. Novosibirsk: Nauka, 1999. 208 p. 325 ptd. ISBN 5-02-031092-1.

Collections of Laws and Statutes

Полный сборник кодексов Российской Федерации: С изменениями и дополнениями на 1 марта 1999 г. [Complete Collection of Codes of the Russian Federation: With Changes and Additions for 1 March 1999]. 768 p. 8000 ptd. ISBN 5-93220-002-2.

Полный сборник кодексов Российской Федерации: С изменениями и дополнениями на 1 мая 1999 г. [Complete Collection of Codes of the Russian Federation: With Changes and Additions for 1 May 1999]. M.: AST, 1999. 928 p. 10000 ptd. ISBN 5-237-02360-6.

Полный сборник кодексов Российской Федерации: С изменениями и дополнениями на 1 сентября 1999 г. [Complete Collection of Codes of the Russian Federation: With Changes and Additions for 1 September 1999]. M.: Slavian. dom knigi, 1999. 800 p. 10000 ptd. ISBN 5-93220-002-2.

Сборник действующих постановлений Пленумов Верховных Судов СССР, РСФСР и Российской Федерации по уголовным делам с комментариями и пояснениями. [Collection of Prevailing Decrees of the Plenums of the Supreme Courts of the USSR, RSFSR and Russian Federation on Criminal Cases with Commentaries and Explanations]. Eds. V. I. Radchenko, A. S. Mikhlin. M.: BEK, 1999. 684 p. 3000 ptd. ISBN 5-85639-266-3.

Сборник кодексов Российской Федерации: Кн.3. [Collection of Codes of the Russian Federation: Book 3]. M.: Delo, 1999. 208 p. 2000 ptd. ISBN 5-7749-0061-4.

Сборник кодексов Российской Федерации: На 1 марта 1999 г. [Collection of Codes of the Russian Federation: For 1 March 1999]. 9th ed. M.: Filin', 1999. 778 p. 10000 ptd. ISBN 5-89568-124-7.

Сборник кодексов Российской Федерации: В 2 книгах. [Collection of Codes of the Russian Federation: In 2 Books]. M.: Delo, 1999. 6000 ptd.

Book 1. 718 p. ISBN 5-7749-0073-8.
Book 2. 624 p. ISBN 5-7749-0049-5.

Сборник постановлений Пленума Высшего Арбитражного Суда Российской Федерации. 1992-1998. [Collection of Decrees of the Plenum of the Supreme Arbitrazh Court of the Russian Federation. 1992-1998]. Ed. A. K. Bolshovaia. M.: Iurid. Dom "Iustitsinform", 1999. 203 p. 10000 ptd. ISBN 5-7205-0393-5, ISBN 5-89568-134-4.

Сборник постановлений Пленумов Верховного Суда и Высшего Арбитражного Суда Российской Федерации по гражданским делам. [Collection of Decrees of the Plenums of the Supreme Court and the Highest Arbitrazh Court of the Russian Federation on Civil Affairs]. Comp. A. P. Sergeev. M.: Prospekt, 1999. 832 p. 5000 ptd. ISBN 5-8369-0033-7.

Сборник законов Российской Федерации. [Collection of Laws of the Russian Federation]. M.: Slavian. dom knigi, 1999. 688 p. 9000 ptd. ISBN 5-93220-005-7.

Сборник законов Российской Федерации: С изменениями и дополнениями на 1 августа 1999 г. [Collection of Laws of the Russian Federation: With Changes and Additions for 1 August 1999]. M.: AST, 1999. 1200 p. 10000 ptd. ISBN 5-237-03015-7.

Законодательство Калининградской области. [Legislation of the Region of Kaliningrad]. Kaliningrad: Iantar. skaz, 1999. 360 p. 1500 ptd.

Legal History

Arkhipov, I. V. *Коммерческое судоустройство и судопроизводство России в XIX веке: Проблемы модернизации.*

[Commercial Court Organisation and Court Organisation in Russia in the 19th Century: Problems of Modernisation]. Saratov: Izd-vo SGU, 1999. 214 p. 500 ptd. ISBN 5-292-02341-8.

Baryshev, V. V. *Правозаступники: Твер. прокуроры. 1764-1917 гг.* [State Advocates: Procurators of Tver. 1764-1917]. Tver, 1999. 80 p. 1000 ptd. ISBN 5-87049-139-8.

Beliaev, I. D. *История русского законодательства: Для вузов.* [History of Russian Legislation: For Institutes of Higher Education]. Spb.: Lan, 1999. 640 ptd. ISBN 5-8114-0141-8.

Belkin, R. S. *История отечественной криминалистики.* [History of National Criminalistics]. M.: NORMA, 1999. 486 p. 3000 ptd. ISBN 5-89123-350-9.

Emelin, A. S. *История государства и права России: Окт. 1917 - дек. 1991 гг.* [History of State and Law of Russia: October 1917 - December 1991]. M.: Shchyt-M, 1999. 229 p. 1000 ptd. ISBN 5-93004-030-3.

Губернаторы Урала. [Governors of the Urals]. Comps. A. D. Kirillov, B. A. Kirillov. Ekaterinburg: Ural. rabochii, 1999. 248 p. 1000 ptd. ISBN 5-85383-150-X.

Khafizova, R. I. *Управление в Уфимской губернии во второй половине XIX - начале XX в.: Учебное пособие.* [Administration in the Ufimskii Province in the Second Half of the 19th to the Beginning of the 20th Centuries: Instructional Manual]. Ufa: Vos. un-t, 1999. 117 p. 200 ptd. ISBN 5-87865-178-5.

Хрестоматия по истории государства и права России: Учебное пособие. [Anthology on the History of State and Law of Russia: Instructional Manual]. Comp. Iu. P. Titov. M.: Prospekt, 1999. 472 p. 10000 ptd. ISBN 5-7896-0036-0.

История государства и права: Учебник. [History of State and Law: Textbook]. Ed. Iu. P. Titov. M.: Prospekt, 1999. 542 p. 10000 ptd. ISBN 5-8369-0063-9.

История отечественного государства и права: Часть 1: Учебник. [History of National State and Law: Part 1: Textbook]. Ed. O. I. Chistiakov. M.: BEK, 1999. 360 p. 10000 ptd. ISBN 5-85639-173-X.

История политических и правовых учений: Учебник для вузов. [History of Political and Legal Doctrines: Textbook]. 2nd. ed. Ed. V. S. Nersesiants. M.: NORMA, INFRA-M, 1999. 727 p. 60000 ptd. ISBN 5-89123-189-1, ISBN 5-86225-633-4.

Also published:

M.: Zertsalo, 1999. 688 p. 10000 ptd. ISBN 5-8078-0054-0.

Kuznetsov, I. N. *История государства и права России: Курс лекций.* [History of State and Law of Russia: Course of Lectures]. Minsk: Amalfeia, 1999. 527 p. 5000 ptd. ISBN 985-441-036-6.

Larkov, N. S., Chernova, I. V. *Полицмейстеры, комиссары, начальники: Руководители правоохранительных органов Том. обл. в XIX-XX вв.* [Commissioners of Police, Commissars, Commanders: Heads of Law Enforcement Agencies of the Region of Tomsk in the 19th to 20th Centuries]. Tomsk: Izd-vo Tom. un-ta, 1999. 183 p. 1000 ptd. ISBN 5-7511-1085-4.

Nemytina, M. V. *Суд в России: вторая половина XIX - начало XX вв.* [The Court in Russia: Second Half of the 19th to the Beginning of the 20th Centuries]. Saratov: SIUI MVD RF, 1999. 256 p. 1000 ptd. ISBN 5-7485-0021-3.

Novogorodtsev, P. I. *Историческая школа юристов: Для вузов.* [Historical School of Jurists: For Institutes of Higher Education]. Comp. Iu. A. Sandulov. Spb.: Lan, 1999. 189 p. 5000 ptd. ISBN 5-8114-0079-9.

Отечественное законодательство XI-XX веков: Ч.1. XI-XIX вв. [National Legislation of the 11th-20th Centuries: Part 1. 11th-19th Centuries]. Ed. O. I. Chistiakov. M.: Iurist', 1999. 463 p. 5000 ptd. ISBN 5-7975-0146-5.

Отечественное законодательство XI-XX веков: Ч.11. XX век: Пособие для семинаров. [National Legislation of the 11th-20th

Centuries: Part 11. 20th Century: Manual for Seminars]. Ed. O. I. Chistiakov. M.: Iurist', 1999. 352 p. 5000 ptd. ISBN 5-7975-0153-8.

Право: история, теория, практика: Выпуск 3. [Law: History, Theory, Practice: Issue 3]. Briansk: Izd-vo BGPU, 1999. 214 p. 300 ptd. ISBN 5-88543-099-3.

Проблемы судебно-правовой реформы в России: история и современность: Выпуск 6. [Problems of Judicial Legal Reform in Russia: History and the Present-Day: Issue 6]. Ed. T. V. Klenova. Samara: Izd-vo Samar. gumanitar. akad., 1999. 246 p. 200 ptd. ISBN 5-86465-020-X.

Российское полицейское (административное) право: Конец XIX - нач. XX в. [Russian Police (Administrative) Law: From the End of the 19th Century to the Beginning of the Twentieth Century]. Comp. & Intro. Iu. N. Starilov. Voronezh: Izd-vo VGU, 1999. 624 p. 1500 ptd. ISBN 5-7455-1065-X.

Smirnov, V. N., Usmanov, R. R. *История адвокатуры Среднего Урала.* [History of the Advokatura of the Central Urals]. Ekaterinburg: Gumanitar. un-t, 1999. 360 p. 4000 ptd. ISBN 5-7741-0033-2.

100-летие инициативы России: от Первой конференции мира 1899 г. к Третьей конференции мира 1999 г.: Сборник материалов. [100th Anniversary of the Initiative of Russia: From the First World Conference of 1899 to the Third World Conference of 1999: Collection of Materials]. Comp. & Ed. V. S. Ivanenko. Spb.: SpbGU, 1999. 167 p. 1000 ptd. ISBN 5-93333-006-X.

Syrykh, V. M. *История государства и права России. Советский и современный периоды: Учебное пособие.* [History of State and Law of Russia. Soviet and Contemporary Periods: Instructional Manual]. M.: Iurist', 1999. 488 p. 10000 ptd. ISBN 5-7975-0101-5.

Utiashev, M. M. *Курс лекций по истории политических и правовых учений.* [Course of Lectures on the History of Political and Legal Doctrines]. Ufa: Poligrafkomb., 1999. 320 p. 1000 ptd. ISBN 5-85051-141-5.

Vernadskii, G. V. *История права: Для вузов.* [History of Law: For Institutes of Higher Education]. Spb.: Spb. un-t MVD Rossii, Lan, 1999. 176 p. 3000 ptd. ISBN 5-0114-0172-8.

Власть и пресса: К истории правового регулирования отношений. 1700-1917. Хрестоматия. [Power and the Media: Towards a History of the Legal Regulation of Relations. 1700-1917. Anthology]. Comp. T. S. Ularionov et al. M.: Izd-vo RAGS, 1999. 237 p. 1000 ptd. ISBN 5-7729-0042-0.

Legal Theory

Alekseev, N. N. *Основы философии права: Для вузов.* [Fundamental Principles of the Philosophy of Law: For Institutes of Higher Education]. Spb.: Lan, 1999. 252 p. 5000 ptd. ISBN 5-8114-0070-5.

Alekseev, S. S. *Философия права.* [Philosophy of Law]. M.: NORMA, 1999. 329 p. 3000 ptd. ISBN 5-89123-149-2.

Alekseev, S. S. *Право: Азбука - теория - философия.* [Law: The Alphabet - Theory -Philosophy]. M.: Statut, 1999. 712 p. 1000 ptd. ISBN 5-8354-0002-0.

Azarkin, N. M. *История юридической мысли России: Курс лекций.* [History of the Legal Thought of Russia: Course of Lectures]. M.: Iurid. lit., 1999. 527 p. 3000 ptd. ISBN 5-7260-0931-2.

Baranov, V. M., Polenina, S. V. *Система права, система законодательства и правовая система: Лекция.* [System of Law, System of Legislation and Legal System: Lecture]. N. Novgorod: Nizhegorod. iurid. in-t MVDRF, 1999. 46 p. 250 ptd.

Belkin, A. R. *Теория доказывания: Научно-методическое пособие.* [Theory of Proof: Instructional Methods Manual]. M.: NORMA, 1999. 429 p. 3000 ptd. ISBN 5-89123-323-1.

Cherdantsev, A. F. *Теория государства и права: Учебник для вузов.* [Theory of State and Law: Textbook for Institutes of Higher Education]. M.: Iurait, 1999. 429 p. 10000 ptd. ISBN 5-85294-078-X.

Chernenko, A. G. *Общероссийская национальная идеология и развитие федерализма в России.* [All-Russian National Ideology and the Development of Federalism in Russia]. Spb.: Aleteia, 1999. 274 p. 5500 ptd.ISBN 5-89329-155-7.

Drobyshevskii, S. A. *Классические теоретические представления о государстве, праве и политике: Учебное пособие для вузов.* [Classic Theoretical Representations on State, Law and Politics: Instructional Manual for Institutes of Higher Education]. Krasnoiarsk: Krasnoiar. gos. un-t, 1999. 376 p. ISBN 5-7638-0135-0.

Efremov, A. F. *Принципы и гарантии законности.* [Principles and Guarantees of Legality]. Samara, 1999. 147 p. 600 ptd. ISBN 5-89716-010-4.

Engibarian, R. V., Kozlov, Iu. K. *Теория государства и права: Учебное пособие.* [Theory of State and Law: Instructional Manual]. M.: Iurist', 1999. 271 p. 5000 ptd. ISBN 5-7975-0184-8.

Gushchin, V. V. *Теория госдударства и права: Вопрос - ответ.* [Theory of State and Law: Question - Answer]. M.: Pravo i Zakon, 1999. 123 p. 5000 ptd. ISBN 5-7858-0033-0.

Khropaniuk, V. N. *Теория государства и права: Учебное пособие для вузов.* [Theory of State and Law: Instructional Manual for Institutes of Higher Education]. Ed. V. G. Strekozov. M.: Interstil, 1999. 377 p. 5000 ptd. ISBN 5-8438-0020-3.

Iugov, A. A. *Правовые основы публичной власти в Российской Федерации.* [Legal Fundamental Principles of Public Authority in the Russian Federation]. Ekaterinburg: Izd-vo UrGIUA, 1999. 124 p. 600 ptd. ISBN 5-7845-0094-5.

Kashanina, T. V. *Происхождение государства и права: Современные трактовки и новые подходы: Учебное пособие.* [Origin of State and Law: Contemporary Interpretations and New Approaches: Instructional Manual]. M.: Iurist', 1999. 335 p. 5000 ptd. ISBN 5-7975-0184-8.

Klimenko, S. V., Chicherin, A. L. *Основы государства и права: Пособие для поступающих в юридические вузы.* [Fundamental Principles of State and Law: Manual for Those Entering Juridical Institutes]. M.: Zertsalo, 1999. 353 p. 8000 ptd. ISBN 5-8078-0003-6.

Komarov, S. A., Malko, A. V. *Теория государства и права: Учебно-методическое пособие.* [Theory of State and Law: Instructional Methods Manual]. M.: NORMA-INFRA-M, 1999. 440 p. 40000 ptd. ISBN 5-89123-313-4.

Kovalev, S. *Прагматика политического идеализма.* [Pragmatics of Political Idealism]. M.: In-t prav cheloveka, 1999. 352 p. 1200 ptd. ISBN 5-8013-0067-8.

Malko, A. V. *Теория государства и права в вопросах и ответах.* [Theory of State and Law in Questions and Answers]. 3rd. rev. ed. M.: Iurist', 1999. 269 p. 10000 ptd. ISBN 5-7975-0158-9.

Morozova, L. A. *Основы государства и права: Пособие.* [Fundamental Principles of State and Law: Manual]. M.: Novaia Volna, 1999. 351 p. 5000 ptd. ISBN 5-7864-0087-5.

Nersesiants, V. S. *Философия права: Учебник для вузов.* [Philosophy of Law: Textbook for Institutes of Higher Education]. M.: NORMA-INFRA-M, 1999. 652 p. 30000 ptd. ISBN 5-89123-098-4, ISBN 5-86225-452-8.

Nersesiants, V. S. *Юриспруденция: Введение в курс общей теории права и государства.* [Jurisprudence: Introduction to the Course on the General Theory of Law and State]. M.: NORMA - INFRA-M, 1999. 288 p. 30000 ptd. ISBN 5-89123-227-8, ISBN 5-86225-732-2.

Общая теория права и государства: Для вузов. [General Theory of Law and State: For Institutes of Higher Education]. Ed. V. V. Lazarev. 3rd. rev. ed. M.: Iurist', 1999. 517 p. 10000 ptd. ISBN 5-7357-0123-1.

Основы права: Учебник. [Fundamental Principles of Law: Textbook]. Ed. A. V. Mitskevich. M.: NORMA-INFRA-M, 1999. 317 p. 50000 ptd. ISBN 5-89123-214-6, ISBN 5-86225-701-2.

Also published:

M.: Vysh. shk., 1999. 319 p. 10000 ptd. ISBN 5-06-003645-6.

Основы права: Учебное пособие для студ. дистанционной формы обучения. [Fundamental Principles of Law: Instructional Manual for Correspondence Courses]. Ed. Z. G. Krylova. M.: RITs MGIU, 1999. 388 p. 350 ptd. ISBN 5-276-00018-2.

Правоведение: Практикум: Учебное пособие. [Jurisprudence: Practical Work: Instructional Manual]. Ed. V. A. Vasenkov. M.: Iurist', 1999. 126 p. 5000 ptd. ISBN 5-7975-0195-3.

Правоведение: Учебное пособие. [Jurisprudence: Instructional Manual]. Ed. S. A. Bogoliubova. M.: Znanie, 1999. 320 p. 20000 ptd. ISBN 5-07-002848-0.

Правовое государство: реальность, мечты, будущее. [Rule-of-Law State: Reality, Aspirations, the Future]. V. M. Boer et al. Spb.: Aleteia, Izd-vo Spb. un-ta MVD Rossii, 1999. 245 p. 2400 ptd. ISBN 5-89329-143-3.

Проблемы теории государства и права: Учебное пособие. [Problems of the Theory of State and Law: Instructional Manual]. Ed. M. N. Marchenko. M.: Prospekt, 1999. 504 p. 10000 ptd. ISBN 5-8369-0007-8.

Protasov, V. N. *Теория государства и права. Проблемы теории права и государства: Вопросы и ответы.* [Theory of State and Law. Problems of the Theory of Law and State: Questions and Answers]. M.: Novy Iurist, 1999. 238 p. 10000 ptd. ISBN 5-7969-0068-4.

Puchkov, O. A. *Социальная свобода. Теоретико-правовые вопросы сущности.* [Social Freedom. Theoretical-Legal Questions of Essence]. Ekaterinburg: Izd-vo UrGIUA, 1999. 161 p. 400 ptd. ISBN 5-7845-0090-2.

Shkatulla, V. I., Nadvikova, V. V., Sytinskaia, M. V. *Основы правовых знаний: Для вузов.* [Fundamental Principles of Legal Knowledge: For Institutes of Higher Education]. M.: Akademiia, 1999. 336 p. 30000 ptd. ISBN 5-7695-0403-X.

Shutak, I. D. *Правовые оговорки: практика применения: Научно-методическое пособие.* [Legal Clauses: Practice of Application:

Instructional Methods Manual]. Spb.: Aleteia, 1999. 155 p. 2200 ptd. ISBN 5-89329-187-5.

Spiridonov. L. I. *Теория государства и права: Учебник.* [Theory of State and Law: Textbook]. M.: Prospekt, 1999. 301 p. 10000 ptd. ISBN 5-7986-0008-4.

Технологии власти и управления в современном государстве. [Technologies of Power and Management in the Contemporary State]. M.: Universitet. gumanitar. litsei, 1999. 250 p. 200 ptd. ISBN 5-88387-031-7.

Теория государства и права: Курс лекций. [Theory of State and Law: Course of Lectures]. 2d. rev. ed. Ed. M. N. Marchenko. M.: Zertsalo, 1999. 475 p. 8000 ptd. ISBN 5-8078-0001-X.

Теория государства и права: Схемы, комментарий. [Theory of State and Law: Diagrams, Commentary]. M.: Iurisprudentsiia, 1999. 77 p. 6000 ptd. ISBN 5-86532-047-5.

Теория государства и права: Учебник. [Theory of State and Law: Textbook]. Ed. V. K. Babaev. M.: Iurist', 1999. 591 p. 10000 ptd. ISBN 5-7975-0239-9.

Tikhomirov, Iu. A., Kotelevskaia, I.V. *Правовые акты: Учебно-практическое пособие.* [Legal Acts: Instructional-Practical Manual]. M.: Izd. g-na Tikhomirova M. Iu., 1999. 381 p. 20000 ptd. ISBN 5-89194-014-0.

Vengerov, A. B. *Теория государства и права: Учебник.* [Theory of State and Law: Textbook]. 3rd. ed. M.: Iurisprudentsiia, 1999. 522 p. 12000 ptd. ISBN 5-8401-0023-4.

Введение в юриспруденцию: Учебное пособие. [Introduction to Jurisprudence: Instructional Manual]. Eds. V. N. Kartashov, L. L. Kruglikov, N. N. Tarusinaia. 2nd. rev. ed. Iaroslav: Iarosl. gos. un-t, 1999. 284 p. 1500 ptd. ISBN 5-230-20486-9.

Legal Education

Aminov, D. I. *Полный курс уголовного права России в таблицах и схемах: Учебное пособие.* [Complete Course on the Criminal Law of Russia in Tables and Diagrams]. Ed. V. P. Revin. M.: Filin', 1999. 427 p. 3000 ptd. ISBN 5-89568-145-X.

Труды Московской государственной юридической академии: No.4. [Scholarly Work of the Moscow State Juridical Academy: No.4]. Ed. O. E. Kutafin. M.: Iurist', 1999. 326 p. 300 ptd. ISBN 5-7975-0174-0.

Учебные программы дисциплин и курсов по специальности «Юриспруденция»: Для вузов. [Educational Programmes of Disciplines and Courses Specialising in "Jurisprudence": For Institutes of Higher Education]. Ed. S. A. Komarov et al. M.: Zertsalo, 1999. 608 p. 3000 ptd. ISBN 5-8078-0045-1.

Varydvin, V. A. *Учебно-методический комплекс. Основы права: Альбом схем, таблиц и определений.* [Instructional Methods System. Fundamental Principles of Law: Album of Diagrams, Tables and Definitions]. 2d. rev. ed. M.: Noosfera, 1999. 164 p. 5000 ptd. ISBN 5-93134-030-0.

Legal Profession

Barshchevskii, M. *Адвокатская этика.* [Advocate Ethics]. Samara: Fedorov, 1999. 288 p. 1000 ptd. ISBN 5-8407-0003-7.

Danilov, E. P. *Справочник адвоката: Консультации, защита в суде, образцы документов.* [An Advocate's Manual: Consultations, Defence in Court, Models of Documents]. 2d. rev. ed. M.: Novy Iurist', 1999. 528 p. 1000 ptd. ISBN 5-7969-0072-2.

Ivakina, N. N. *Основы судебного красноречия: Риторика для юристов: Учебное пособие.* [Fundamental Principles of Judicial Eloquence: Rhetoric for Jurists: Instructional Manual]. M.: Iurist', 1999. 383 p. 5000 ptd. ISBN 5-7975-0150-3.

Kolganova, M. V. *Введение в юридическую специальность: Краткий курс лекций.* [Introduction to the Legal Profession: A Short Course of Lectures]. M.: Finstatinform, 1999. 85 p. 1000 ptd. ISBN 5-7866-0100-5.

Melnikovskii, M. S. *Некоторые вопросы методики и тактики осуществления адвокатом защиты осужденных в порядке надзора: Методическое пособие.* [Certain Questions of the Methodology and Tactics of the Effectuation by the Advocate of the Defence of Convicted Persons in the Supervision Procedure: Methods Manual]. M.: DE-IURE, 1999. 46 p. 1000 ptd. ISBN 5-8549-048-9.

Rossinskaia, E. R. *Профессия - эксперт.* [Profession - An Expert]. M.: Iurist', 1999. 192 p. 3000 ptd. ISBN 5-7975-0128-7.

Sotov, P. V., Kamenetskii, R. A. *Адвокатура и нотариат: Учебно-практическое пособие.* [The Advocatura and Notariat: Instructional Manual]. M.: Prospekt, Kodeks, 1999. 400 p. 10000 ptd. ISBN 5-8369-0001-9.

Uporov, I. V. *Профессия - юрист.* [Profession - A Jurist]. M.: AST; Rostov n/D.: Feniks, 1999. 416 p. 10000 ptd. ISBN 5-222-00789-8.

Biography

Briachikhin, A. M. *Автобиография префекта.* [Autobiography of a Prefect]. M.: Kontakt RL, 1999. 200 p. 10000 ptd. ISBN 5-86502-035-8.

Getsevich, I. *Наедине со всеми: Геннадий Райков. Без ретуши. Выступления, интервью, размышления.* [In Private with Everyone: Genadii Raikov. Without Retouching. Speeches, Interviews, Reflections]. Ekaterinburg: Ural. rabochii, 1999. 151 p. 25000 ptd. ISBN 5-85383-147-X.

Iakubovskaia, I. *Генерал Дима: Карьера. Тюрьма. Любовь.* [General Dima: Career. Prison. Love]. M.: Kollektsiia "Sovershenno sekretno", 1999. 255 p. 20000 ptd. ISBN 5-89048-049-9.

Pustogarov, V. V. *Ф. Ф. Мартенс - юрист, дипломат.* [F. F. Martens - Jurist, Diplomat]. 2d. rev. ed. M.: Mezhdunar. otnosheniia, 1999. 287 p. 2500 ptd. ISBN 5-7133-0975-4.

Skripilev, E. A. *В. Д. Спасович - король русской адвокатуры.* [V. D. Spasovich -King of the Russian Advokatura]. In-t gosudarstva i prava RAN. Ed. & intro. G. M. Reznik. M., 1999. 101 p. 2500 ptd. ISBN 5-88720-060-X.

Civil Law

Актуальные проблемы гражданского права. [Urgent Problems of Civil Law]. Ed. M. I. Braginskii. M.: Statut, 1999. 464 p. 5000 ptd. ISBN 5-89398-017-4.

Alekseev, S. S. *Гражданское право в современную эпоху.* [Civil Law in the Contemporary Epoch]. M.: Iurait, 1999. 40 p. 3000 ptd. ISBN 5-85294-082-8.

Egorov, Iu. P. *Сделки в гражданском праве: Для вузов.* [Transactions in Civil Law: For Institutes of Higher Education]. Novosibirsk: Nauka, Sib. izd. firma RAN, 1999. 160 p. 500 ptd. ISBN 5-02-032271-7.

Гражданский кодекс Российской Федерации. [Civil Code of the Russian Federation]. Comp. D. V. Murzin. M.: NORMA-INFRA-M, 1999. 1024 p. 60000 ptd. ISBN 5-89123-353-3, ISBN 5-16-000024-0.

Гражданский кодекс Российской Федерации: Ч. 1, 2. [Civil Code of the Russian Federation: Parts 1 & 2]. M.: OLMA-Press; Novosibirsk: IUKEA, 1999. 559 p. 11000 ptd. ISBN 5-86750-096-9.

Also published:
M.: NORMA-INFRA-M, 1999. 555 p. 8000 ptd. ISBN 5-89123-387-8, ISBN 5-816-000107-7.

Гражданский кодекс Российской Федерации: Чч.1, 2. С постатейными материалами из практики Высшего Арбитражного Суда Российской Федерации. [Civil Code of the Russian Federation: Parts 1 & 2. With Article by Article Materials from the Practice of the Highest Arbitrazh Court of the Russian Federation]. Comp. D. V. Murzin. M.: NORMA-INFRA-M, 1999. 832 p. 60000 ptd. ISBN 5-89123-304-5, ISBN 5-86225-951-1.

Гражданский кодекс Российской Федерации: Чч. 1 и 2. Официальный текст по состоянию на 1 декабря 1998 г. [Civil Code of the Russian Federation: Parts 1 and 2. Official Text as of 1

December 1998]. M.: NORMA-INFRA-M, 1999. 555 p. 6000 ptd. ISBN 5-89123-317-7.

Гражданский кодекс Российской Федерации: Чч.1 и 2. Официальный текст по состоянию на 1 марта 1999 г. [Civil Code of the Russian Federation: Parts 1 & 2. Official Text as of 1 March 1999]. M.: NORMA-INFRA-M, 1999. 560 p. 10000 ptd. ISBN 5-89123-338-X, ISBN 5-86225-984-8.

Гражданский кодекс Российской Федерации: Чч. 1 и 2. С постатейными материалами из практики Высшего Арбитражного Суда РФ. [Civil Code of the Russian Federation: Parts 1 and 2. With Article by Article Materials from the Practice of the Supreme Arbitrazh Court of the Russian Federation]. M.: NORMA-INFRA-M, 1999. 819 p. 6000 ptd. ISBN 5-89123-304-5, ISBN 5-86225-951-1.

Гражданский кодекс Российской Федерации: Ч.2. Комментарий. Гл.30. Купля-продажа. Кн.1. [Civil Code of the Russian Federation: Part 2. Commentary. Chapter 30. Contract of Sale. Book 1]. Eds. T. E. Abova, A. Iu. Kabalkin. M.: BEK, 1999. 235 p. 3000 ptd. ISBN 5-85639-242-6.

Гражданский кодекс Российской Федерации в схемах. [Civil Code of the Russian Federation in Diagrams]. Ed. T. M. Medvedeva. M.: Gorodets, Formula prava, 1999. 101 p. 5000 ptd. ISBN 5-89391-019-2.

Гражданское право: Часть 2: Учебник. [Civil Law: Part 2: Textbook]. Ed. A. G. Kalpin. M.: Iurist', 1999. 542 p. 50000 ptd. ISBN 5-7975-0223-2.

Гражданское право: Часть 3. Учебник. [Civil Law: Part 3. Textbook]. Eds. A. P. Sergeev, Iu. K. Tolstoi. M.: Prospekt, 1999. 591 p. 10000 ptd. ISBN 5-8369-0035-3.

Гражданское право: Учебник. [Civil Law: Textbook]. Eds. A. P. Sergeev, Iu. K. Tolstoi. 3rd. rev. ed. M.: Prospekt, 1999. 20000 ptd.

Part 1. 631 p. ISBN 5-8369-0013-2.
Part 2. 782 p. ISBN 5-8369-0014-0.

Vol.1. 4th rev. ed. 610 p. ISBN 5-8369-0051-5.
Vol.2. 720 p. 20000 ptd. ISBN 5-8369-0052-3.
Vol.3. 2nd. rev. ed. 621 p. ISBN 5-8369-0053-1.

Гражданское право России: Часть 1. [Civil Law of Russia: Part 1]. Eds. Z. I. Tsybulenko, P. V. Ramzaev. 2nd. rev. ed. M.: Iurist', 1999. 163 p. 10000 ptd. ISBN 5-7975-0220-8.

Гражданское законодательство: Сборник нормативных актов. [Civil Legislation: Collection of Normative Acts]. Comp. A. P. Sergeev. M.: Kodeks, Prospekt, 1999. 10000 ptd.
Part 1. 688 p. ISBN 5-8369-0002-7.
Part 2. 720 p. ISBN 5-8369-0003-5.

Гражданское законодательство России: Ч.1: Сборник нормативных правовых актов и документов. [Civil Legislation of Russia: Part 1: Collection of Normative Legal Acts and Documents]. Ed. Z. I. Tsybulenko. M.: Iurist', 1999. 620 p. 10000 ptd. ISBN 5-7975-0196-1.

Grishaev, T. P. *Гражданское право. Часть первая в вопросах и ответах: Учебное пособие.* [Civil Law. Part One in Questions and Answers: Instructional Manual]. M.: Iurist', 1999. 141 p. 10000 ptd. ISBN 5-7975-0242-9.

Gusev, A. N. *Постатейный комментарий к части первой Гражданского кодекса Российской Федерации.* [Article by Article Commentary to the First Part of the Civil Code of the Russian Federation]. 2d. rev. ed. M.: INFRA-M, 1999. 773 p. ISBN 5-86225-900-7.

Gusev, A. N. *Постатейный комментарий к части второй Гражданского кодекса Российской Федерации.* [Article by Article Commentary to the Second Part of the Civil Code of the Russian Federation]. 3rd. rev. ed. M.: INFRA-M, 1999. 820 p. 30000 ptd. ISBN 5-86225-625-3.

Комментарий к Гражданскому кодексу Российской Федерации, части первой (постатейный). [Commentary to the Civil Code of the Russian Federation, Part 1 (Article by Article)]. Ed. O. N. Sadikov.

M.: KONTRAKT, INFRA-M, 1999. XXII, 777 p. 60000 ptd. ISBN 5-90785-017-2, ISBN 5-86225-669-5.

Комментарий к Гражданскому кодексу Российской Федерации, части второй (постатейный). [Commentary to the Civil Code of the Russian Federation, Part Two (Article by Article)]. 3rd. rev. ed. Ed. O. R. Sadikov. M.: Kontrakt, INFRA-M, 1999. 781 p. 48000 ptd. ISBN 5-900785-26-2.

Коммерческое право России: Учебно-методическое пособие. [Commercial Law of Russia: Instructional Methods Manual]. Ed. B. I. Putinskii. M.: Gorodets, 1999. 144 p. 5000 ptd. ISBN 5-89391-051-6.

Korneeva, I. L. *Практикум по гражданскому праву: Ч.2.* [Practical Work on Civil Law: Part 2]. M.: Iurist', 1999. 196 p. 5000 ptd. ISBN 5-7975-0125-2.

Kruglova, N. Iu. *Коммерческое право: Учебник.* [Commercial Law: Textbook]. M.: Rus. delovaia lit., 1999. 848 p. ISBN 5-89247-035-0.

Lebedev, K. K. *Практикум по коммерческому праву: Учебно-методическое и практическое пособие.* [Practical Work on Commercial Law: Instructional Methods and Practical Manual]. Spb.: Izd-vo Spb. un-ta, 1999. 424 p. 5000 ptd. ISBN 5-93333-007-8.

Nadeev, R. K., Korolev, A. N. *Путеводитель по Гражданскому кодексу Российской Федерации, Гражданскому кодексу РСФСР и Основам гражданского законодательства Союза ССР и республик: По состоянию на 1 марта 1999 г.* [Guide to the Civil Code of the Russian Federation, the RSFSR Civil Code and the Fundamental Principles of the Civil Legislation of the USSR and Republics: For 1 March 1999]. M., 1999. 182 p. 5000 ptd. ISBN 5-7018-0044-4.

Практикум по гражданскому праву: Ч. 1. [Practical Work on Civil Law: Part 1]. Eds. A. G. Kalpin, A. Iu. Kabalkin, V. V. Dolinskaia. M.: Iurist', 1999. 172 p. 5000 ptd. ISBN 5-7975-0046-9.

Reshetnikova, I. V., Iarkov, V. V. *Гражданское право и гражданский процесс в современной России.* [Civil Law and Civil Procedure in

Contemporary Russia]. Ekaterinburg. M.: NORMA, 1999. 302 p. 15000 ptd. ISBN 5-89123-233-2.

Российское гражданское право: Учебник. [Russian Civil Law: Textbook]. Eds. Z. G. Krylova, E. P. Gavrilov. M.: IurInfoR, 1999. 416 p. 5000 ptd. ISBN 5-89158-019-5.

Teliukina, M. V. *Гражданское право: Т.1: Схемы.* [Civil Law: Vol.1: Diagrams]. Ed. E. A. Sukhanov. M.: BEK, 1999. 120 p. 3000 ptd. ISBN 5-85639-259-0.

Tikhomirov, M. Iu. *Доверенности.* [Powers of Attorney]. M.: Izd. g-na Tikhomirova M. Iu., Iurinformtsentr, 1999. 29 p. 3000 ptd. ISBN 5-89194-026-4.

Tkachuk, I. B. *Коммерческая тайна: Организация защиты, расследование посягательств.* [Commercial Secret: Organisation of Defence, Investigation of Infringements]. M.: Shchyt-M, 1999. 165 p. 1000 ptd. ISBN 5-93004-044-3.

Ownership and Privatisation

Chernoiarov, A. D. *Защита прав на жилую недвижимость.* [Defence of Rights to a Dwelling Immovable]. Novosibirsk: RIF-servis, 1999. 214 p. 10000 ptd. ISBN 5-85298-032-3.

Erdelevskii, A. M. *Комментарий к Федеральному закону «О государственной регистрации прав на недвижимое имущество и сделок с ним».* [Commentary to the Federal Law "On State Registration of Rights to Immovable Property and on Transactions with It"]. M.: BEK, 1999. 211 p. 2000 ptd. ISBN 5-89639-260-4.

Ershova, I. V. *Имущество и финансы предприятия. Правовое регулирование: Практическое пособие.* [Property and Finances of an Enterprise. Legal Regulation: Practical Manual]. M.: Iurist', 1999. 397 p. 5000 ptd. ISBN 5-7975-0176-7.

Федеральный закон «О государственной регистрации прав на недвижимое имущество и сделок с ним»: Комментарий в схемах и таблицах. [Federal Law "On the State Registration of Rights to Immovable Property and Transactions with It": Commentary in Diagrams and Tables]. Tiumen: Izd-vo TiumGU, 1999. 140 p. 500 ptd. ISBN 5-88081-154-9.

Goremykin, V. A., Bugulov, E. R. *Недвижимость: регистрация прав и сделок, ипотечное кредитование в схемах.* [Immovable Property: Registration of Rights and Transactions, Mortgage Credit in Diagrams]. 2d. ed. M.: Filin', 1999. 144 p. 5000 ptd. ISBN 5-89568-113-1.

Государственная регистрация прав на недвижимое имущество и сделок с ним: правовая форма: В 3 ч. [State Registration of Rights to Immovable Property and Transactions with It: Legal Form: In 3 Parts]. Tiumen: Izd-vo TiumGU, 1999. 500 ptd. ISBN 5-88081-154-9.
Part 1. 171 p.
Part 2. 162 p.
Part 3. 233 p.

Гражданско-правовые документы для оформления сделок с недвижимостью. [Civil Law Documents for Formalising Transactions with an Immovable]. Ed. M. Iu. Tikhomirov. M.: Izd. g-na Tikhomirova M. Iu., Iurinformtsentr, 1999. 86 p. 3000 ptd. ISBN 5-89194-024-8.

Комментарий к Федеральному закону «О государственной регистрации прав на недвижимое имущество и сделок с ним». [Commentary to the Federal Law "On the State Registration of Rights to Immovable Property and Transactions with It"]. M.: NORMA-INFRA-M, 1999. 523 p. 50000 ptd. ISBN 5-89123-240-5.

Комментарий к Федеральному закону «Об ипотеке (залоге недвижимости)». [Commentary to the Federal Law "On Mortgage (Pledge of an Immovable)"]. Ed. I. D. Grachev. M.: NORMA-INFRA-M, 1999. 325 p. 30000 ptd. ISBN 5-89123-349-5, ISBN 5-16-000021-6.

Lonchakov, A. P. *Административно-правовая организация механизма управления собственностью в сфере экономики: Учебное пособие.* [Administrative Legal Organisation of the Mechanism for the Management of Ownership in the Sphere of the

Economy: Instructional Manual]. Khabarovsk: DVIUI KHGTU, 1999. 249 p. 2000 ptd. ISBN 5-7389-0050-2.

Mattei, U., Sukhanov, E. A. *Основные положения права собственности.* [Basic Provisions of the Right of Ownership]. M.: Iurist', 1999. 383 p. 5000 ptd. ISBN 5-7975-0155-4.

Mikheeva, L. Iu. *Доверительное управление имуществом.* [Trust Management of Property]. M.: Iurist', 1999. 176 p. 3000 ptd. ISBN 5-7975-0264-X.

Наложение ареста на имущество. Оценка и распределение активов. [Imposition of Arrest on Property. Valuation and Distribution of Assets]. Eds. V. F. Ukolov, A. M. Omarov. M.: Luch, Mol. gvardiia, 1999. 111 p. 500 ptd. ISBN 5-235-02362-5.

О приватизации жилищного фонда в Российской Федерации. [On the Privatisation of the Housing Fund in the Russian Federation]. M.: Izd. g-na Tikhomirova M.Iu., 1999. 13 p. 3000 ptd. ISBN 5-89194-015-9.

Shilokhvost, O. Iu., *Отступное в гражданском праве России.* [Release Money in the Civil Law of Russia]. M.: Statut, 1999. 251 p. 5000 ptd. ISBN 5-8354-0025-X.

Sklovskii, K. I. *Собственность в гражданском праве.* [Ownership in Civil Law]. M.: Delo, 1999. 511 p. 3000 ptd. ISBN 5-7749-0141-6.

Skvortsov, O. Iu. *Приватизационное право: Учебное пособие.* [Privatisation Law: Instructional Manual]. M.: ZAO "Biznes-shkola "Intel-Sintez", 1999. 272 p. 3000 ptd. ISBN 5-87057-173-1.

Вопросы государственной регистрации прав на недвижимое имущество и сделок с ним: Сборник. Выпуск 5. [Questions of the State Registration of Rights to Immovable Property and Transactions with It: Collection. Issue 5]. Comp. E. A. Kindeeva et al. Ed. V. V. Ogorodnikov. M.: Violanta, 1999. 399 p. 6000 ptd. ISBN 5-88803-011-2.

Zakharova, N. N. *Комментарий к Федеральному закону «Об ипотеке (залоге недвижимости)»: Постатейный.* [Commentary to the Federal Law "On Mortgage (Pledge of an Immovable)": Article by Article]. M.: Iurait, 1999. 192 p. 6000 ptd. ISBN 5-85294-076-3.

Законодательство о государственной регистрации прав на недвижимое имущество и сделок с ним. [Legislation on the State Registration of Rights on Immovable Property and Transactions With It]. Comp. P. V. Krasheninnikov. 2d. rev. ed. M.: Spark, 1999. 143 p. 8000 ptd. ISBN 5-88914-123-6.

Economic Societies and Partnerships

Anokhin, V. T. *Предпринимательское право.* [Entrepreneurial Law]. M.: VLADOS, 1999. 400 p. 10000 ptd. ISBN 5-691-00354-2.

Bashkinskas, V. Iu., Dedov, D. I., Karelina, S. A. *Правовое регулирование деятельности акционерных обществ: Учебное пособие.* [Legal Regulation of the Activity of Joint-Stock Societies: Instructional Manual]. Ed. E. P. Gubin. M.: Zertsalo, 1999. 241 p. 5000 ptd. ISBN 5-8078-0029-X.

Blek, B., Krekman, P., Tarasova, A. *Комментарий Федерального закона «Об акционерных обществах».* [Commentary to the Federal Law "On Joint-Stock Societies"]. M.: Labirint, 1999. 720 p. 3000 ptd. ISBN 5-87604-098-3.

Chukovskaia, E. A. *Аудиовизуальный бизнес: Договорное регулирование. Учебное пособие для вузов.* [Audio-Visual Business: Contractual Regulation. Instructional Manual for Institutes of Higher Education]. M.: Ros-Konsult, 1999. 331 p. 4000 ptd. ISBN 5-89805-005-1.

Dashevskaia, L. M. *Правовые основы хозяйственной деятельности предприятий.* [Legal Fundamental Principles of the Economic Activity of Enterprises]. M.: Kolos, 1999. 224 p. 2000 ptd. ISBN 5-10-003493-9.

Ershova, I. V., Ivanova, T. M. *Предпринимательское право: Учебное пособие.* [Entrepreneurial Law: Instructional Manual]. M.: Iurisprudentsiia, 1999. 336 p. 10000 ptd. ISBN 5-8401-0006-4.

Федеральный Закон «О несостоятельности (банкротстве): Постатейный комментарий. [Federal Law "On Insolvency (Bankruptcy)": Article by Article Commentary]. Ed. V. V. Vitrianskii. M.: Statut, 1999. 417 p. 15000 ptd. ISBN 5-89398-018-2.

Федеральный закон «О садоводческих, огороднических и дачных некоммерческих объединениях граждан». [Federal Law "On Horticultural, Market Gardening and Suburban Non-Commercial Citizens' Associations"]. M.: Druzhba narodov, 1999. 96 p. 5000 ptd. ISBN 5-285-00339-3.

Федеральный закон Российской Федерации «О несостоятельности (банкротстве)»: Официальный текст. [Federal Law of the Russian Federation "On Insolvency (Bankruptcy)": Official Text]. 3rd. ed. M.: Filin', 1999. 128 p. 5000 ptd. ISBN 5-89568-087-9.

Гражданское и предпринимательское право: Сборник документов. Ч.2. [Civil and Entrepreneurial Law: Collection of Documents. Part 2]. Ed. T. V. Bogachevaia. Comp. M. Iu. Savranskii. M.: TON, Ostozhie, 1999. 896 p. 7000 ptd. ISBN 5-86095-125-6.

Юридические консультации по вопросам применения Закона Российской Федерации «О садоводческих, огороднических и дачных некоммерческих объединениях граждан». [Legal Consultations on Questions of the Application of the Russian Federation Law "On Horticultural, Market Gardening and Suburban Non-Commercial Citizens' Associations"]. M.: Druzhba narodov, 1999. 96 p. 5000 ptd. ISBN 5-285-00341-5.

Kashanina, T. V. *Корпоративное право: Учебник для вузов.* [Corporate Law: Textbook for Institutes of Higher Education]. M.: NORMA-INFRA-M, 1999. 802 p. 30000 ptd. ISBN 5-89123-174-3.

Комментарий к Федеральному закону «Об акционерных обществах». [Commentary to the Federal law "On Joint-Stock Societies"]. 2d. rev. ed. Ed. M. Iu. Tikhomirov. M.: Izd. g-na Tikhomirova M. Iu., 1999. 392 p. 20000 ptd. ISBN 5-89194-016-7.

Комментарий к Федеральному закону «Об обществах с ограниченной ответственностью». [Commentary to the Federal

Law "On Limited Responsibility Societies"]. Eds. A. A. Ignatenko, S. N. Movchana. M.: Filin', 1999. 384 p. 5000 ptd. ISBN 5-89568-142-5.

Laptev, V. V. *Акционерное право.* [Joint-Stock Society Law]. M.: Kontrakt, INFRA-M, 1999. 246 p. 6000 ptd. ISBN 5-86225-993-7.

Larin, V. V. *Акционерное право.* [Joint-Stock Law]. Spb.: Izd-vo Ros. nats. b-ki, 1999. 268 p. 3000 ptd. ISBN 5-8192-0042-X.

Meteleva, Iu. A. *Правовое положение акционера в акционерном обществе.* [Legal Status of the Stockholder in the Joint-Stock Society]. M.: Statut, 1999. 191 p. 7000 ptd. ISBN 5-8354-0005-5.

Научно-практический комментарий к части первой Гражданского кодекса Российской Федерации для предпринимателей. [Scientific-Practical Commentary to Part One of the Civil Code of the Russian Federation for Entrepreneurs]. M. I. Braginskii et al. 2d. rev. ed. M.: Spark, Red. zhurn. "Khoz-vo i pravo", 1999. 736 p. 10000 ptd. ISBN 5-88914-115-5.

О лицензировании отдельных видов деятельности: Федеральный закон. [On Licensing Certain Types of Activity: Federal Law]. M.: INFRA-M, 1999. 21 p. 3000 ptd. ISBN 5-86225-698-9.

Об обществах с ограниченной ответственностью: Федеральный закон от 8 февраля 1998 г. No.14-ФЗ. [On Limited Responsibility Societies: Federal Law of 8 February 1998. No.14-F3]. M.: Iurisprudentsiia, 1999. 48 p. 5000 ptd. ISBN 5-86532-048-3.
Also published:
M.: Iurait, 1999. 47 p. 5000 ptd. ISBN 5-85294-033-X.

Petukhov, V. N. *Корпорации в российской промышленности: законодательство и практика: Научно-практическое пособие.* [Corporations in Russian Industry: Legislation and Practice]. M.: Gorodets, 1999. 208 p. 2000 ptd. ISBN 5-89391-052-4.

Pliev, E. G. *Правовые проблемы предпринимательства в России.* [Legal Problems of Entrepreneurship in Russia]. M.: Prospekt, 1999. 119 p. 1000 ptd. ISBN 5-8369-0038-8.

Предпринимательское (хозяйственное) право: Сборник нормативных актов: Учебное пособие для вузов. [Entrepreneurial (Economic) Law: Collection of Normative Acts: Instructional Manual for Institutes of Higher Education]. Comp., Ed. and Intro. I. V. Doinikov. 3rd. rev. ed. M.: Bylina, 1999. 623 p. 10000 ptd. ISBN 5-88528-2420.

Предпринимательское (хозяйственное) право: Учебник. В 2 томах. Том 1. [Entrepreneurial (Economic) Law: Textbook. In 2 Volumes. Vol.1]. Ed. O. M. Oleinik. M.: Iurist', 1999. 727 p. 50000 ptd. ISBN 5-7975-0231-3.

Проблемы правоприменительной практики в предпринимательской деятельности. [Problems of Law Application Practice in Entrepreneurial Activity]. Eds. A. V. Chernykh, D. V. Goloverov. M.: Kn. mir, 1999. 223 p. ISBN 5-8041-0047-5.

Tosunian, G. A., Vikulin, A. Iu. *Постатейный комментарий к Федералному закону «О несостоятельности (банкротстве) кредитных организаций».* [Article by Article Commentary to the Federal Law "On the Insolvency (Bankruptcy) of Credit Organisations"]. M.: BEK, 1999. 332 p. 3000 ptd. ISBN 5-85639-273-6.

Учредительные и внутренние документы общества с ограниченной ответственностью. [Constitutive and Internal Documents of a Limited Responsibility Society]. M.: M. Iu. Tikhomirov, 1999. 76 p. 3000 ptd. ISBN 5-89194-020-5.

Управление и корпоративный конторль в акционерном обществе: Практическое пособие. [Management and Corporative Control in a Joint-Stock Society: Practical Manual]. Ed. E. P. Gubin. M.: Iurist', 1999. 247 p. 5000 ptd. ISBN 5-7975-0147-3.

Устав и внутренние документы садоводческого (огороднического, дачного) некоммерческого партнерства. [Charter and Internal Documents of a Horticultural (Market Garden, Country) Non-Commercial Partnership]. M.: M. Iu. Tikhomirov, 1999. 52 p. 3000 ptd. ISBN 5-89194-021-3.

Закон города Москвы о социальном партнерстве. [Law of the City of Moscow on Social Partnership]. M.: Informart, 1999. 16 p. 5000 ptd.

Zaleskii, V. V., Kallistratova, R. F. *Комментарий к Федеральному закону «О некоммерческих организациях».* [Commentary to the Federal Law "On Non-Commercial Organisations"]. 2d. rev. ed. M.: Iurait, 1999. 260 p. 3000 ptd. ISBN 5-85294-064-X.

Zhilinskii, S. E. *Предпринимательское право (правовая основа предпринимательской деятельности): Учебник для вузов.* [Entrepreneurial Law (Legal Basis of Entrepreneurial Activity): Textbook for Institutes of Higher Education]. 2nd. rev. ed. M.: NORMA-INFRA-M, 1999. 661 p. 6000 ptd. ISBN 5-89123-354-1, ISBN 5-16-000028-3.

Zinchenko, S. A., Shapsugov, D. Iu., Korkh, S. E. *Предпринимательство и статус его субъектов в современном российском праве.* [Entrepreneurship and the Status of Its Subjects in Contemporary Russian Law]. Rostov n/D.: SKAGS, 1999. 198 p. 1000 ptd. ISBN 5-89546-037-2.

Consumer Protection

Good, R. *Руководство к Унифицированным правилам для гарантий по требованию.* [Guide to Unified Rules for Guarantees on Demand]. Trans. from English. M.: Konsaltbankir, 1999. 166 p. 1100 ptd. ISBN 5-85187-055-9, ISBN 5-85187-085-0.

Комментарий к Закону РФ «О защите прав потребителей». Разъяснения «О некоторых вопросах, связанных с применением закона РФ «О защите прав потребителей»: Официальный текст. [Commentary to the Russian Federation Law "On the Defence of Consumers' Rights". Explanations "On Certain Questions, Connected with the Adoption of the Russian Federation Law "On the Defence of Consumers' Rights": Official Text]. M.: IVTS "Marketing", 1999. 32 p. 5000 ptd. ISBN 5-7856-0097-8.

О потребительской кооперации (потребительских обществах, их союзах) в Российской Федерации: Закон Российской

Федерации: Официальный текст. [On Consumer Cooperation (Consumer Societies, Their Unions) in the Russian Federation: Law of Russian Federation: Official Text]. M.: Marketing, 1999. 40 p. 3000 ptd. ISBN 5-7856-0112-5.

Odintsov, S. *Правовое регулирование деятельности дистрибьютора в сфере многоуровневого (сетевого) маркетинга.* [Legal Regulation of Activity of the Distributor in the Sphere of Multi-Level (Computer Network) Marketing]. M.: BINOM, 1999. 314 p. 4000 ptd. ISBN 5-7989-0148-3.

Pisarevskii, E. L. *Туристская деятельность: Проблемы правового регулирования.* [Tourist Activity: Problems of Legal Regulation]. Vladivostok: In-t mezhdunar. turizma, 1999. 283 p. 1000 ptd. ISBN 5-93304-002-9.

Rogozhin, M. Iu. *Документы делового общения.* [Business Relations Documents]. M.: Rus. delovaia lit., 1999. 204 p. 3000 ptd. ISBN 5-89247-027-X.

Защита прав потребителей: Разъяснения по применению закона Российской Федерации «О защите прав потребителей». [Defence of Consumers' Rights: Explanations on the Application of the Russian Federation Law "On the Defence of Consumers' Rights]. M.: INFRA-M, 1999. 26 p. 3000 ptd. ISBN 5-86225-745-4.

Защита прав потребителей: Сборник законодательных и нормативных актов Российской Федерации. [Defence of Consumers' Rights: Collection of Legislative and Normative Acts of the Russian Federation]. M.: Novaia Volna, 1999. 128 p. 5000 ptd. ISBN 5-7864-0074-3.

Securities

Belov, V. A. *Вексельное законодательство России: Научно-практический комментарий.* [Bill of Exchange Legislation of Russia: Scientific Practical Commentary]. 2d. rev. ed. M.: IurInfoR, 1999. 549 p. 10000 ptd. ISBN 5-89158-026-8.

Iuldashbaeva, L. R. *Правовое регулирование оборота*

эмиссионных ценных бумаг (акций, облигаций). [Legal Regulation of the Circulation of Emission Securities (Stocks, Obligations)]. M.: Statut, 1999. 204 p. 5000 ptd. ISBN 5-8354-0018-7.

Novoselova, L. A. *Вексель в хозяйственном обороте.* [The Bill of Exchange in Economic Turnover]. 3rd. rev. ed. M.: Statut, 1999. 221 p. 3000 ptd. ISBN 5-8354-0017-9.

О рынке ценных бумаг. [On the Securities' Market]. M.: Izdanie g-na Tikhomirova M. Iu., 1999. 51 p. 3000 ptd. ISBN 5-89194-015-9.

Obligations

Braginskii, M. I. *Договор хранения.* [Storage Contract]. M.: Statut, 1999. 157 p. 5000 ptd. ISBN 5-8354-0020-9.

Braginskii, M. I. *Договор подряда и подобные ему договоры.* [Independent-Work Contract and Similar Contracts]. M.: Statut, 1999. 254 p. 10000 ptd. ISBN 5-8354-0003-9.

Braginskii, M. I., Vitrianskii, V. V. *Договорное право: Книга 1.* [Contractual Law: Book 1]. 2nd. rev. ed. M.: Statut, 1999. 841 p. 5000 ptd. ISBN 5-8354-0016-0.

Договорные споры: Сборник документов. [Contractual Disputes: Collection of Documents]. Ed. M. Iu. Tikhomirov. M.: Izd. g-na Tikhomirova M. Iu., 1999. 208 p. 3000 ptd. ISBN 5-89194-032-9.

Договоры: Образцы документов, комментарий, практика разрешения споров. [Contracts: Models of Documents, Commentary, Practice of Settling Disputes]. Ed. M. Iu. Tikhomirov. M.: Izd. g-na Tikhomirova M. Iu., 1999. 376 p. 30000 ptd. ISBN 5-89194-030-2.

Gongalo, B. M. *Обеспечение исполнения обязательств.* [Securing the Performance of Obligations]. M.: Spark, 1999. 152 p. 2000 ptd. ISBN 5-88914-110-4.

Kasso, L. A. *Понятие о залоге в современном праве.* [Concept of Pledge in Contemporary Law]. M.: Statut, 1999. 284 p. 7000 ptd. ISBN 5-89398-025-5.

Lunts, L. A. *Деньги и денежные обязательства в гражданском праве.* [Money and Monetary Obligations in Civil Law]. M.: Statut, 1999. 352 p. 5000 ptd. ISBN 5-8354-0012-8.

Научно-практический комментарий к Федеральному закону (залог недвижимости): Постатейный. [Scientific-Practical Commentary to the Federal Law (Pledge of Immovable): Article by Article]. Ed. M. G. Masevich. M.: Kontrakt, INFRA-M, 1999. 292 p. 3000 ptd. ISBN 5-900785-32-7, ISBN 5-86225-850-7.

Научно-практический комментарий к Федеральному закону «Об ипотеке (залоге недвижимости)» (постатейный). [Scientific-Practical Commentary to the Federal Law "On Mortgage (Pledge of Immovable)" (Article by Article)]. Ed. M. G. Masevich. M.: KONTRAKT, INFRA-M, 1999. 292 p. 3000 ptd. ISBN 5-86225-850-7.

Novikova, I. Iu. *Аренда зданий и сооружений: Правовое регулирование. Налогообложение.* [Lease of Buildings and Installations: Legal Regulation. Taxation]. Comps. O. V. Volkova, S. D. Kazancheva. M.: Sovr. ekonomika i pravo, 1999. 106 p. ISBN 5-250-00-826-X.

О лизинге: Федеральный закон Российской Федерации. Официальный текст. [On Finance Leasing: Federal Law of the Russian Federation. Official Text]. M.: Marketing, 1999. 28 p. 3000 ptd. ISBN 5-7856-0074-9.

Samokhvalova, Iu. N. *Лизинг в России: правовые основы, бухгалтерский учёт, налогообложение.* [Finance Leasing in Russia: Legal Fundamental Principles, Accountancy, Taxation]. Eds. V. F. Ukolov, A. M. Omarov. M.: Luch. Mol. gvardiia, 1999. 110 p. 500 ptd. ISBN 5-235-02361-7.

Sarbash, S. V. *Договор банковского счета: проблемы доктрины и судебной практики.* [Banking Account Contract: Problems of Doctrine and Judicial Practice]. M.: Statut, 1999. 270 p. 5000 ptd. ISBN 5-8354-0010-1.

Сборник договоров: Все виды договоров, предусмотренные новым ГК РФ. [Collection of Contracts: All Types of Contracts

Provided for by the New Civil Code of the Russian Federation]. Comp. A. N. Dolzhenko et al. M.: Prospekt, 1999. 560 p. 15000 ptd. ISBN 5-8369-0028-0.

Сборник договоров с дискетой. [Collection of Contracts with Diskette]. Comp. A. N. Dolzhenko. 2d. rev. ed. M.: Prospekt, 1999. 232 p. 10000 ptd. ISBN 5-8369-0034-5.

Сборник типовых договоров. [Collection of Standard Contracts]. 3rd. rev. ed. Comp. V. M. Prudnikov. M.: INFRA-M, 1999. 318 p. 100000 ptd. ISBN 5-86225-534-6.

Seregin, V. P., Khalevinskaia, E. D. *Организация, учёт и налогообложение лизинговых операций.* [The Organisation, Registration and Taxation of Finance Leasing Operations]. M.: Iurist', 1999. 174 p. 1000 ptd. ISBN 5-7975-0168-6.

Smirnov, V. V., Lukina, Z. P. *Комментарий к Федеральному закону об ипотеке (залоге недвижимости).* [Commentary to the Federal Law on Mortgage (Pledge of Immovable)]. M.: Fond "Pravovaia kultura", 1999. 245 p. 5000 ptd. ISBN 5-93094-080-0.

Споры о возмещении имущественного ущерба и компенсации морального вреда: Сборник документов. [Disputes on Compensation for Property Damage and Compensation for Moral Harm: Collection of Documents]. Comp. O. M. Ogloblina. Ed. M. Iu. Tikhomirov. M.: Iurinform-tsentr, 1999. 155 p. 3000 ptd. ISBN 5-89194-037-X.

Свод хозяйственных договоров и документооборота предприятий с юридическим комментарием: В 2 томах. [Digest of Economic Contracts and Circulation of Documents of Enterprises with a Legal, Arbitrazh and Tax Commentary: In 2 Volumes]. Ed. A. V. Bryzgalin. 2nd. rev. ed. M.: Tsentr "Nalogi in fin. pravo", Analitika-Press, 1999. 30000 ptd.

Vol.1. 613 p. ISBN 5-7916-0063-1.
Vol.2. 581 p. ISBN 5-7916-0064-X.

Tikhomirov, M. Iu. *Гражданско-правовые договоры.* [Civil Law Contracts]. M.: Izd. g-na Tikhomirova, 1999. 141 p. 3000 ptd. ISBN 5-89194-022-1.

Vitrianskii, V. V. *Договор аренды и его виды: прокат, фрахтование на время, аренда зданий, сооружений и предприятий, лизинг.* [Contract of Lease and Its Types: Hire, Chartering for Time, Lease of Buildings, Installations and Enterprises, Leasing]. M.: Statut, 1999. 299 p. 5000 ptd. ISBN 5-8354-0021-7.

Inheritance Law

Danilov, E. P. *Наследование: Консультации. Образцы документов. Судебные споры.* [Inheritance: Consultations. Models of Documents. Judicial Disputes]. M.: Novy Iurist', 1999. 239 p. 8000 ptd. ISBN 5-7969-0059-5.

Tolstoi, Iu. K. *Наследственное право: Учебное пособие.* [Inheritance Law: Instructional Manual]. M.: Prospekt, 1999. 222 p. 5000 ptd. ISBN 5-8369-0042-6.

Vlasov, Iu. N., Kalinin, V. V. *Наследование по закону и по завещанию.* [Inheritance According to the Law and According to Testaments]. M.: Iurait, 1999. 247 p. 5000 ptd. ISBN 5-85294-072-0.

Intellectual Property

Makagonova, N. V. *Авторское право: Учебное пособие.* [Author's Right: Instructional Manual]. Ed. E. P. Gavrilov. M.: Iurid. lit., 1999. 287 p. 3000 ptd. ISBN 5-7260-0932-0.

Melnikov, V. M. *Актуальные вопросы развития законодательства Российской Федерации о товарных знаках.* [Urgent Questions on the Development of the Legislation of the Russian Federation on Trademarks]. M.: INITS, 1999. 24 p. 180 ptd.

Расследование неправомерного доступа к компьютерной информации: Научно-практическое пособие. [Investigation of Unlawful Access to Computer Information: Scientific-Practical Manual]. Ed. N. G. Shurukhnova. M.: Shchyt-M, 1999. 254 p. 1500 ptd. ISBN 5-93004-035-4.

Sergeev, A. P. *Право интеллектуальной собственности в Российской Федерации: Учебник.* [Law of Intellectual Property in the Russian Federation: Textbook]. 2nd. rev. ed. M.: Prospekt, 1999. 751 p. ISBN 5-8369-0032-9.

Теоретические и практические аспекты охраны промышленной собственности в Российской Федерации. [Theoretical and Practical Aspects of the Protection of Industrial Ownership in the Russian Federation]. Ed. A. D. Korchagin. M.: INITS Rospatent, 1999. 552 p. 900 ptd.

Family Law

Antokolskaia, M. V. *Семейное право: Учебник.* [Family Law: Textbook]. 2nd. rev. ed. M.: Iurist', 1999. 336 p. 10000 ptd. ISBN 5-7975-0234-8.

Korolev, Iu. A. *Семейное право России: Учебное пособие.* [Family Law of Russia: Instructional Manual]. M.: Iurid. lit., 1999. 335 p. 5000 ptd. ISBN 5-7260-0937-1.

Kuznetsov, V. F., Kuznetsova, O. V. *Проблемы применения семейного кодекса.* [Problems of the Application of the Family Code]. 2nd. rev. ed. Cheliabinsk: CHGU, 1999. 211 p. 310 ptd. ISBN 5-230-20051-0.

Kuznetsova, I. M. *Семейное право.* [Family Law]. M.: Iurist', 1999. 118 p. 10000 ptd. ISBN 5-7975-0254-2.

Muratova, S. A. *Семейное право: Схемы, комментарий.* [Family Law: Diagrams, Commentary]. M.: Iurisprudentsiia, 1999. 153 p. 7000 ptd. ISBN 5-8401-0004-8.

Muratova, S. A., Tarsamaeva, N. Iu. *Семейное право: Учебное пособие.* [Family Law: Instructional Manual]. M.: Novy Iurist, 1999. 272 p. 6000 ptd. ISBN 5-7969-0061-7.

Насилие в семье: Как бороться с ним государству. [Violence in the Family: How the State Should Fight Against It]. Trans. from English. M.: Glas, 1999. 191 p. ISBN 5-7172-0043-9.

Pchelintseva, L. M. *Комментарий к Семейному кодексу Российской Федерации.* [Commentary to the Family Code of the

Russian Federation]. M.: NORMA-INFRA-M, 1999. 689 p. 6000 ptd. ISBN 5-89123-333-9, ISBN 5-86225-994-5.

Pchelintseva, L. M. *Практикум по семейному праву.* [Practical Work on Family Law]. 2d. rev. ed. M.: NORMA-INFRA-M, 1999. 248 p. 30000 ptd. ISBN 5-89123-314-2.

Pchelintseva, L. M. *Семейное право России: Учебник для вузов.* [Family Law of Russia: Textbook for Institutes of Higher Education]. M.: NORMA-INFRA-M, 1999. 672 p. 60000 ptd. ISBN 5-89123-287-1, ISBN 5-86225-929-5.

Права ребёнка: Сборник международных и российских законодательных актов. [Rights of the Child: Collection of International and Russian Legislative Acts]. M.: Novaia Volna, 1999. 127 p. 5000 ptd. ISBN 5-7864-0099-9.

Семейный кодекс Российской Федерации. [Family Code of the Russian Federation]. M., Spb.: Gerda, 1999. 112 p. 5000 ptd. ISBN 5-7978-0032-2.

Also published:

M.: Iurist', 1999. 85 p. 10000 ptd. ISBN 5-7975-0209-7.

Семейный кодекс Российской Федерации. Федеральный закон «Об актах гражданского состояния»: Официальные тексты по состоянию на 15 апреля 1999 г. [Family Code of the Russian Federation. Federal Law "On Certificates of Registration": Official Texts as of 15 April 1999]. M.: Tandem, EKMOS, 1999. 96 p. 3000 ptd. ISBN 5-88124-022-7.

Семейный кодекс Российской Федерации: С изменениями и дополнениями на 15 февраля 1999 г. [Family Code of the Russian Federation: With Changes and Additions for 15 February 1999]. M.: Prospekt, 1999. 72 p. 7000 ptd. ISBN 5-7896-0075-1.

Семейный кодекс Российской Федерации: С изменениями и дополнениями на 1 мая 1999 г. [Family Code of the Russian Federation: With Changes and Additions for 1 May 1999]. M.: Prospekt, 1999. 72 p. 5000 ptd. ISBN 5-8369-0023-X.

Семейный кодекс Российской Федерации: С изменениями и дополнениями на 15 августа 1999 г. [Family Code of the Russian Federation: With Changes and Additions for 15 August 1999]. M.: Prospekt, 1999. 72 p. 5000 ptd. ISBN 5-8369-0040-X.

Семейный кодекс Российской Федерации: С изменениями и дополнениями на 15 сентября 1999 г. [Family Code of the Russian Federation: With Changes and Additions for 15 September 1999]. M.: Prospekt, 1999. 72 p. 10000 ptd. ISBN 5-8369-0040-X.

Tarusina, N. N. *Очерки теории российского семейного права.* [Essays on the Theory of Russian Family Law]. Iaroslav: IAGU, 1999. 93 p. 200 ptd. ISBN 5-8397-0006-1.

Закон о защите детства: Законодательство Российской Федерации о защите прав ребенка. [Law on the Defence of Childhood: Legislation of the Russian Federation on Defence of the Rights of the Child]. Comps. E. M. Rybinskii, N. A. Ivanova. M.: NII detstva Ros. det. fonda, 1999. 352 p. 4000 ptd. ISBN 5-85201-347-1.

Защита прав ребёнка. [Defence of Children's Rights]. M.: Ros. blagotvorit. fond "Niet alkogolizmu i narkomanii" ("NAN"), 1999. 120 p. 1500 ptd. ISBN 5-88516-035-X.

Housing Law

Danilov, E. P. *Жилищные споры.* [Housing Disputes]. M.: Pravo i zakon, 1999. 349 p. 5000 ptd. ISBN 5-7858-0031-4.

Dubovoi, N. *Жилищно-коммунальный комплекс района в условиях экономической реформы: Кн.2. Правовые основы экономических реформ в жилищно-коммунальном хозяйстве.* [Municipal Housing Complex of the District under the Terms of Economic Reform: Book 2. Legal Fundamental Principles of Economic Reforms in the Municipal Housing Economy]. M.: Triada, Ltd, 1998-1999. 1500 ptd.

Part 1. 448 p. ISBN 5-86344-084-8.
Part 2. 572 p. ISBN 5-86344-085-6.
Part 3. 638 p. ISBN 5-86344-086-4.
Part 4. 607 p. ISBN 5-86344-086-4.

240 страниц о недвижимости. [240 Pages on Immovable Property]. M.: Dom. Advokat, 1999. 240 p. (Dom. advokat. Zhilishchnaia entsyklopedia. Issue 4). 100000 ptd. ISBN 5-89156-008-9.

Krasheninnikov, P. V. *Сделки с жилыми помещениями.* [Transactions with Dwellings]. M.: Statut, 1999. 286 p. 5000 ptd. ISBN 5-8354-0006-3.

Netrevozhko, T. A. *Квартира: покупка, продажа, обмен ...: Руководство по операциям с недвижимостью: 200 практических советов.* [The Flat: Purchase, Sale, Exchange: Guide to Operations with Immovable Property: 200 Items of Practical Advice]. 2nd rev. ed. M.: Kn. mir, 1999. 319 p. 3000 ptd. ISBN 5-8041-0019-X.

Судебная практика по жилищным спорам: Сборник постановлений, решений и определений федеральных судов. [Judicial Practice on Housing Disputes: Collection of Decrees, Decisions and Rulings of Federal Courts]. Comp. P. V. Krasheninnikov et al. M.: NORMA-INFRA-M, 1999. 585 p. 6000 ptd. ISBN 5-89123-143-3.

Titov, A. A. *Комментарий к Закону РФ «Об основах федеральной жилищной политики» (постатейный).* [Commentary to the RF Law "On the Fundamental Principles of the Federal Housing Policy" (Article by Article)]. Ed. V. B. Isakov. M.: Iurait, 1999. 301 p. 10000 ptd. ISBN 5-85294-067-4.

Titov, A. A. *Комментарий к Жилищному кодексу РСФСР: Постатейный.* [Commentary to the RSFSR Housing Code: Article by Article Commentary]. Ed. V. B. Isakov. M.: Iurait, 1999. 310 p. 10000 ptd. ISBN 5-85294-065-8.

Titov, A. A. *Комментарий к жилищному законодательству Российской Федерации: Постатейный комментарий к основным законам: Закону РФ «Об основах федеральной жилищной политики». Жилищному кодексу РСФСР. Закону РФ «О приватизации жилищного фонда в Российской Федерации».* [Commentary to the Housing Legislation of the Russian Federation: Article by Article Commentary to the Fundamental Laws: Law of the Russian Federation "On the Fundamental Principles of Federal Housing Policy". RSFSR Housing Code. Law of the Russian Federation "On the Privatisation of the Housing Fund in the Russian Federation"]. Ed. V. B. Isakov. M.: Iurait, 1999. 603 p. 10000 ptd. ISBN 5-85294-066-6.

Жилищное законодательство России: Сборник нормативных документов с комментарий. [Housing Legislation of Russia: Collection of Normative Documents with Commentary]. Comp. D. V. Primakov. M.: Biznes-Inform, 1999. 351 p. 4000 ptd. ISBN 5-89563-001-4.

Жилищный кодекс. [Housing Code]. M.: Izdanie g-na Tikhomirova M. Iu., 1999. 77 p. 3000 ptd. ISBN 5-89194-015-9.

Жилищный кодекс РСФСР: Официальный текст по состоянию на 1 февраля 1999 г. [RSFSR Housing Code: Official Text as of 1 February 1999]. Intro. P. V. Krasheninnikov. M.: NORMA-INFRA-M, 1999. 77 p. 4000 ptd. ISBN 5-89123-336-3.

Жилищный кодекс РСФСР: По состоянию на 15 февраля 1999 г. Закон Российской Федерации «Об основах федеральной жилищной политики»: По состоянию на 15 февраля 1999 г. [RSFSR Housing Code: As of 15 February 1999. Law of Russian Federation "On the Fundamental Principles of Housing Policy": As of 15 February 1999]. M.: OLMA-Press, Novosibirsk: IUKEA, 1999. 112 p. 11000 ptd. ISBN 5-224-00276-1, ISBN 5-86750-100-0.

Жилищный кодекс РСФСР: С изменениями и дополнениями на 15 февраля 1999 г. [RSFSR Housing Code: With Changes and Additions for 15 February 1999]. M.: Prospekt, 1999. 72 p. 7000 ptd. ISBN 5-7896-0076-X.

Жилищный кодекс РСФСР: С изменениями и дополнениями на 1 июня 1999 г. [RSFSR Housing Code: With Changes and Additions for 1 June 1999]. M.: Prospekt, 1999. 72 p. 10000 ptd. ISBN 5-8369-0050-7.

Жилищный кодекс РСФСР: С изменениями и дополнениями на 15 октября 1999. [RSFSR Housing Code: With Changes and Additions for 15 October 1999]. M.: Prospekt, Kodeks, 1999. 72 p. 10000 ptd. ISBN 5-8369-0050-7.

Жилищные споры: Сборник документов. [Housing Disputes: Collection of Documents]. Ed. M. Iu. Tikhomirov. M.: Izd. g-na Tikhomirova M. Iu., 1999. 152 p. 3000 ptd. ISBN 5-89194-034-5.

Competition and Anti-Monopoly Law

Конкурентное право Российской Федерации: Учебное пособие для вузов. [Competition Law of the Russian Federation: Instructional Manual for Institutes of Higher Education]. N. V. Vasileva et al. Eds. N. I. Klein, N. E. Fonarevaia. M.: Logos, 1999. 431 p. 10000 ptd. ISBN 5-88439-128-5.

О конкуренции и ограничении монополистической деятельности на товарных рынках. [On Competition and the Limitation of Monopolistic Activity on Goods' Markets]. M.: Izd. g-na Tikhomirova M. Iu., 1999. 40 p. 2000 ptd. ISBN 5-89194-105-9.

Banking and Financial Law

Бюджетный кодекс Российской Федерации: От 31 июля 1998 г. Официальный текст. [Budget Code of the Russian Federation: From 31 July 1998. Official Text]. M.: NORMA-INFRA-M, 1999. 144 p. 3000 ptd. ISBN 5-89123-295-2, ISBN 5-86225-937-6.

Бюджетный кодекс Российской Федерации: С изменениями и дополнениями на 15 сентября 1999 г. [Budget Code of the Russian Federation: With Changes and Additions for 15 September 1999]. M.: Prospekt, 1999. 157 p. 5000 ptd. ISBN 5-8369-0009-4.

Бюджетный кодекс Российской Федерации: С изменениями и дополнениями на 15 ноября 1999 г. [Budget Code of the Russian Federation: With Changes and Additions for 15 November 1999]. M.: Prospekt, 1999. 160 p. 5000 ptd. ISBN 5-8369-0009-4.

Erdelevskii, A. M. *Финансовые услуги, вексель, недвижимость: анализ и комментарий законодательства и судебной практики.* [Financial Services, Bill of Exchange, Immovable Property: Analysis and Commentary to the Legislation and Judicial Practice]. M.: BEK, 1999. 299 p. 2000 ptd. ISBN 5-85639-255-8.

Финансовое право: Учебник. [Financial Law: Textbook]. Ed. N. I. Khimichev. 2nd rev. ed. M.: Iurist', 1999. 20000 ptd. ISBN 7975-0256-9.

Фонды по защите прав вкладчиков и акционеров. [Funds for the Defence of the Rights of Depositors and Stockholders]. Eds. V. F. Ukolov, A. M. Omarov. M.: Luch. Mol. gvardiia, 1999. 108 p. 500 ptd. ISBN 6-235-02360-9.

Girev, V. N., Zemlin, A. I. *Финансовое право: Практикум.* [Financial Law: Practical Work]. M.: Iurisprudentsiia, 1999. 143 p. 8000 ptd. ISBN 5-8401-0013-7.

Gracheva, E. Iu. *Финансовое право: Схемы и комментарий.* [Financial Law: Diagrams and Commentary]. M.: Iurisprudentsiia, 1999. 96 p. 7000 ptd. ISBN 5-86532-050-3.

Gracheva, E. Iu. *Финансовое право: Учебное пособие.* [Financial Law: Instructional Manual]. 3rd. rev. ed. M.: Iurisprudentsiia, 1999. 98 p. 8000 ptd. ISBN 5-8401-0020-X.

Gracheva, E. Iu., Sokolova, E. D. *Финансовое право: Вопросы и ответы.* [Financial Law: Questions and Answers]. M.: Iurisprudentsiia, 1999. 189 p. 8000 ptd. ISBN 5-8401-0005-6.

Karaseva, M. V. *Финансовое право: Общая часть. Учебник.* [Financial Law: General Part. Textbook]. M.: Iurist', 1999. 253 p. 10000 ptd. ISBN 5-7975-0204-6.

Комментарий к Бюджетному кодексу Российской Федерации (вводный). [Commentary to the Budget Code of the Russian Federation (Introductory)]. Eds. M. V. Romanovskii, O. V. Vrublevskaia. M.: Iurait, 1999. 221 p. 5000 ptd. ISBN 5-85294-069-0.

Kravtsova, S. Iu. *Правовой режим уставного капитала банка.* [Legal Regime of the Charter Capital of a Bank]. M.: Delo, 1999. 117 p. 1000 ptd. ISBN 5-7749-0150-5.

Положение о составе затрат с постатейными материалами. [Statute on the Elements of Expenditure with Article by Article

Materials]. 2d. ed. M.: INFRA-M, 1999. 120 p. 3000 ptd. ISBN 5-16-000009-7.

Правовые основы обеспечения прав вкладчиков. [Legal Fundamental Principles of Ensuring the Rights of Depositors]. Eds. V. F. Ukolov, A. M. Omarov. M.: Luch. Mol. gvardiia, 1999. 110 p. 500 ptd. ISBN 5-235-02361-7.

Правовые проблемы организации рынка ипотечного кредитования в России. [Legal Problems of the Organisation of the Mortgage Credits Market in Russia]. Ed. V. S. Em. M.: Statut, 1999. 256 p. 10000 ptd. ISBN 5-8354-0008-X.

Currency Legislation

О валютном регулировании и валютном контроле. [On Currency Regulation and Currency Control]. M.: Izd. g-na Tikhomirova M. Iu., Iurinformtsentr, 1999. 16 p. 3000 ptd. ISBN 5-89194-025-6.

Sapozhnikov, N. V. *Валютные операции коммерческих банков. Правовое регулирование: Практическое пособие.* [Currency Operations of Commercial Banks. Legal Regulation: Practical Manual]. M.: Iurist', 1999. 254 p. 3000 ptd. ISBN 5-7975-0161-9.

Insurance

Alenichev, V. V. *Страховое законодательство России: Том 1. Зарождение, становление и развитие страхового дела X-XX вв.* [Russian Insurance Legislation: Vol.1. Birth, Formation and Development of the Insurance Business from the 10th-20th Centuries]. Eds. I. A. Isaev, V. V. Shakhov. M.: IUKIS, 1999. 623 p. 300 ptd. ISBN 5-86030-018-2.

Fogelson, Iu. *Введение в страховое право: Учебно-практическое пособие.* [Introduction to Insurance Law: Instructional Practical Manual]. M.: BEK, 1999. 255 p. 3000 ptd. ISBN 5-85639-256-6.

Fogelson, Iu. B. *Комментарий к страховому законодательству.* [Commentary to Insurance Legislation]. M.: Iurist', 1999. 284 p. 5000 ptd.

Об обязательном социальном страховании от несчастных случаев на производстве и профессиональных заболеваний: Федеральный закон Российской Федерации от 24 июля 1998 г. No.125-ФЗ. [On Obligatory Social Insurance from Production Accidents and Occupational Disease: Federal Law of the Russian Federation of 24 July 1998. No.125-F3]. M.: Aprokhim, 1999. 31 p. 3000 ptd. ISBN 5-89785-024-0.

Об организации страхового дела в Российской Федерации. [On the Organisation of Insurance Business in the Russian Federation]. M.: Izd. g-na Tikhomirova M. Iu., 1999. 29 p. 2000 ptd. ISBN 5-89194-015-9.

Bookkeeping and Audit Law

О бухгалтерском учете: Федеральный закон. [On Accountancy: Federal Law]. M.: INFRA-M, 1999. 14 p. 3000 ptd. ISBN 5-86225-692-X.

Положение по ведению бухгалтерского учёта и бухгалтерской отчётности в Российской Федерации: Утверждено Приказом Министерства финансов Российской Федерации (вводится в действие с 1 января 1999 г.). Официальный текст. [Statute on Conducting Bookkeeping Registration and Bookkeeping Accountability in the Russian Federation: Confirmed by Order of the Finance Ministry of the Russian Federation (Enters into Operation from 1 January 1999). Official Text]. M.: Marketing, 1999. 34 p. 5000 ptd. ISBN 5-7856-0073-0.

Правовые основы бухгалтерского учёта и аудиторской деятельности: Учебник. [Legal Fundamental Principles of Accountancy and Auditor Activity: Textbook]. Ed. S. G. Chaadaev. M.: Iurist', 1999. 415 p. 10000 ptd. ISBN 5-7975-0141-4.

Tolkachenko, A. A. *Судебная бухгалтерия: Учебно-практическое пособие.* [Forensic Bookkeeping: Instructional Practical Manual]. M.: Pravovoe prosveshchenie, 1999. 122 p. 5000 ptd. ISBN 5-89-661-009-2.

Agrarian Law

Аграрное законодательство Российской Федерации: Сборник нормативных правовых актов и документов. [Agrarian Legislation of the Russian Federation: Collection of Normative Legal Acts and Documents]. Comp. M. S. Pashova. M.: Iurist', 1999. 701 p. 5000 ptd. ISBN 5-7975-0175-9.

Demianenko, V. N., Demianenko, V. V. *Сельскохозяйственно-кооперативное право: Курс лекций.* [Agricultural-Cooperative Law: Course of Lectures]. Saratov: Sarat. gos. akad. prava, 1999. 259 p. 500 ptd. ISBN 5-7924-0068-7.

Проблемы правового регулирования государственного протекционизма аграрного сектора экономики в России. [Problems of the Legal Regulation of State Protectionism of the Agrarian Sector of the Economy in Russia]. Ed. G. G. Faizullin. Ufa: Poligrafkomb., 1999. 415 p. 1000 ptd. ISBN 5-85051-144-X.

Land Law

Chubukov, G. V. *Земельное право России: Курс лекций.* [Land Law of Russia: Course of Lectures]. M.: MAEP, 1999. 128 p. 1000 ptd. ISBN 5-93417-001-5.

Документы в земельных правоотношениях. [Documents in Land Relations]. Ed. M. Iu. Tikhomirov. M.: Iurinformtsentr, 1999. 55 p. 3000 ptd. ISBN 5-89194-039-6.

Erofeev, B. V. *Земельное право.* [Land Law]. 3rd rev. ed. M.: MTSUPL, 1999. 559 p. 5000 ptd. ISBN 5-86095-206-6.

Ikonitskaia, I. A. *Земельное право Российской Федерации.* [Land Law of the Russian Federation]. In-t gosudarstva i prava RAN. M., 1999. 127 p. 1600 ptd. ISBN 5-88720-058-8.

Vedenin, N. N. *Земельное право: Вопросы и ответы.* [Land Law: Questions and Answers]. M.: Novy Iurist, 1999. 104 p. 5000 ptd. ISBN 5-7969-0063-3.

Also published:

M.: Iurisprudentsiia, 1999. 112 p. 6000 ptd. ISBN 5-8401-0017-X. (2nd. rev. ed.)

Земельное право: Учебник для вузов. [Land Law: Textbook for Institutes of Higher Education]. Ed. S. A. Bogoliubov. M.: NORMA-INFRA-M, 1999. 388 p. 30000 ptd. ISBN 5-89123-228-6, ISBN 5-86225-734-9.

Земельный кодекс. [Land Code]. M.: Izdanie g-na Tikhomirova M. Iu., 1999. 61 p. 3000 ptd. ISBN 5-89104-015-9.

Земельные споры: Сборник документов. [Land Disputes: Collection of Documents]. Ed. M. Iu. Tikhomirov. M.: Izd. g-na Tikhomirova M. Iu., 1999. 376 p. 30000 ptd. ISBN 5-89194-030-2.

Земля и право: Сборник нормативных актов. [Land and Law: Collection of Normative Acts]. Ed. V. Kh. Uliukaev. M.: Bylina, 1999. 511 p. 3000 ptd. ISBN 5-88528-247-1.

Environmental and Natural Resource Law

Bogoliubov, S. A. *Экологическое право: Учебник для вузов.* [Ecological Law: Textbook for Institutes of Higher Education]. M.: NORMA-INFRA-M, 1999. 433 p. 50000 ptd. ISBN 5-89123-259-6, ISBN 5-86225-839-6.

Brinchuk, M. M. *Экологическое право: Учебник.* [Ecological Law: Textbook]. M.: Iurist', 1999. 351 p. 10000 ptd. ISBN 5-7975-0237-2.

Экологическое право России: Сборник материалов научно-практических конференций 1995-1998 гг. [Ecological Law of Russia: Collection of Materials from Scientific-Practical Conferences from 1995-1998]. Comps. I. A. Ignatieva, A. K. Golichenkov. M.: Zertsalo, 1999. 394 p. 2000 ptd. ISBN 5-8078-0044-3.

Erofeev, B. V. *Экологическое право: Учебник для вузов.* [Ecological Law: Textbook for Institutes of Higher Education]. M.: Iurisprudentsiia, 1999. 445 p. 8000 ptd. ISBN 5-86532-044-0.

Kleandrov, M. I. *Нефтегазовое законодательство в системе*

российского права. [Oil and Gas Legislation in the System of Russian Law]. Eds. V. V. Laptev, V. F. Iakovlev. Novosibirsk: Nauka, Sib. izd. firma RAN, 1999. 144 p. 500 ptd. ISBN 5-02-031550-8.

Комментарий к Федеральному закону «Об экологической экспертизе». [Commentary to the Federal Law "On Ecological Expertise"]. Ed. M. M. Brinchuk. M.: BEK, 1999. 203 p. 5000 ptd. ISBN 5-85639-262-0.

Комментарий к Закону Российской Федерации «Об охране окружающей природной среды». [Commentary to the Russian Federation Law "On the Protection of the Environment"]. Ed. S. A. Bogoliubov. M.: NORMA-INFRA-M, 1999. 368 p. 20000 ptd. ISBN 5-89123-067-4.

Kuznetsova, N. V. *Экологическое право.* [Ecological Law]. 2nd. rev. ed. M.: Iurisprudentsiia, 1999. 156 p. 7000 ptd. ISBN 5-8401-0022-6.

Novikova, E. V. *Частное право и экологическое законодательство: влияние и соотношение.* [Private Law and Ecological Legislation: Influence and Correlation]. M.: Iurist', 1999. 63 p. 1000 ptd. ISBN 5-7975-0286-0.

Основы экологического права: Учебное пособие. [Fundamental Principles of Ecological Law: Instructional Manual]. Ed. I. A. Eremichev. M.: MIUI MVD Rossii, Shchyt-M, 1999. 117 p. 3000 ptd. ISBN 5-93004-049-4.

Сборник законодательных актов об охране окружающей среды. [Collection of Legislative Acts on the Protection of the Environment]. Orel: Izdatel Pikalin, 1999. 312 p. 500 ptd.

Vedenin, N. N. *Экологическое право: Вопросы и ответы.* [Ecological Law: Questions and Answers]. M.: Iurisprudentsiia, 1999. 126 p. 7000 ptd. ISBN 5-8401-0014-5.

Водный кодекс Российской Федерации: Официальный текст по состоянию на 15 февраля 1999 г. [Water Code of the Russian Federation: Official Text for 15 February 1999]. M.: NORMA-INFRA-M, 1999. 87 p. 2000 ptd. ISBN 5-89123-298-7, ISBN 5-86225-943-0.

Водный кодекс Российской Федерации: С изменениями и дополнениями по состоянию на 1 октября 1999 г. [Water Code of the Russian Federation: With Changes and Additions for 1 October 1999]. 4th ed. M.: NORMA-INFRA-M, 1999. 78 p. 2000 ptd. ISBN 5-89123-298-7, ISBN 5-86225-943-0.

Transport Law

Egiazarov, V. A. *Транспортное право: Учебное пособие.* [Transport Law: Instructional Manual]. M.: Iurid. lit., 1999. 272 p. 3000 ptd. ISBN 5-7260-0930-4.

Если вас остановил инспектор: Ваши права. [If an Inspector Stops You: Your Rights]. M.: Avers, 1999. 81 p. 100000 ptd. ISBN 5-7198-0041-7.

Iaroshik, O. D., Ruslanova, I. N. *Справочник по проблемам дорожно-транспортного происшествия: Дорожно-транспортное происшествие: Кто виноват? Что делать?* [Manual on the Problems of Road Transport Accidents: The Road Transport Accident: Who is to Blame? What is to be Done?]. M.: Atlasy avtomobilei, 1999. 191 p. 30000 ptd. ISBN 5-8245-0004-5.

Volgin, V. V. *Дорожно-транспортные происшествия. От причины до расплаты: Практическое пособие.* [Road Transport Accidents. From Cause to Payment: Practical Manual]. M.: Livr, 1999. 112 p. 10000 ptd. ISBN 5-89104-057-3.

Воздушный кодекс Российской Федерации: С изменениями и дополнениями по состоянию на 1 октября 1999 г. [Air Code of the Russian Federation: With Changes and Additions for 1 October 1999]. 4th ed. M.: NORMA-INFRA-M, 1999. 75 p. 3000 ptd. ISBN 5-89123-330-4, ISBN 5-86225-990-2.

Забайкальская транспортная ...: Штрихи к истории Забайкал. трансп. милиции. [Beyond the Baikal Transport ...: Features of the History of Beyond the Baikal Transport]. Ed. V. G. Prudnikov. Comp. E. O. Khavkin. Chita, Poisk, 1999. 304 p. 3000 ptd. ISBN 5-93119-026-0.

Maritime Law

Кодекс торгового мореплавания Российской Федерации. [Merchant Shipping Code of the Russian Federation]. M.: B-chka "Ros. gazety", 1999. 191 p. 10000 ptd.

Also published:

M.: Kontrakt RL, Red. gazety "Morskie vesti Rossii", 1999. 239 p. 5000 ptd. ISBN 5-86502-036-6.

Кодекс торгового мореплавания Российской Федерации: Принят Государственной Думой 31 марта 1999 г. [Merchant Shipping Code of the Russian Federation: Adopted by the State Duma on 31 March 1999]. Spb.: ZAO "TSNIIMF", 1999. 335 p. 1500 ptd. ISBN 5-8072-0022-5.

Air Law

Воздушный кодекс Российской Федерации: Официальный текст по состоянию на 1 ноября 1998 г. [Air Code of the Russian Federation: Official Text as of 1 November 1998]. M.: NORMA-INFRA-M, 1999. 75 p. 2000 ptd. ISBN 5-89123-299-5, ISBN 5-86225-944-9.

Воздушный кодекс Российской Федерации: Официальный текст по состоянию на 1 января 1999 г. [Air Code of the Russian Federation: Official Text as of 1 January 1999]. M.: NORMA-INFRA-M, 1999. 75 p. 3000 ptd. ISBN 5-89123-330-4, ISBN 5-86225-990-2.

Communications and Mass Media Law

Краткий юридический справочник для журналистов. [A Short Legal Manual for Journalists]. Comp. D. Ibodov. M.: Galeriia, 1999. 136 p. 600 ptd. ISBN 5-8137-0024-2.

О средствах массовой информации. Об информации, информатизации и защите информации. [On the Mass Media. On Information, Informatisation and the Defence of Information]. M.: Izd. g-na Tikhomirova M. Iu., 1999. 47 p. 3000 ptd. ISBN 5-89194-027-2.

Rassolov, M. M. *Информационное право: Учебное пособие.*

[Informational Law: Instructional Manual]. M.: Iurist', 1999. 400 p. 5000 ptd. ISBN 5-7975-0179-1.

Labour Law

Ershov, V. V., Ershova, E. A. *Трудовой договор: Учебное пособие.* [Labour Contract: Instructional Manual]. M.: Delo, 1999. 351 p. 5000 ptd. ISBN 5-7749-0128-9.

Golenko, E. N., Kovalev, V. I. *Трудовое право: Схемы и комментарий.* [Labour Law: Diagrams and Commentary]. M.: Iurisprudentsiia, 1999. 176 p. 7000 ptd. ISBN 5-86532-050-5.

Кодекс законов о труде Российской Федерации. [Code of Laws on Labour of the Russian Federation]. M.: NORMA-INFRA-M, 1999. 134 p. 6000 ptd. ISBN 5-86225-998-8.
Also published:
M.: Novaia Volna, 1999. 126 p. 5000 ptd. ISBN 5-7864-0032-8.

Кодекс законов о труде Российской Федерации: Официальный текст по состоянию на 15 мая 1999 г. [Code of Laws on Labour of the Russian Federation: Official Text as of 15 May 1999]. M.: Tandem, EKMOS, 1999. 79 p. 3000 ptd. ISBN 5-88124-050-2.

Кодекс законов о труде Российской Федерации: Официальный текст по состоянию на 15 ноября 1999 г. [Code of Laws on Labour of the Russian Federation: Official Text for 15 November 1999]. M.: TANDEM, EKMOS, 1999. 80 p. 5000 ptd. ISBN 5-88124-050-2.

Кодекс законов о труде Российской Федерации: По состоянию на 15 февраля 1999 г. [Code of Laws on Labour of the Russian Federation: As of 15 February 1999]. M.: OLMA-Press, Novosibirsk: IUKEA, 1999. 160 p. 11000 ptd. ISBN 5-224-00281-8, ISBN 5-86750-123-X.

Кодекс Законов о труде Российской Федерации: По состоянию на 1 июля 1999 г. [Code of Laws on Labour of the Russian Federation: For 1 July 1999]. M.: Iurist', 1999. 100 p. 10000 ptd. ISBN 5-7975-0232-1.
Also published:

M.: Prospekt, 1999. 95 p. 15000 ptd. ISBN 5-8369-0005-1. (With Changes and Additions for 15 September 1999].

Кодекс законов о труде Российской Федерации: С изменениями и дополнениями на 1 февраля 1999 г. [Code of Laws on Labour of the Russian Federation: With Changes and Additions for 1 February 1999]. M.: Prospekt, 1999. 93 p. 10000 ptd. ISBN 5-7896-0044-1.

Кодекс законов о труде Российской Федерации: С изменениями и дополнениями на 1 апреля 1999 г. [Code of Laws on Labour of the Russian Federation: With Changes and Additions for 1 April 1999]. M.: Prospekt, 1999. 95 p. 1000 ptd. ISBN 5-8369-0005-1.

Кодекс законов о труде Российской Федерации: С изменениями и дополнениями на 15 августа 1999 г. [Code of Laws on Labour of the Russian Federation: With Changes and Additions for 15 August 1999]. M.: Prospekt, 1999. 95 p. 10000 ptd. ISBN 5-8369-0005-1.

Коллективный договор. [Collective Contract]. Comp. A. V. Verkhovtsev. M.: INFRA-M, 1999. 64 p. 3000 ptd. ISBN 5-16-000017-8.

Комментарий к Кодексу Законов о Труде Российской Федерации. [Commentary to the Code of Laws on Labour of the Russian Federation]. Ed. K. N. Gusov. 3rd. rev. ed. M.: Prospekt, 1999. 605 p. 20000 ptd. ISBN 5-7986-0020-3.

Also published:
M.: Prospekt, 1999. 621 p. 15000 ptd. ISBN 5-8369-0024-8. (4th ed.)

Комментарий к Кодексу законов о труде Российской Федерации (постатейный). [Commentary to the Code of Laws on Labour of the Russian Federation (Article by Article)]. Comp. A. B. Borisov. M.: Knizh. mir, 1999. 824 p. ISBN 5-8041-0045-9.

Комментарий к Кодексу законов о труде Российской Федерации: С изменениями и дополнениями на 5 мая 1999 г. [Commentary to the Code of Laws on Labour of the Russian Federation: With Changes and Additions for 5 May 1999]. Iu. N. Korshunov et al. M.: Spark, 1999. 576 p. 12000 ptd. ISBN 5-88914-121-X.

Комментарий к Кодексу законов о труде Российской Федерации: Текст Кодекса законов о труде РФ приводится по состоянию на 30 сентября 1998 г. [Commentary to the Code of Laws on Labour of the Russian Federation: Text of the RF Code of Laws on Labour from 30 September 1998]. 2d. rev. ed. M.: INFRA-M, 1999. XVI, 784 p. 60000 ptd. ISBN 5-86225-942-2.

Московское трехсторонние соглашение на 1999 год между Правительством Москвы, московскими объединениями профсоюзов и московскими объединениями предпринимателей (работодателей). [Moscow Three-Sided Agreement for 1999 Between the Government of Moscow, Moscow Associations of Trade Unions and Moscow Associations of Entrepreneurs (Employers)]. M.: Infomart, 1999. 16 p. 20000 ptd.

Netesov, A. V. *Современный трудовой договор (контракт): Нормативные акты.* [Contemporary Labour Contract: Normative Acts]. M.: Spb.: Gerda, 1999. 286 p. 5000 ptd. ISBN 5-7978-0051-9.

Об основах охраны труда в Российской Федерации: Федеральный закон. Официальный текст. [On the Fundamental Principles of the Protection of Labour in the Russian Federation: Federal Law. Official Text]. M.: Marketing, 1999. 26 p. 5000 ptd. ISBN 5-7856-0104-4.

Об основах охраны труда в Российской Федерации: Федеральный закон Российской Федерации от 17 июля 1999 г. No.181-ФЗ. [On the Fundamental Principles of the Protection of Labour in the Russian Federation: Federal Law of the Russian Federation of 17 July 1999. No.181-F3]. M.: Aprokhim, 1999. 27 p. 2000 ptd. ISBN 5-89785-027-5.

Практикум по российскому трудовому праву: Для вузов. [Practical Work on Russian Labour Law: For Institutes of Higher Education]. A. A. Abramova et al. M.: NORMA-INFRA-M, 1999. 688 p. 30000 ptd. ISBN 5-89123-343-6, ISBN 5-86225-906-6.

Pustozerova, V. M. *Комментарий КЗоТ РФ: С изменениями и дополнениями.* [Commentary to the Code of Laws on Labour of the Russian Federation: With Changes and Additions]. M.: PRIOR, 1999.

512 p. 14000 ptd. ISBN 5-7990-0151-6.

Рабочее место: права и право. [Place of Work: Rights and the Law]. A. Gerasimov et al. M.: Dom. advokat, 1999. 208 p. 20000 ptd. ISBN 5-89156-009-7.

Российское трудовое право: Учебник. [Russian Labour Law: Textbook]. Ed. A. D. Zaikin. M.: NORMA-INFRA-M, 1999. 415 p. 50000 ptd. ISBN 5-89123-127-1, ISBN 5-86225-538-9.

Sannikova, L. V. *Договор найма труда в России.* [Contract for Hired Labour in Russia]. M.: MT-Press, 1999. 120 p. 3000 ptd. ISBN 5-86567-024-8.

Сборник нормативных актов о труде. [Collection of Normative Acts on Labour]. Comp. N. P. Sharilo. M.: Iurid. lit., 1999. 704 p. 5000 ptd. ISBN 5-7260-0904-5.

Сборник нормативно-правовых документов по охране труда. [Collection of Normative Legal Documents on the Protection of Labour]. Ed. Iu. I. Kadochnikov. Tiumen: Tium. izd. dom, 1999. 472 p. 10000 ptd. ISBN 5-88131-111-6.

Тарифно-квалификационные характеристики по должностям служащих. [Tariff Qualification Characteristics for Employees' Posts]. M.: INFRA-M, 1999. 108 p. 40000 ptd. ISBN 5-86225-402-1.

Tikhomirov, M. Iu. *Трудовые договоры (контракты): Образцы документов, комментарий, нормативные акты.* [Labour Contracts: Models of Documents, Commentary, Normative Acts]. M.: Izdanie g-na Tikhomirova M. Iu., 1999. 324 p. 20000 ptd. ISBN 5-89194-009-4.

Tikhomirov, M. Iu. *Трудовые контракты.* [Labour Contracts]. M.: Izd. g-na Tikhomirova M. Iu., 1999. 54 p. 3000 ptd. ISBN 5-89194-023-X.

Труд молодежи: Комментарий к КЗоТ. [The Labour of Youth: Commentary to the Code of Laws on Labour]. M.: INFRA-M, 1999. 107 p. 3000 ptd. ISBN 5-16-000041-0.

Труд женщин. [Women's Labour]. M.: INFRA-M, 1999. 64 p. 3000 ptd. ISBN 5-16-000040-2.

Трудовое и социальное право России: Для вузов. [Labour and Social Law of Russia: For Institutes of Higher Education]. Ed. L. N. Anisimov. M.: VLADOS, Mosk. gos. sotsialny un-t, 1999. 431 p. 10000 ptd. ISBN 5-691-00347-X.

Трудовое право: Учебник. [Labour Law: Textbook]. Ed. O. V. Smirnov. 3rd. rev. ed. M.: Prospekt, 1999. 512 p. 10000 ptd. ISBN 5-8369-0031-0.

Трудовое право России: Учебник для вузов. [Labour Law of Russia: Textbook for Institutes of Higher Education]. Eds. R. Z. Livshitz, Iu. P. Orlovskii. M.: NORMA-INFRA-M, 1999. 473 p. 60000 ptd. ISBN 5-89123-175-1, ISBN 5-86225-672-5.

Трудовое законодательство: Сборник нормативных актов по состоянию на 15 августа 1999 г. [Labour Legislation: Collection of Normative Acts for 15 August 1999]. Comp. K. N. Gusov. 4th rev. ed. M.: Prospekt, 1999. 406 p. 5000 ptd. ISBN 5-8369-0039-6.

Трудовой кодекс Российской Федерации: Проект федерального закона. [Labour Code of the Russian Federation: Draft of the Federal Law]. M.: Marketing, 1999. 171 p. 5000 ptd. ISBN 5-7856-0105-2.

Трудовые споры: Сборник документов. [Labour Disputes: Collection of Documents]. Ed. M. Iu. Tikhomirov. Comp. O. M. Ogliblin. M.: Izd. g-na Tikhomirova M. Iu.. Iurinformtsentr, 1999. 200 p. 3000 ptd. ISBN 5-89194-035-3.

Vlasov, V. I., Krapivin, O. M. *Комментарий к законодательству о занятости и трудоустройстве населения.* [Commentary to the Legislation on the Employment and Arrangement of Labour of the Population]. M.: NORMA-INFRA-M, 1999. 357 p. 30000 ptd. ISBN 5-89123-362-2, ISBN 5-86225-916-3.

Zaikin, A. D., Remizov, K. S. *Экономико-правовое регулирование труда и заработной платы: Учебник для вузов.* [Economical-Legal Regulation of Labour and Wages: Textbook for Institutes of

Higher Education]. M.: NORMA-INFRA-M, 1999. 315 p. 30000 ptd. ISBN 5-89123-345-2, ISBN 5-16-000010-0.

Законодательство о труде: надзор и контроль. [Legislation on Labour: Supervision and Control]. Comp. A. V. Verkhovtsev. M.: INFRA-M, 1999. 72 p. 3000 ptd. ISBN 5-16-000093-3.

Заработная плата: Комментарий к КЗоТ. [Wages: Commentary to the Code of Laws on Labour]. Comp. A. V. Verkhovtsev. 2nd. rev. ed. M.: INFRA-M, 1999. 144 p. 18000 ptd. ISBN 5-86225-917-1.

Social Security

Azarova, E. G., Kondratieva, Z. A. *Комментарий к Закону Российской Федерации «О государственных пенсиях в Российской Федерации» (постатейный): Текст Закона по состоянию на 1 декабря 1998 г.* [Commentary to the Russian Federation Law "On State Pensions in the Russian Federation" (Article by Article): Text of Law as of 1 December 1998]. M.: NORMA-INFRA-M, 1999. 215 p. 3000 ptd. ISBN 5-89123-322-3, ISBN 5-86225-979-1.

Чернобыль 13: Права и льготы: Сборник нормативных документов о социальной защите граждан, подвергшихся воздействию радиации вследствие катастрофы на Чернобыл. АЕС, ядерных испытаний на Семипалатин. полигоне, аварии в 1957 году на ПО «Маяк» и сбросов радиоактив. отходов в реку Теча. [Chernobyl 13: Rights and Privileges: Collection of Normative Documents on the Social Defence of Citizens Subjected to the Effect of Radiation as a Consequence of the Disaster at the Chernobyl Nuclear Plant, the Nuclear Tests at the Semipalatinsk Site, the Accident in 1957 at the Industrial Combine "Maiak" and the Disposal of Radioactive Waste in the River Techa]. Comps. V. N. Kurashov, N. G. Kurashova. Posad: Melekess, 1999. 242 p. 1000 ptd.

Golenko, E. N., Kovalev, V. I. *Право социального обеспечения: Схемы и комментарии.* [Law of Social Security: Diagrams and Commentaries]. M.: Iurisprudentsiia, 1999. 182 p. 8000 ptd. ISBN 5-8401-0002-1.

Государственное социальное страхование. [State Social

Security]. Comp. A. V. Verkhovtsev. M.: INFRA-M, 1999. 144 p. 3000 ptd. ISBN 5-16-000091-7.

Machulskaia, E. E. *Практикум по праву социального обеспечения: Для вузов.* [Practical Work on the Right to Social Security: For Institutes of Higher Education]. M.: NORMA-INFRA-M, 1999. 240 p. 30000 ptd. ISBN 5-89123-275-8.

Machulskaia, E. E. *Право социального обеспечения: Для вузов.* [Right to Social Security: For Institutes of Higher Education]. 2d. rev. ed. M.: Knizh. mir, 1999. 239 p. (Vysh. shkola). 4000 ptd. ISBN 5-8041-0006-8.

Constitutional Law

Baglai, M. V. *Конституционное право Российской Федерации: Учебник.* [Constitutional Law of the Russian Federation: Textbook]. 2nd. rev. ed. M.: NORMA-INFRA-M, 1999. 776 p. 60000 ptd. ISBN 5-89123-329-0, ISBN 5-86225-989-9.

Chirkin, V. E. *Государствоведение: Учебник.* [Constitutional Law: Textbook]. M.: Iurist', 1999. 398 p. 5000 ptd. ISBN 5-7975-0164-3.

Ermakov, V. G. *Федерация как форма государственного устройства России.* [The Federation as a Form of State Structure of Russia]. M.: Bylina, 1999. 192 p. 550 ptd. ISBN 5-88528-238-2.

Федеральный конституционный закон «О правительстве Российской Федерации»: Комментарий. [Federal Constitutional Law "On the Government of the Russian Federation": Commentary]. Ed. L. A. Okunkov. M.: Iurid. lit., 1999. 480 p. 3000 ptd. ISBN 5-7260-0929-0.

Glotov, S. A. *Конституционно-правовые проблемы сотрудничества России и Совета Европы.* [Constitutional and Legal Problems of the Cooperation of Russia and the Council of Europe]. Saratov: Izd-vo Sarat. Gos. Akad. Prava, 1999. 544 p. 2500 ptd. ISBN 5-7924-0062-X.

Katkov, D. B., Korchigo, E. V. *Конституционное право России:*

Учебное пособие. [Constitutional Law of Russia: Instructional Manual]. Ed. Iu. A. Vedeneev. M.: Iurisprudentsiia, 1999. 288 p. 8000 ptd. ISBN 5-8401-0007-2.

Koliushin, E. I. *Конституционное (государственное) право России: Курс лекций.* [Constitutional (State) Law of Russia: Course of Lectures]. M.: Izd-vo Mosk. un-ta, 1999. 381 p. 3000 ptd. ISBN 5-211-04088-0.

Конституция Российской Федерации. [Constitution of the Russian Federation]. M.: Novy Iurist, 1999. 46 p. 10000 ptd. ISBN 5-7969-0066-8.

Also published:
Spb.: Litera, 1999. 48 p. 15000 ptd. ISBN 5-86617-034-5.
M.: Iurait, 1999. 46 p. 10000 ptd. ISBN 5-85294-008-9.
M.: NORMA-INFRA-M, 1999. 75 p. 24000 ptd. ISBN 5-89123-308-8.
M.: Filin', 1999. 64 p. 5000 ptd. ISBN 5-89568-138-7.
M.: Prospekt, 1999. 48 p. 40000 ptd. ISBN 5-7896-0085-9.
M.: Delo, 1999. 40 p. 5000 ptd. ISBN 5-7749-0151-3.
M.: AST 1999. 63 p. 20000 ptd. ISBN 5-237-02346-0.

Конституция Российской Федерации: Принята 12 декабря 1993 г. [Constitution of the Russian Federation: Adopted 12 December 1993]. Intro. V. B. Isakov. M., 1999. 184 p. 5000 ptd. ISBN 5-7918-0043-6.

Конституция Российской Федерации: Принята всенарод. голосованием 12 декабря 1993 г. Официальный текст по состоянию на 1 февраля 1999 г. [Constitution of the Russian Federation: Adopted by All-People's Voting on 12 December 1993. Official Text for 1 February 1999]. M.: NORMA-INFRA-M, 1999. 75 p. 8000 ptd. ISBN 5-89123-337-1, ISBN 5-86225-983-X.

Also published:
Spb.: Izd. Dom A. Gromova, 1999. 63 p. 10000 ptd. ISBN 5-89138-007-2.

Конституционное право: Учебник. [Constitutional Law: Textbook]. Ed. V. V. Lazarev. M.: Iurist', 1999. 592 p. 10000 ptd. ISBN 5-7975-0259-3.

Конституционное право России: Схемы, комментарии. Пособие. [Constitutional Law of Russia: Diagrams, Commentaries. Manual]. M.: Iurisprudentsiia, 1999. 64 p. 7000 ptd. ISBN 5-86532-043-2.

Конституционное право в вопросах в ответах. [Constitutional Law in Questions and Answers]. Ed. A. V. Malko. M.: Iurist', 1999. 228 p. 10000 ptd. ISBN 5-7975-0162-7.

Конституционное законодательство России. [Constitutional Legislation of Russia]. Ed. Iu. A. Tikhomirov. M.: Gorodets - Formula prava, 1999. 382 p. ISBN 5-89391-045-1.

Kozlova, E. I., Kutafin, O. E. *Конституционное право.* [Constitutional Law]. M.: Iurist', 1999. 304 p. 10000 ptd. ISBN 5-7975-0201-1.

Mikhailov, D. *Конституционное право граждан на жилище в Российской Федерации.* [Constitutional Rights of Citizens to Housing in the Russian Federation]. M.: Ves' Mir, 1999. 59 p. 500 ptd. ISBN 5-7777-0078-0.

Российский конституционализм: проблемы и решения: Материалы международных конфер. [Russian Constitutionalism: Problems and Decisions: Materials from International Conferences]. M.: In-t gosudarstva i prava RAN, 1999. 247 p. 1200 ptd. ISBN 5-8339-0004-2.

Rudinskii, F. M. *«Дело КПСС» в Конституционном Суде: Записки участника процесса.* ["Case of the Communist Party of the Soviet Union" in the Constitutional Court": Notes of a Participant of the Trial]. M.: Bylina, 1999. 503 p. 2000 ptd.

Сборник нормативных актов по конституционному праву Российской Федерации: Том 4. [Collection of Normative Acts on the Constitutional Law of the Russian Federation: Vol.4]. Comps. A. P. Vorobiev, P. G. Shchekochikhin. Ed. P. G. Shchekochikhin. Ekaterinburg. FGUIPP "Ural. rabochii", 1999. 1045 p. 2000 ptd. ISBN 5-85383-159-3.

Vol.5. Ekaterinburg: Ural. rabochii, 1999. 956 p. 2000 ptd. ISBN

5-85383-163-1.

Shaio, A. *Самоограничение власти: Краткий курс конституционализма.* [Self-Limitation of Power: A Short Course on Constitutionalism]. Trans. from Hungarian. M.: Iurist', 1999. 292 p. 3000 ptd. ISBN 5-7975-0235-6.

Parliament

Elchev, V. A. *Аппарат Государственной Думы и законотворческий процесс.* [Apparatus of the State Duma and the Law Creation Process]. M.: Pamiatniki ist. mysli, 1999. 256 p. 1000 ptd. ISBN 5-88451-073-X.

Gagut, L. *Государственная Дума.* [State Duma]. M.: Rus, 1999. 96 p. 1000 ptd. ISBN 5-89655-014-6.

Государственная Дума: Стенограмма заседаний. [State Duma: Record of Sessions]. M.: Izvestiia, 1999. 500 ptd.

Vol.7 (30). 1996. Spring Session. 21 June - 17 July. 704 p.
Vol.9 (32). 1996. Autumn Session. 2-16 October. 751 p.
Vol.10 (33). 1996. Autumn Session. 18 October-11 November. 687 p.
Vol.11 (34). 1996. Autumn Session. 13-29 November. 640 p.
Vol.12 (35). 1996. Autumn Session. 4-15 December. 736 p.
Vol.13 (36). 1996. Autumn Session. 18-28 December. 671 p.
Vol.14 (37). 1997. Spring Session. 15 January-5 February. 816 p.
Vol.15 (38). 1997. Spring Session. 7-20 February. 704 p.
Vol.17 (40). 1997. Spring Session. 19 March-4 April. 671 p.
Vol.18 (41). 1997. Spring Session. 9-24 April. 831 p.
Vol.49 (72). 1999. Spring Session. 13-15 May. 528 p.

Grankin, I. V. *Парламент России.* [Russia's Parliament]. M.: Konsaltbankir, 1999. 304 p. 1000 ptd. ISBN 5-85187-089-3.

Комментарий к Гражданскому законодательству Российской Федерации о хозяйственных обществах. [Commentary to the Civil Legislation of the Russian Federation on Economic Societies]. M.: Izd. g-na Tikhomirova, 1999. 462 p. 20000 ptd. ISBN 5-89194-019-1.

Lapaeva, V. V. *Право и многопартийность в современной России.* [The Law and Multi-Party System in Contemporary Russia]. M.: NORMA, 1999. 296 p. 3000 ptd.

Okunkov, L. A. Roshchin, V. A. *Вето Президента: Научно-практическое пособие.* [The President's Veto: Scientific-Practical Manual]. M.: Gorodets, Formula prava, 1999. 347 p. 1500 ptd. ISBN 5-89391-043-5.

Парламентское право России. [Russian Parliamentary Law]. Eds. I. M. Stepanov, T. Ia. Khabrievaia. M.: Iurist', 1999. 391 p. 5000 ptd. ISBN 5-7975-0127-9.

Правила оформления документов в Государственной Думе Федерального Собрания Российской Федерации. [Rules for the Formulation of Documents in the State Duma of the Federal Assembly of the Russian Federation]. M.: Izd. Gos. Dumy, 1999. 79 p. 1500 ptd.

Сборник документов и материалов Специальной комиссии Государственной Думы Федерального Собрания Российской Федерации по оценке соблюдения процедурных правил и фактической обоснованности обвинения, выдвинутого против Президента Российской Федерации, и их рассмотрения Государственной Думой 13-15 мая 1999 года. [Collection of Documents and Materials of the Special Commission of the State Duma of the Federal Assembly of the Russian Federation for the Appraisal of Observance of Procedural Rules and the Actual Justification of the Accusation Brought Against the President of the Russian Federation and Their Examination by the State Duma on 13-15 May 1999]. Comps. V. D. Filimonov, T. V. Lazarev, P. P. Lopata. Ed. V. D. Filimonov. M.: Izd. Gos. Dumy, 1999. 999 p. 1000 ptd. ISBN 5-86656-093-3.

Shokhin, A. *Шестая Государственная Дума: законотворчество и политика.* [Sixth State Duma: Law Creation and Politics]. M., 1999. 183 p. 3000 ptd.

Vasetskii, N. A., Krasnov, Iu. K. *Парламентаризм в действии: Государственная Дума Федерального Собрания РФ в 1994-1998 гг.* [Parliamentarism in Action: State Duma of the Federal Assembly of the Russian Federation in 1994-1998]. M.: Izd. Gos. Dumy, 1999. 55 p. 1000 ptd.

Zorin, V. Iu., Amanzholova, D. A., Kuleshov, S. V. *Национальный вопрос в Государственных Думах России.* [The National Question in the State Dumas of Russia]. M.: Rus. mir, 1999. 520 p. 3000 ptd. ISBN 5-85810-048-1.

Elections

Astafichev, P. A. *Избирательное право России: современное состояние и перспективы развития.* [Electoral Law of Russia: Contemporary Condition and Development Prospects]. Orel: ORAGS, 1999. 201 p. 500 ptd. ISBN 5-93179-016-0.

Avakian, T. A. *Выборы-99 депутатов Государственной Думы: правила и процедуры.* [Elections-99 of Deputies of the State Duma: Rules and Procedures]. M.: Mezhdunar. obshchesv. fond "Interligal", 1999. 112 p.

Barashkov, Iu. *Депутат СССР.* [A Deputy of the USSR]. 2d. rev. ed. Arkhangelsk: Pravda Severa, 1999. 287 p. 300 ptd. ISBN 5-85879-110-8.

Федеральный закон «О выборах депутатов Государственной Думы Федерального Собрания Российской Федерации». [Federal Law "On Elections of Deputies of the State Duma of the Federal Assembly of the Russian Federation"]. M.: Tsentr. izbirat. komissiia Ros. Federatsii, 1999. 256 p. 200000 ptd.

Also published:

M.: Tsentr. izbirat. komissii Ros. Federatsii, 1999. 256 p. 1000 ptd.

Федеральный закон «Об основных гарантиях избирательных прав и права на участие в референдуме граждан Российской Федерации»: С изменениями и дополнениями внесенными Федеральным законом от 30 марта 1999 г. No.55-ФЗ «О внесении изменений и доп. в Федеральный закон «Об основных гарантиях избирательных прав и права на участие в референдуме граждан Российской Федерации». [Federal Law "On the Basic Guarantees of Electoral Rights and Rights of Citizens to Participate in the Referendum of the Russian Federation": With Changes and Additions Introduced by the Federal Law of 30 March 1999 No.55-F3 "On the Introduction of Changes and Additions to the Federal Law "On the Basic Guarantees of Electoral Rights and Rights of Citizens to Participate in the Referendum of the Russian Federation"]. M.: Tsentr. izbirat. komis. Ros. Federatsii, 1999. 160 p. 1000 ptd.

Khalipov, V. F., Khalipova, E. V., Shishkin, A. N. *Выборы и власть.* [Elections and Power]. M.: Sovershenstvo, 1999. 378 p. 10000 ptd. ISBN 5-8089-0032-8.

Ignatenko, V. V., Ishchenko, E. P. *Юридическая ответственность за нарушения избирательного законодательства.* [Legal Responsibility for the Violation of Electoral Legislation]. M.: RTSOIT, 1999. 96 p. 3000 ptd. ISBN 5-93639-002-0.

Ishchenko, A. E., Ishchenko, E. P. *Выбираю в первый раз: Молодому избирателю об основах российского избирательного права и избирательного процесса.* [I Am Voting for the First Time: For the Young Voter About the Fundamental Principles of Russian Electoral Law and the Electoral Process]. M.: RTSOIT, 1999. 25 p. 5000 ptd. ISBN 5-93639-044-7.

Iusov, S. V., Tkachev, V. N., Kharkovskii, A. I. *Избирательные споры в ходе федеральных, региональных и местных выборов 1993-1999 годов.* [Electoral Disputes in the Course of Federal, Regional and Local Elections in the Years 1993-1999]. M.: Prospekt, 1999. 80 p. 500 ptd. ISBN 5-8369-0075-2.

Избирательное право и избирательный процесс в Российской Федерации: Для вузов. [Electoral Law and the Electoral Process in the Russian Federation: For Institutes of Higher Education]. S. A. Avakian et al. M.: NORMA, 1999. 841 p. 30000 ptd. ISBN 5-89123-311-8.

Избирательное право России: В документах. Том 1. Федеральные нормативно-правовые акты. [Russian Electoral Law: In Documents. Vol.1. Federal Normative Legal Acts]. Ed. O. E.

Kutafin. M.: Mosk. gos. iurid. akad., 1999. 638 p. 1000 ptd. ISBN 5-86095-191-4.

Избирательное право России (в документах): Т.2. Региональные нормативно-правовые акты. [Electoral Law of Russia (in Documents): Vol.2. Regional Normative-Legal Acts]. Comps. N. A. Mikhaleva, A. A. Iashin. M.: Mosk. gos. iurid. akad., 1999. 868 p. 1000 ptd. ISBN 5-86095-192-2.

Избирательное право России: В документах. Т.3. Нормативно-правовые акты Центральной избирательной комиссии Российской Федерации. [Electoral Law of Russia: In Documents. Vol.3. Normative-Legal Acts of the Central Electoral Commission of the Russian Federation]. Ed. O. E. Kutafin. M.: Mosk. gos. iurid. akad., 1999. 836 p. 1000 ptd. ISBN 5-86095-193-0.

Комментарий к Федеральному закону «Об основных гарантиях избирательных прав и права на участие в референдуме граждан Российской Федерации»: С изменениями и дополнениями внесенными Федерал. законом от 30 марта 1999 г. No.55-ФЗ. [Commentary to the Federal Law "On the Basic Guarantees of Electoral Rights and Rights of Citizens of the Russian Federation to Participate in the Referendum": With Changes and Additions Introduced by the Federal Law of 30 March 1999. No.55-F3]. Eds. V. I. Vasiliev, A. A. Veshniakov, V. I. Lysenko. M.: NORMA, 1999. 760 p. 5000 ptd. ISBN 5-89123-394-0.

Kornienko, V., Vagin, O. *Технологии выборных кампаний.* [Technologies of Electoral Campaigns]. Ed. V. Zhirinovskii. 2d. rev. ed. M.: Izd. LDPR, 1999. 72 p. 3000 ptd.

Kovler, A. I. *Кандидат и его команда: Организационная структура избирательной кампании: Методическое пособие.* [The Candidate and His Team: The Organisational Structure of the Electoral Campaign: Methods Manual]. 2nd. rev. ed. M.: RTSOIT, 1999. 32 p. 3000 ptd. ISBN 5-93639-003-9.

Kovler, A. I., Zotova, Z. M. *Стратегия избирательной кампании и ее планирование.* [The Strategy of the Electoral Campaign and Its Planning]. M.: RTSOIT, 1999. 73 p. 3000 ptd. ISBN 5-93639-001-2.

Lesnin, I. V. *Технология политического успеха, или Как победить на местных выборах.* [Technology of Political Success or How to Win in Local Elections]. Volgograd: Peremena, 1999. 79 p. 150 ptd. ISBN 5-88234-346-1.

Об основных гарантиях избирательных прав и права на участие в референдуме граждан Российской Федерации: Федеральный закон от 19 сентября 1997 г. No.124-ФЗ. [On the Basic Guarantees of Electoral Rights and Rights to Participate in the Referendum of Citizens of the Russian Federation: Federal Law of 19 September 1997. No.124-F3]. M.: Iurisprudentsiia, 1999. 120 p. 6000 ptd. ISBN 5-8401-0015-3.

Общероссийские избирательные объединения накануне выборов депутатов Государственной Думы Федерального Собрания Российской Федерации третьего созыва: Справочник. [All-Russian Electoral Associations on the Eve of Elections of Deputies of the State Duma of the Federal Assembly of the Russian Federation of the Third Convocation: Manual]. Ed. O. K. Zastrozhnaia. M.: Ves' Mir, 1999. 183 p. 6500 ptd. ISBN 5-7777-0053-5.

Практика проведения демократических выборов в Московской области: Учебное пособие. [Practice of Conducting Democratic Elections in the Moscow Region: Instructional Manual]. Ed. V. I. Smirnovaia. M.: Sovr. tetradi, 1999. 143 p. 2000 ptd. ISBN 5-88289-114-0.

Регламент Центральной избирательной комиссии Российской Федерации. [Reglament of the Central Electoral Commission of the Russian Federation]. M.: Tsentr. izbirat. komis. Ros. Federatsii, 1999. 55 p. 500 p.

Русские выборы. [Russian Elections]. M.: RIA "Novosti", 1999. 174 p. 5000 ptd.

Сборник нормативных актов Центральной избирательной комиссии Российской Федерации по вопросам выборов депутатов Государственной Думы Федерального Собрания Российской Федерации: Выпуск 2. [Collection of Normative Acts of the Central Electoral Commission of the Russian Federation on

Questions of the Elections of Deputies of the State Duma of the Federal Assembly of the Russian Federation: Issue 2]. M.:Izd. Tsentr. izbirat. komissii RF, 1999. 80 p. 5000 ptd.

Suntsov, A. P. *Избирательная система субъекта Российской Федерации.* [Electoral System of the Subject of the Russian Federation]. Tiumen: Tium. iurid. in-t MVD RF, 1999. 163 p. 150 ptd.

Rights of Man and Citizen

Andrichenko, L. V., Belousova, E. V. *В помощь вынужденным переселенцам.* [With Aid for Forced Immigrants]. M.: Zvenia, 1999. 64 p. 15000 ptd. ISBN 5-7870-0024-2.

Конвенция о защите прав человека и основных свобод: С поправками, внесенными Протоколом No.11. Вступил в силу 1 ноября 1996 г. [Convention on the Defence of Human Rights and Basic Freedoms: With Amendments Introduced by Protocol No.11. Entered into Force on 1 November 1996]. Comps. V. B. Isakov et al. M.: Iurait, 1999. 189 p. 3000 ptd. ISBN 5-85294-077-1.

Mironov, O. O. *Доклад о деятельности Уполномоченного по правам человека в Российской Федерации в 1998 году.* [Report on the Activity of the Plenipotentiary for Human Rights in the Russian Federation in 1998]. M.: Respublika, 1999. 78 p. 5000 ptd. ISBN 5-250-02731-8.

Mironov, O. O. *О соблюдении прав граждан, страдающих психическими расстройствами.* [On the Observance of the Rights of Citizens Suffering from Psychological Disorders]. M.: Respublika, 1999. 63 p. 2000 ptd. ISBN 5-250-02735-0.

О соблюдении прав человека и гражданина в Российской Федерации в 1998 году. [On the Observance of the Rights of a Person and Citizen in the Russian Federation in 1998]. M.: Iurid. lit., 1999. 45 p. 1045 ptd. ISBN 5-7260-0926-6-2.

Об обжаловании в суд действий и решений, нарушающих права и свободы граждан. [On the Appeal to Court on Actions and

Decisions which Violate the Rights and Freedoms of Citizens]. M.: Izd. g-na Tikhomirova M. Iu., 1999. 50 p. 3000 ptd. ISBN 5-89194-015-9.

Права человека: Учебник для вузов. [Human Rights: Textbook for Institutes of Higher Education]. Ed. E. A. Lukasheva. M.: NORMA-INFRA-M, 1999. 573 p. 30000 ptd. ISBN 5-89123-352-5, ISBN 5-16-00023-2.

Права человека в России: проблемы гарантий на современном этапе. [Human Rights in Russia: Problems of Guarantees in the Contemporary Stage]. Ed. P. V. Anisimov. Volgograd: VIUI MVD Rossii, 1999. 130 p. 100 ptd. ISBN 5-7899-0068-2.

Проблема обеспечения прав граждан на доступ к правовой информации: Материалы международного «круглого стола». Москва, Государственная Дума, 25-26 ноября 1997 г. [The Problem of Safeguarding the Rights of Citizens for Access to Legal Information: Materials from the International "Round Table". Moscow, State Duma, 25-26 November 1997]. M.: Izd. Gos. Dumy, 1999. 583 p. 1500 ptd. ISBN 5-89686-008-0.

В помощь вынужденным переселенцам. [To the Aid of Forced Immigrants]. L. V. Andrichenko, E. V. Belousova. Ed. M. E. Petrosian. M.: Zvenia, 1999. 63 p. 15000 ptd. ISBN 5-7870-0024-2.

Subjects of the Federation

Административно-территориальное устройство Республики Башкортостан на 1 января 1999 года. [Administrative-Territorial Structure of the Republic of Bashkortostan for 1 January 1999]. Ufa: Bashkortostan, 1999. 411 p. 15000 ptd. ISBN 5-85051-142-3.

Goshuliak, V. V. *Конституционное и уставное законодательство субъектов Российской Федерации.* [Constitutional and Charter Legislation of Subjects of the Russian Federation]. M.: NORMA, 1999. 439 p. 500 ptd.

Государственная и муниципальная кадровая политика Республики Адыгея в современных условиях. [State and Municipal

Personnel Policy of the Republic of Adigeia under Contemporary Conditions]. A. A. Dzharimov et al. Maikop; Rostov n/D.: Sev.-Kavkaz. akad. gos. sluzhby, 1999. 214 p. ISBN 5-89546-035-6.

Комментарий к Федеральному закону о гарантиях прав коренных малочисленных народов Российской Федерации. [Commentary to the Federal Law on the Guarantees of Rights of Indigenous Small Nations of the Russian Federation]. Ed. B. S. Krylov. M.: Izd. g-na Tikhomirova M. Iu., Iurinformtsentr, 1999. 152 p. 5000 ptd. ISBN 5-89194-040-X.

Kriazhkov, V. A. *Конституционное правосудие в субъектах Российской Федерации: Правовые основы и практика.* [Constitutional Justice in the Subjects of the Russian Federation: Legal Fundamental Principles and Practice]. M.: Formula prava, 1999. 768 p. 1000 ptd. ISBN 5-8467-0001-2.

Lebedev, A. N. *Статус субъекта Российской Федерации: Основы концепции, конституционная модель, практика.* [Status of a Subject of the Russian Federation: Fundamental Principles of Concept, Constitutional Model, Practice]. M.: In-t gosudarstva i prava RAN, 1999. 197 p. ISBN 5-8339-0003-4.

Проблемы реализации суверенитета Республики Башкортостан (1557-1998 гг.): Документы. Нормативные акты. [Problems of the Realisation of the Sovereignty of the Republic of Bashkortostan (1557-1998): Documents. Normative Acts]. Comp. M. K. Malikov. Sterlitamak: Izd-vo Bashkir. un-ta, 1999. 511 p. 1000 ptd. ISBN 5-7477-0261-0.

Сборник законов Иркутской области: В 2 ч. [Collection of Laws from the Irkutsk Region: In 2 Parts]. Comp. E. V. Lopatina. Irkutsk: Vost.-Sib. kn. izd-vo, 1999. 500 ptd.

Ч.1. Законодательство о финансах и кредите и экономическое законодательство: С изменениями и дополнениями на 13.01.99. [Part 1. Legislation on Finances and Credit and Economic Legislation: With Changes and Additions for 13 January 1999]. 336 p.

Ч.2. Государственное устройство области: С измене-

ниями и дополнениями на 13.01.99. [Part 2. State Structure of a Region: With Changes and Additions for 13 January 1999]. 414p. ISBN 5-7424-0766-1.

Sergevnin, S. *Субъект федерации: статус и законодательная деятельность.* [Subject of the Federation: Status and Legislative Activity]. Spb.: Izd-vo in-ta, 1999. 215 p. 1500 ptd. ISBN 5-86247-025-5.

Статус малочисленных народов России: Кн.2. Правовые акты. [The Status of Small (in Numbers) Nations of Russia: Book 2. Legal Acts]. Comp. V. A. Kriazhkov. M.: Izd. g-na Tikhomirova M. Iu., 1999. 396 p. 1500 ptd. ISBN 5-89194-018-3.

Законы Тюменской области. 1994-1998: В 2 томах. [Laws of the Tiumen Region. 1994-1998: In 2 Volumes]. Comps. B. U. Agishev et al. 2nd. rev. ed. Tiumen: Izd. Tiumen. obl. Dumy, 1999. 2000 ptd.

Vol.1. 632 p. ISBN 5-88131-125-6.

Vol.2. 488 p. ISBN 5-88131-126-4.

Local Government

Frenkel, Z. G. *Волостное самоуправление: Его значение, задачи и взаимоотношения с кооперацией.* [Volost Self-Government: Its Significance, Tasks and Mutual Relationships with Cooperation]. Intro. & Commentary: T. M. Govorenkovaia. Pereizd. M.: Munitsipal. vlast, 1999. 302 p. 3000 ptd. ISBN 5-938158-002-6.

Градостроительный кодекс Российской Федерации: Официальный текст. Введен в действие с 11 мая 1998 г. [Urban Construction Code of the Russian Federation: Official Text. Entered into Operation from 11 May 1998]. M.: NORMA-INFRA-M, 1999. 90 p. 2000 ptd. ISBN 5-89123-366-5, ISBN 5-86225-859-0.

Компетенция органов местного самоуправления: Сборник извлечений из законов Российской Федерации. По состоянию на 1 ноября 1998 г. [Competence of Agencies of Local Self-Government: Collection of Excerpts of Laws of the Russian Federation. As of 1 November 1998]. Comp. V. A. Shchepachev. Orenburg: Kn. izd-vo, 1999. 704 p. 2000 ptd. ISBN 5-88788-050-3.

Korolev, S. V. *Теория муниципального управления.* [Theory of Municipal Administration]. M.: In-t gosudarstva i prava RAN, 1999. 143 p. 900 ptd. ISBN 5-7856-0123-0.

Местное самоуправление: российский путь. [Local Self-Government: The Russian Way]. Iu. G. Volkov et al.: Ed. G. V. Dylnov. Saratov: Region. Privolzh. izd-vo "Det. kn.", 1999. 312 p. 1000 ptd. ISBN 5-8270-0224-0.

Местное самоуправление в Санкт-Петербурге и Литве. [Local Self-Government in St. Petersburg and Lithuania]. Ed. M. B. Gorny. Spb.: Norma, 1999. 166 p. 500 ptd. ISBN 5-87857-029-7.

Местное самоуправление в современной России: права, обязанности и деятельность представительных органов власти. [Local Self-Government in Contemporary Russia: Rights, Duties and Activity of Representative Agencies of Power]. A. S. Avtonomov et al. M.: Fond razvitiia parlamentarizma v Rossii, Ves' Mir, 1999. 79 p. 10000 ptd. ISBN 5-7777-0076-4.

Муниципальное право Российской Федерации: Хрестоматия. [Municipal Law of the Russian Federation: Anthology]. Comp. & Intro. E. V. Belousovaia. M.: Iurist', 1999. 543 p. 5000 ptd. ISBN 5-7975-0261-5.

Основы местного самоуправления и муниципального управления: В 2 ч. Учебное пособие. [Fundamental Principles of Local Self-Government and Municipal Administration: In 2 Parts. Instructional Manual]. M.: Munitsipalnaia vlast, 1999. 1000 ptd. ISBN 5-93158-004-2.

Part 1. *Российское и зарубежное наследие.* [Russian and Foreign Legacy]. 209 p.

Part 2. *Правовые, организационные и финансовые основы самоуправления.* [Legal, Organisational and Financial Fundamental Principles of Local Self-Government]. 158 p.

Ovchinnikov, I. I. *Местное самоуправление в системе народовластия.* [Local Self-Government in the System of Sovereignty]. M.: In-t gosudarstva i prava RAN, 1999. 329 p. 1000 ptd. ISBN 5-8339-0006-9.

Порядок и условия прохождения муниципальной службы: Учебно-методическое пособие. [Procedure and Conditions of Municipal Service: Instructional-Methods Manual]. Eds. A. F. Murashko, O. L. Savranskaia, V. A. Stoliarovaia. M.: RITS "Munitsipal. vlast", 1999. 149 p. 10000 ptd. ISBN 5-93158-006-9.

Postovoi, N. V. *Муниципальное право: Вопросы и ответы.* [Municipal Law: Questions and Answers]. M.: Novy Iurist, 1999. 117 p. 5000 ptd. ISBN 5-7969-0058-7.

Район в городе. [District in the City]. A. V. Petrov et al. M.: Tsentr, 1999. 192 p. 5000 ptd. ISBN 5-88860-058-X.

Сборник документов органов самоуправления города Чебоксары, устанавливающих порядок управления муниципальной собственностью. [Collection of Documents of Organs of Self-Government of the City of Cheboksary, which Establish the Procedure for the Administration of Municipal Ownership]. Cheboksary: Chuvash. kn. izd-vo, 1999. 781 p. 1000 ptd. ISBN 5-7670-1120-6.

Школа муниципального служащего. 1-13 ноября 1998 г. [School of the Municipal Employee. 1-13 November 1998]. Obninsk: Metod. materialy. Ed. & Comp. A. E. Balobanov. M.: Mosk. obshchestv. nauch. fond, 1999. 253 p. 1000 ptd. ISBN 89554-088-0.

Shugrina, E. S. *Муниципальное право.* [Municipal Law]. M.: Delo, 1999. 496 p. 5000 ptd. ISBN 5-7749-0144-0.

Собрание нормативных правовых актов Орловской области: Выпуск 1-2. Том 1. [Collection of Normative Legal Acts of the Orlov Region: Issue 1-2. Vol.1]. Ed. A. S. Aksiutich et al. Orel: ORAGS, 1999. 765 p. 1000 ptd. ISBN 5-93179-018-7.

Становление местного самоуправления в Российской Федерации. [Formation of Local Self-Government in the Russian Federation]. Ed. & Comp. O. L. Savranskaia. M.: Mosk. obshestv. nauch. fond, 1999. 377 p. 2000 ptd. ISBN 5-89554-066-X.

Стратегический выбор города: научное обоснование и механизм реализации: На примере г. Тольятти, Самар. обл.

[Strategic Choice of a City: Scientific Justification and Mechanism for Realisation: After the Example of the City of Toliatti, Samar. Region]. Eds. V. E. Rokhchin, S. F. Zhilkin. Spb.: ISEP RAN, 1999. 182 p. 1000 ptd. ISBN 5-85991-023-1.

Vasiliev, V. I. *Местное самоуправление: Учебное и научно-практическое пособие.* [Local Self-Government: Instructional and Scientific-Practical Manual]. M.:Izd. g-na Tikhomirova M. Iu., 1999. 453 p. 5000 ptd. ISBN 5-89194-017-5.

Vydrin, I. V., Kokotov, A. N. *Муниципальное право России: Учебник для вузов.* [Municipal Law of Russia: Textbook for Institutes of Higher Education]. M.: NORMA-INFRA-M, 1999. 359 p. 50000 ptd. ISBN 5-86225-520-6.

Законы города Москвы. Постановления Московской городской Думы. 1998. [Laws of the City of Moscow. Decrees of the Moscow Municipal Duma. 1998]. Ed. A. V. Petrov. M.: In-t zakonodatelstva i sravnit. pravovedeniia pri Pravitelstve RF, 1999. 519 p. 3000 ptd. ISBN 5-85299-006-X.

Zamotaev, A. A. *Местное самоуправление: основные понятия и термины.* [Local Self-Government: Basic Concepts and Terms]. M.: Munitsipalnaia Vlast, 1999. 396 p. 2000 ptd. ISBN 5-93158-001-8.

State Symbols

Государственные символы и награды Российской Федерации. [State Symbols and Awards of the Russian Federation]. Comp. Iu. L. Kusher. M.: Knizh. palata, 1999. 171 p. 3000 ptd. ISBN 5-7000-0476-3.

Administrative Law

Административная ответственность: Сборник нормативных правовых актов. [Administrative Responsibility: Collection of Normative Legal Acts]. Comps. P. V. Anisimov, V. D. Simuzhin. Volgograd: VIUI MVD Rossii, 1999. 188 p. 300 ptd. ISBN 5-7899-0054-2.

Административное право: Для вузов. [Administrative Law: For

Institutes of Higher Education]. Eds. Iu. M. Kozlov, L. L. Popov. M.: Iurist', 1999. 726 p. 10000 ptd. ISBN 5-7975-0138-4.

Agapov, A. B. *Учебник административного права.* [Textbook of Administrative Law]. M.: Gorodets, 1999. 558 p. 6000 ptd. ISBN 5-89391-040-0.

Alekhin, A. P., Karmolitskii, A. A., Kozlov, Iu. M. *Административное право Российской Федерации: Для вузов.* [Administrative Law of the Russian Federation: For Institutes of Higher Education]. 2d. rev. ed. M.: Zertsalo, 1999. 672 p. 8000 ptd. ISBN 5-8078-0043-5.

Bakhrakh, D. N. *Административная ответственность: Пособие.* [Administrative Responsibility: Manual]. M.: Iurisprudentsiia, 1999. 111 p. 7000 ptd. ISBN 5-86532-049-1.

Belova, S. I. *Административно-правовое регулирование архивного дела в Российской Федерации: Учебное пособие.* [Administrative Legal Regulation of Archive Matters in the Russian Federation: Instructional Manual]. Saratov: Sarat. iurid. in-t, 1999. 68 p. 200 ptd. ISBN 5-7485-0023-X.

Безопасность России: Правовые, социально-экономические и научно-технические аспекты. [Russia's Security: Legal, Socio-Economic and Scientific-Technical Aspects]. M.: MGF "Znanie", 1999. 667 p. 1000 ptd. ISBN 5-87633-044-2.

Chukovenkov, A. Iu., Iankovaia, V. F. *Оформление документов: Комментарий к ГОСТ, 730-97 «Унифицированные системы документации. Унифицированная система организационно-распорядительной документации. Требования к оформлению документов».* [Formalisation of Documents: Commentary to the All-Union State Standard, 730-97 "Unified Systems of Documentation. Unified System of Organisational-Administrative Documentation"]. M.: Delo, 1999. 232 p. 10000 ptd. ISBN 5-7749-0149-1.

Ежегодник 98: Государственная служба России. [Annual 98: State Service of Russia]. Ed. F. D. Demidov. M.: Izd-vo, RAGS, 1999. 318 p. 500 ptd. ISBN 5-7729-0041-2.

Государственная служба: Для вузов. [State Service: For Institutes of Higher Education]. Ed. A. V. Obolonskii. M.: Delo, 1999. 440 p. 5000 ptd. ISBN 5-7749-0153-X.

Государственная служба: Сборник нормативных документов. [State Service: Collection of Normative Documents]. M.: Delo, 1999. 430 p. 3000 ptd. ISBN 5-7749-0157-2.

Государственный служащий: культура поведения и деловой этикет. [State Employee: Behavioural Culture and Professional Etiquette]. 2d. ed. Ed. E. V. Okhotskii. M.: Izd-vo RAGS, 1999. 335 p. 1000 ptd. ISBN 5-7729-0037-4.

Iakimov, A. Iu. *Статус субъекта административной юрисдикции и проблемы его реализации: Монограмма.* [Status of a Subject of Administrative Jurisdiction and Problems of Its Realisation: Monogram]. M.: Prospekt, 1999. 199 p. 1000 ptd. ISBN 5-8369-0004-3.

Институты административного права. [Institutes of Administrative Law]. Eds. I. L. Bachilo, N. Iu. Khamanev. M.: In-t gosudarstva i prava RAN, 1999. 264 p. 1000 ptd. ISBN 5-8339-0008-5.

Khalafin, A. *Как прописаться в Москве: Консультации юриста.* [How to Register in Moscow: A Jurist's Advice]. M.: Poznavat. kn. plius, 1999. 175 p.

Кодекс об административных правонарушениях: С изменениями и дополнениями на 15 сентября 1999 г. [Code on Administrative Violations of Law: With Changes and Additions for 15 September 1999]. M.: Kodeks, Prospekt, 1999. 198 p. 10000 ptd. ISBN 5-8369-0011-6.

Кодекс РСФСР об административных правонарушениях. [RSFSR Code on Administrative Violations of Law]. 12th ed. M.: NORMA-INFRA-M, 1999. 256 p. 6000 ptd. ISBN 5-89123-291-X, ISBN 5-86225-933-3.

Кодекс РСФСР об административных правонарушениях: Официальный текст. По состоянию на 1 февраля 1999 г. [RSFSR

Code on Administrative Violations of Law: Official Text as of 1 February 1999]. M.: NORMA-INFRA-M, 1999. 284 p. 6000 ptd. ISBN 5-89123-291-X.

Кодекс РСФСР об административных правонарушениях: Официальный текст. По состоянию на 22 марта 1999 г. [RSFSR Code on Administrative Violations of Law: Official Text. As of 22 March 1999]. M.: Filin', 1999. 279 p. 5000 ptd. ISBN 5-89568-140-9.

Кодекс РСФСР об административных правонарушениях: Официальный текст по состоянию на 15 мая 1999 г. [RSFSR Code on Administrative Violations of Law: Official Text from 15 May 1999]. M.: TANDEM, EKMOS, 1999. 160 p. 3000 ptd. ISBN 5-88124-051-2.

Also published:
M.: Prospekt, Kodeks, 1999. 198 p. 10000 ptd. ISBN 5-8369-0011-6.

Кодекс РСФСР об административных правонарушениях: По состоянию на 15 февраля 1999 г. [RSFSR Code on Administrative Violations of Law: As of 15 February 1999]. M.: OLMA-Press, Novosibirsk: IUKEA, 1999. 288 p. 11000 ptd. ISBN 5-86750-081-0.

Комментарий к Федеральному закону «Об основах государственной службы Российской Федерации» и законодательству о государственной службе зарубежных государств. [Commentary to the Federal Law "On the Fundamental Principles of State Service of the Russian Federation" and to the Legislation on the State Service of Foreign States]. Ed. L. A. Okunkov. M.: Kontrakt, INFRA-M, 1999. 368 p. 20000 ptd. ISBN 5-900785-23-8, ISBN 5-86225-737-3.

Комментарий к Кодексу РСФСР об административных правонарушениях. [Commentary to the RSFSR Code on Administrative Violations of Law]. Eds. I. I. Veremeenko, N. G. Salishchevaia, M. S. Studenkinaia. 3rd. rev. ed. M.: Prospekt, 1999. 907 p. 20000 ptd. ISBN 5-7986-0022-X.

Korenevskii, Iu. V. *Как обжаловать приговор суда.* [How to Appeal Against the Judgement of a Court]. M.: Ucheb.-konsultativ. tsentr

"IurInfoR", 1999. 178 p. 5000 ptd. ISBN 5-89158-017-9.

Kozlov, Iu. M. *Административное право России: Учебно-методическое пособие.* [Administrative Law of Russia: Instructional Methods Manual]. Ed. B. I. Putinskii. M.: Gorodets, 1999. 144 p. 5000 ptd. ISBN 5-89391-051-6.

Kunitsyn, A. R. *Образцы заявлений и жалоб в суд: Практическое пособие.* [Samples of Applications and Appeals to Court: Practical Manual]. M.: Soleks, 1999. 290 p. 5000 ptd. ISBN 5-900216-25-X.

Lukianenko, A. E., Lukianenko, V. I., Novikov, A. V. *Управление персоналом государственных органов: система организации и функционирования.* [Management of the Personnel of State Agencies: System of Organisation and Functioning]. M.: Nauka, 1999. 573 p. ISBN 5-02-008341-0.

Mironov, M. A. *Власть и народ: обратная связь: Вопросы теории и практики организации работы с обращениями граждан в современных условиях.* [Power and the Nation: A Retroactive Bond: Questions of the Theory and Practice of the Organisation of Work with Citizens' Appeals under Contemporary Conditions]. M.: Iurd. lit., 1999. 312 p. 1000 ptd. ISBN 5-7260-0928-2.

Настольная книга государственного служащего: Комментарий к Федеральному закону «Об основах государственной службы Российской Федерации». [A Civil Servant's Manual: Commentary to the Federal Law "On the Fundamental Principles of the Civil Service of the Russian Federation"]. Ed. V. I. Shkatulla. M.: Ekonomika, 1999. 678 p. 5000 ptd. ISBN 5-282-01935-3.

Научно-практический комментарий к Федеральному закону «О защите населения и территорий от чрезвычайных ситуаций природного и техногенного характера»: С постатейными материалами. [Scientific-Practical Commentary to the Federal Law "On the Defence of the Population and Territories from Extraordinary Situations of a Natural and Technogenic Character": With Article by Article Materials]. Ed. A. P. Moskalets. M.: MCHS Rossii, 1999. 410 p. 500 ptd.

Nozdrachev, A. F. *Государственная служба: Учебник.* [The State Service: Textbook]. M.: Statut, 1999. 592 p. 10000 ptd. ISBN 5-8354-0015-4.

Российское административное право: Часть общая. Книга 1. Сборник нормативных актов. [Russian Administrative Law: General Part. Book 1. Collection of Normative Acts]. Comp. N. M. Konin et al. Saratov: SGAP, 1999. 544 p. 1000 ptd. ISBN 5-7924-0056-3.

Российское служебное право: Сборник нормативных актов. Учебное пособие. [Russian Employment Law: Collection of Normative Acts. Instructional Manual]. Comp. Iu. N. Starilov. Voronezh: Izd-vo Voronezh. gos. un-ta, 1999. 800 p. 1000 ptd. ISBN 5-7455-1044-7.

Soloviev, O. M., Iarulin, I. F. *Институты государства и гражданского общества: Учебное пособие.* [Institutes of State and Civil Society: Instructional Manual]. Khabarovsk: Izd-vo KHGTU, 1999. 123 p. 300 ptd. ISBN 5-7389-0232-7.

Справочник по административно-территориальному устройству Московской области. [Manual on the Administrative and Territorial Structure of the Moscow Region]. M.: RIO Upr. izdatelstv poligrafii i knizh. torgovli Mosk. obl., 1999. 334 p. 1500 ptd. ISBN 5-89752-019-4.

Turusov, A. A. *Осторожно: КоАП - защищайтесь!: Административные правонарушения.* [Be Careful: The Code on Administrative Violations of Law - Defend Yourselves!: Administrative Violations of Law]. M.: AST: Rostov n/D: Feniks, 1999. 319 p. 10000 ptd. ISBN 5-222-00801-0.

Учиться государственной службе. [To Study the Civil Service]. Ed. V. V. Bakushev. M.: Svarog i Ko., 1999. 1050 p. ISBN 5-93070-012-5.

Taxation

Evstigneev, E. N. *Основы налогообложения и налогового права: Учебное пособие.* [Fundamental Principles of Taxation and Tax Law:

Instructional Manual]. M.: INFRA-M, 1999. 119 p. 6000 ptd. ISBN 5-86225-992-9.

Guev, A. N. *Постатейный комментарий Налогового Кодекса Российской Федерации.* [Article by Article Commentary to the Tax Code of the Russian Federation]. M.: IUKANG, 1999. 957 p. 600 ptd. ISBN 5-900749-08-8.

Комментарий изменений к Налоговому кодексу Российской Федерации, части первой (постатейный). [Commentary to the Changes to the First Part (Article by Article) of the Tax Code of the Russian Federation]. Ed. A. V. Bryzgalin. M.: Nalogi i fin. pravo, Analitika-Press, 1999. 229 p. 50000 ptd. ISBN 5-7916-0069-0.

Комментарий к Налоговому кодексу Российской Федерации, части первой (постатейный). [Commentary to the Tax Code of the Russian Federation, Part One, Article by Article]. Ed. A. V. Bryzgalin. M.: Nalogi i finansovoe pravo, Analitika-Press, 1999. 397 p. 30000 ptd. ISBN 5-7916-0051-8.

Also published:
M.: Knizh. mir, 1999. 184 p. 10000 ptd. ISBN 5-8041-0041-6.
M.: NORMA-INFRA-M, 1999. 425 p. 60000 ptd. ISBN 5-89123-373-8, ISBN 5-86225-928-7.
M.: Knizh. mir, 1999. 327 p. 5000 ptd. ISBN 5-8041-0054-8.

Kulesh, V. A. *Налоговая адвокатура, или Как защищаться от финансовых санкций.* [Tax Advocatura, or How to Defend Oneself from Financial Sanctions]. 2d. rev. ed. M.: Biznes-shkola "Intel-Sintez", 1999. 242 p. 2500 ptd. ISBN 5-87057-135-9.

Налог с продаж: Закон. Инструкция. Разъяснения. [Tax from Sales: Law. Instruction. Explanations]. M.: INFRA-M, 1999. 32 p. 3000 ptd. ISBN 5-86225-826-4.

Налог с продаж в Москве: Вводится в действие с 1 июля 1999 г.: Закон города Москвы «О налоге с продаж». Ответы на вопросы. [Tax from Sales in Moscow: Enters into Operation from 1 July 1999: Law of the City of Moscow "On Tax from Sales". Answers to Questions]. M.: Sovr. ekonomika i pravo, 1999. 32 p. 3000 ptd. ISBN 5-8411-0006-8.

Налоговый кодекс. Налог с продаж: Официальный текст закона. Комментарий к закону. [Tax Code. Tax from Sales: Official Text of the Law. Commentary to the Law]. M.: In-t nalogovogo prava, 1999. 64 p. 5000 ptd. ISBN 5-93212-004-5.

Налоговый кодекс Российской Федерации. [Tax Code of the Russian Federation]. M.: NIPKTS VOSKHOD, 1999. 101 p. ISBN 5-93055-010-7.

Налоговый кодекс Российской Федерации: Ч.1. [Tax Code of the Russian Federation: Part 1]. M.: Prospekt, 1999. 96 p. 5000 ptd. ISBN 5-7896-0082-4.

Also published:
M.: Delo, 1999. 96 p. 5000 ptd. ISBN 5-7749-0139-4.
M.: NORMA-INFRA-M, 1999. 142 p. 10000 ptd. ISBN 5-89123-321-5, ISBN 5-86225-879-3.
M.: OLMA-Press, Novosibirsk: IUKEA, 1999. 144 p. 11000 ptd. ISBN 5-224-00262-1, ISBN 5-86750-121-3.
M.: Izd. g-na Tikhomirova M. Iu., 1999. 93 p. 3000 ptd. ISBN 5-89194-015-9.
M.: Statut, 1999. 125 p. 10000 ptd. ISBN 5-5-8354-0001-2.
M.: Nalogi i finansovoe pravo, Analitik-Press, 1999. 150 p. 5000 ptd. ISBN 5-7916-0055-0.
M.: Finansy i statistika, 1999. 136 p. 4000 ptd. ISBN 5-279-02076-1.
M.: Spb.: Gerda, 1999. 126 p. 5000 ptd. ISBN 5-7978-0050-0.
M.: Filin', 1999. 144 p. 5000 ptd. ISBN 5-89568-136-0.
M.: Slavian. dom knigi, 1999. 128 p. 8000 ptd. ISBN 5-93220-006-5.
Ulianovsk: Knigochei, 1999. 7000 ptd. ISBN 5-855525-017-2.
Ufa: Bashkortostan, 1999. 93 p. 10000 ptd. ISBN 5-8258-0130-8.
M.: Ucheb.-inform. tsentr pri Gos. nalogovoi inspektsii po g. Moskve, 1999. 112 p. 5000 ptd. ISBN 5-86297-106-8.

Налоговый кодекс Российской Федерации: Ч.1: Федеральный закон «О введении в действие части первой Налогового кодекса РФ». Комментарии. [Tax Code of the Russian Federation: Part 1: Federal Law "On the Introduction into Operation of Part 1 of the Russian Federation Tax Code". Commentaries]. Tiumen: Slovo, 1999. 128 p. 5000 ptd. ISBN 5-93030-015-1.

Налоговый кодекс Российской Федерации: Ч.1. Официальный текст по состоянию на 8 февраля 1999 г. [Tax Code of the Russian Federation: Part 1. Official Text as of 8 February 1999]. M.: Filin', 1999. 139 p. 5000 ptd. ISBN 5-89568-136-0.

Налоговый кодекс Российской Федерации: Часть 1: Официальный текст по сост. на 15 августа 1999 г. [Tax Code of the Russian Federation: Part 1: Official Text for 15 August 1999]. M.: INFRA-M, 1999. 107 p. 12000 ptd. ISBN 5-86225-926-0.

Налоговый кодекс Российской Федерации: Часть 1: По состоянию на 15 сентября 1999 г. [Tax Code of the Russian Federation: Part 1: For 15 September 1999]. M., Spb.: Izd. Torgovy Dom "Gerda", 1999. 158 p. 10000 ptd. ISBN 5-7978-0050-0.

Налоговый кодекс Российской Федерации: Ч.1. Постатейный комментарий. [Tax Code of the Russian Federation: Part 1. Article by Article Commentary]. Ed. V. I. Sloma. M.: Statut, 1999. 396 p. 30000 ptd. ISBN 5-89398-024-7.

Налоговый кодекс Российской Федерации: Часть 1: Принят Государственной Думой 16 июля 1998 г.: Одобрен Советом Федерации 17 июля 1998 г. [Tax Code of the Russian Federation: Part 1: Adopted by the State Duma on 16 July 1998: Approved by the Soviet of the Federation on 17 July 1998]. M.: Politekh-4, 1999. 165 p. 5000 ptd. ISBN 5-86297-120-3.

Налоговый кодекс Российской Федерации: Ч.1. С изменениями и дополнениями. [Tax Code of the Russian Federation: Part 1. With Changes and Additions]. Spb.: Izd. Dom A. Gromova, 1999. 142 p. 7500 ptd. ISBN 5-89138-009-9.

Налоговый кодекс Российской Федерации: Часть 1. С изменениями и дополнениями на 15 июля 1999 г. [Tax Code of the Russian Federation: Part 1. With Changes and Additions for 15 July 1999]. Ed. N. M. Golovanov. Spb.: Iurid. tsentr "Press", 1999. 288 p. 5000 ptd. ISBN 5-93292-003-3.

Налоговый кодекс Российской Федерации: Часть 1. С изменениями и дополнениями на 1 августа 1999 г. [Tax Code of the

Russian Federation: Part 1: With Changes and Additions for 1 August 1999]. M.: OLMA-Press: Novosibirsk: IUKEA, 1999. 159 p. 20000 ptd. ISBN 5-224-00601-5, ISBN 5-93316-013-7.

Налоговый кодекс Российской Федерации: Часть 1. С изменениями и дополнениями на 1 октября 1999 г. [Tax Code of the Russian Federation: Part 1. With Changes and Additions for 1 October 1999]. M.: Prospekt, Kodeks, 1999. 128 p. 10000 ptd. ISBN 5-8369-0055-8.

Налоговый кодекс Российской Федерации: Часть 1. С постатейными комментарии к изменениям и дополнениям. [Tax Code of the Russian Federation: Part 1. With Article by Article Commentaries to Changes and Additions]. Comp. V. R. Zakharin. M.: DiS, 1999. 200 p. 5000 ptd. ISBN 5-8018-0069-7.

Налоговый кодекс в схемах: Официальный текст и комментарий. [Tax Code in Diagrams: Official Text and Commentary]. M.: In-t issled. po nalogovomu pravu, 1999. 240 p. 5000 ptd. ISBN 5-93212-003-7.

Налоговые споры: Сборник документов. [Tax Disputes: Collection of Documents]. Ed. M. Iu. Tikhomirov. M.: Iurinformtsentr, Izd. g-na Tikhomirova M. Iu., 1999. 231 p. 3000 ptd. ISBN 5-89194-031-0.

Nikonov, A. A. *Комментарий к изменениям в Налоговый кодекс РФ.* [Commentary to the Changes to the Tax Code of the Russian Federation]. M.: "Glavbukh", 1999. 147 p. 8000 ptd. ISBN 5-88759-065-3.

Panskov, V. G. *Комментарии к Налоговому кодексу Российской Федерации: Ч.1. Вводится в действие с 1 января 1999 г.* [Commentaries to the Tax Code of the Russian Federation: Part 1. Enters into Operation from 1 January 1999]. M.: Finansy i statistika, 1999. 62 p. 3000 ptd. ISBN 5-279-02074-5.

Also published:

M.: Finansy i statistika, 1999. 78 p. 5000 ptd. ISBN 5-279-02164-4. (2d. rev. ed.)

Petrova, G. V. *Налоговое право: Учебник для вузов.* [Tax Law:

Textbook for Institutes of Higher Education]. M.: NORMA-INFRA-M, 1999. 271 p. 30000 ptd. ISBN 5-89123-181-6, ISBN 5-86225-638-5.

Подоходный налог с физических лиц. [Income Tax from Physical Persons]. M.: Marketing, 1999. 268 p. 5000 ptd. ISBN 5-7856-0131-1.

Shatalov, S. D. *Комментарий к Налоговому кодексу Российской Федерации части первой (постатейный): Учебное пособие для вузов.* [Commentary to the First Part (Article by Article) of the Tax Code of the Russian Federation: Instructional Manual for Institutes of Higher Education]. M.: MTSFER, 1999. 637 p. ISBN 5-7709-0109-8.

Customs Law

Комментарий к Таможенному кодексу Российской Федерации. [Commentary to the Customs Code of the Russian Federation]. Eds. V. A. Maksimtsev, B. N. Gabrichidze. M.: NORMA, INFRA-M, 1999. 495 p. ISBN 5-89123-100-X, ISBN 5-86225-457-9.

Российское таможенное право: Учебник. [Russian Customs Law: Textbook]. Ed. B. N. Gabrichidze. M.: NORMA, INFRA-M, 1999. 511 p. 60000 ptd. ISBN 5-89123-097-6, ISBN 5-86225-451-X.

Таможенное дело в Саратовском крае: К 10-летию либерализации внешнеэкономической деятельности. [Customs Matters on the Territory of Saratov: For the 10th Anniversary of the Liberalisation of Foreign Economic Activity]. G. A. Kartashov et al. Saratov: KADR, 1999. 167 p. 1000 ptd.

Таможенное право: Курс лекций: В 2 томах. [Customs Law: Course of Lectures: In 2 Volumes]. Ed. V. G. Draganov. M.; Ekonomika, 1999. 10000 ptd. ISBN 5-282-01983-3.

Vol.1. General Part. 406 p.

Vol.2. Particular Part. 656 p.

Таможенное право: Нормативные акты по Таможенному законодательству. [Customs Law: Normative Acts on Customs Legislation]. M.: TargO, 1999. 819 p. 500 ptd. ISBN 5-8141-0005-2.

Таможенный энциклопедический справочник: В 2 томах.

[Customs Encyclopedic Manual: In 2 Volumes]. Ed. I. Iu. Krasnianskii. M.: Letopisets, 1999. 828 p. 3000 ptd. ISBN 5-93186-002-9.

Таможенный кодекс Российской Федерации: Официальный текст по состоянию на 1 декабря 1998 г. [Customs Code of the Russian Federation: Official Text as of 1 December 1998]. M.: NORMA-INFRA-M, 1999. 279 p. 3000 ptd. ISBN 5-89123-319-3, ISBN 5-86225-973-2.

Таможенный кодекс Российской Федерации: По состоянию на 15 февраля 1999 г. Федеральный закон «О службе в таможенных органах Российской Федерации». [Customs Code of the Russian Federation: As of 15 February 1999. Federal Law "On Service in the Customs Agencies of the Russian Federation"]. M.: OLMA-Press, Novosibirsk, 1999. 336 p. 11000 ptd. ISBN 5-224-00279-6.

Таможенный кодекс Российской Федерации: С изменениями и дополнениями на 15 февраля 1999 г. [Customs Code of the Russian Federation: With Changes and Additions for 15 February 1999]. M.: Prospekt, 1999. 220 p. 5000 ptd. ISBN 5-7896-0074-3.

Таможенный кодекс Российской Федерации: С изменениями и дополнениями на 15 октября 1999 г. [Customs Code of the Russian Federation: With Changes and Additions for 15 October 1999]. M.: Prospekt, Kodeks, 1999. 220 p. 5000 ptd. ISBN 5-8369-0047-7.

Таможенный тариф Российской Федерации. [Customs Tariff of the Russian Federation]. M.: ZAO "Gruppa TARGO", 1999. 905 p. 500 ptd. ISBN 5-8141-0004-4.

Таможня в системе государственной внешнеэкономической политики России: региональный аспект. [Customs in the System of the Russian State Foreign Economic Policy: Regional Aspect]. Ed. S. G. Gorshenin. Orenburg: Kn. izd-vo, 1999. 299 p. 1000 ptd. ISBN 5-88788-060-0.

Public Education and Culture

Электронные документы в корпоративных сетях: второе пришествие Гутенберга. [Electronic Documents in Corporate

Networks: The Second Coming of Gutenburg]. S. V. Klimenko et al. M.: Ankei, Eko-Trendz, 1999. 271 p. ISBN 5-88405-014-3.

Fagradiants, I. V. *Переписка с официальными лицами и учреждениями: Образцы писем.* [Correspondence with Officials and Institutions: Models of Letters]. Trans. from German. In German & Russian. M.: ETS, 1999. 207 p. 1000 ptd. ISBN 5-76455-028-0.

Glushchenko, P. P., Chaban, Iu. M. *Сам себе адвокат: Практическое пособие.* [Be Your Own Advocate: Practical Manual]. 2nd. rev. ed. Spb.: Politekhnika, 1999. 246 p. 5000 ptd. ISBN 5-7325-0497-4.

Kirsanova, M. V., Aksenov, Iu. M. *Курс делопроизводства: Учебное пособие.* [Clerical Work Course: Instructional Manual]. 2d. ed. M.: INFRA-M; Novosibirsk: NGAEiU, 1999. 271 p. 50000 ptd. ISBN 5-86225-521-4, ISBN 5-7014-0007-7.

Kuznetsov, S. L. *Делопроизводство на компьютере: Компьютерные технологии в делопроизводстве.* [Clerical Work on a Computer: Computer Technologies in Clerical Work]. 2d. rev. ed. M.: Biznes-shkola “Intel-Sintez”, 1999. 200 p. 5000 ptd. ISBN 5-87057-160-X.

Об образовании: Закон Российской Федерации. [On Education: Law of the Russian Federation]. M.: INFRA-M, 1999. 52 p. 3000 ptd. ISBN 5-86225-782-9.

Образовательное право: Учебно-методическое пособие. [Educational Law: Instructional Methods Manual]. Eds. V. M. Syrykh, V. I. Shkatulla. Ufa: Vost. un-t, 1999. 119 p. 1000 ptd. ISBN 5-87865-190-4.

Sotov, P. V., Tikhomirov, A. N. *Делопроизводство.* [Clerical Work]. M.: Prospekt, 1999. 80 p. 10000 ptd. ISBN 5-7896-0079-4.

Religion

Gerosa, L. *Каноническое право в католической церкви.* [Canon Law in the Catholic Church]. Trans. from Italian. M.: Khristian. Rossiia,

1999. 379 p. 2000 ptd. ISBN 5-87468-043-8.

Русская Православная Церковь и право: Комментарий. [The Russian Orthodox Church and the Law. Commentary]. Ed. M. V. Ilichev. M.: BEK, 1999. 464 p. 6000 ptd. ISBN 5-85639-271-X.

Public Health and Safety

Andrianov, V. I., Sokolov, A. V. *Охранные устройства для дома и офиса.* [Protective Equipment for the Home and Office]. Spb.: Lan, 1999. 302 p. 10000 ptd. ISBN 5-8114-0040-X.

О санитарно-эпидемиологическом благополучии населения: Федеральный закон. [On the Sanitary and Epidemiological Welfare of the Population: Federal Law]. M.: INFRA-M, 1999. 40 p. 3000 ptd. ISBN 5-86225-579-6.

Panchenko, A. I. *Учись защищать себя.* [Learn to Defend Yourself]. M.: Mir bezopasnosti, 1999. 80 p. 2000 ptd. ISBN 5-89258-012-1.

Shikin, A. S. *Как уберечь себя от взрыва.* [How to Guard Against an Explosion]. M.: Mir bezopasnosti, 1999. 79 p. 2000 ptd. ISBN 5-89258-013-X.

Police Agencies

Административная деятельность органов внутренних дел. [Administrative Activity of Internal Affairs Agencies]. Ed. A. P. Korenev. 3rd. rev. ed. M.: Shchyt-M, 1999. 281 p. 1500 ptd. ISBN 5-93004-047-8.

Bagaets, A. M. *Война не окончена: Книга об истории и людях транспортной милиции Кузбасса.* [The War is Not Over: A Book on the History and People of the Kuzbas Transport Police]. Novosibirsk: Kn. izd-vo, 1999. 272 p. 1000 ptd. ISBN 5-7620-0834-7.

Beloglazov, A. V., Mingaleev, I. I., Krylova, G. G. *Страницы истории: Казан. милиция.* [Pages of History: Police of Kazan]. Kazan: Liana, 1999. 159 p. 1000 ptd. ISBN 5-7497-0004-6.

Боевой пост - на магистралях: 80 лет транспортной милиции. [Battle Post - On the Highways: 80 Years of the Transport Police]. Ed. & Comp. S. V. Katkov. Saratov: Letopis, 1999. 159 p. 2500 ptd.

Chislov, A. I. *Профессионализм и деятельность сотрудников милиции.* [Professionalism and the Activity of Police Personnel]. Ed. V. P. Salnikov. Spb.: Sankt-Peterburg. un-t MVD Rossii, Akad. prava, ekonomiki i bezopasnosti zhiznedetelnosti, 1999. 174 p. 3000 ptd. ISBN 5-93598-002-9.

Dziliev, M. I. *Рынок и насилие: Пособие для руководителей силовых и охранных структур, служб безопасности и предпринимателей.* [The Market and Force: Manual for Directors of Power and Protection Structures, the Security Forces and Entrepreneurs]. M.: Izd. dom "Mir bezopastnosti", 1999. 319 p. 3000 ptd. ISBN 5-89258-021-0.

Fokin, V. M. *Правоохранительные органы Российской Федерации: Учебник для вузов.* [Law Enforcement Agencies of the Russian Federation: Textbook for Institutes of Higher Education]. Ed. M. I. Lepikhov. M.: Bylina, 1999. 219 p. 3000 ptd. ISBN 5-88528-236-6.

Gutsenko, K. F., Kovalev, M. A. *Правоохранительные органы: Хрестоматия.* [Law Enforcement Agencies: Anthology]. Ed. K. F. Gutsenko. M.: Zertsalo, 1999. 368 p. 5000 ptd. ISBN 5-8078-0051-6.

Gutsenko, K. F., Kovalev, M. A. *Правоохранительные органы: Учебник для вузов.* [Law Enforcement Agencies: Textbook for Institutes of Higher Education]. 4th. rev. ed. M.: Zertsalo, 1999. 416 p. 8000 ptd. ISBN 5-8078-0033-8.

Mak-Mak, V. P. *Служба безопасности предприятия: Правовые аспекты деятельности.* [Security Service of the Enterprise: Legal Aspects of Activity]. M.: Mir bezopasnosti, 1999. 159 p. 2000 ptd. ISBN 5-89258-015-6.

Marshunov, M. N. *Комментарии к законам «Об оружии», «О частной детективной и охранной деятельности»: Научно-*

практические рекомендации. [Commentaries to the Laws "On Weapons", "On Private Detective and Protection Activity": Scientific-Practical Recommendations]. M., Spb.: Gerda, 1999. 248 p. 5000 ptd. ISBN 5-7978-0016-0.

Marshunov, M. N. *Комментарий к Закону Российской Федерации «О милиции»: Научно-практические рекомендации.* [Commentary to the Russian Federation Law "On the Police": Scientific-Practical Recommendations]. M., Spb.: Gerda, 1999. 248 p. 5000 ptd. ISBN 5-7978-0008-X.

О милиции: Сборник нормативных актов. [About the Police: Collection of Normative Acts]. M.: Iurait, 1999. 128 p. 3000 ptd. ISBN 5-85294-015-1.

О милиции: Закон РСФСР. [About the Police: RSFSR Law]. 2d. ed. M.: Novy Iurist', 1999. 32 p. 8000 ptd. ISBN 5-7969-0075-7.

О милиции: Закон РСФСР от 18 апреля 1991 г. No.1026-1. [On the Police: RSFSR Law of 18 April 1991. No.1026-1]. M.: Iurisprudentsiia, 1999. 32 p. 7000 ptd. ISBN 5-8401-0016-1.

Основы управления в органах внутренних дел: Учебник. [Fundamental Principles of Administration in the Internal Affairs Agencies: Textbook]. Ed. A. P. Korenev. 3rd. rev. ed. M.: MIUI MVD Rossii, Shchyt-M, 1999. 354 p. 5000 ptd. ISBN 5-93004-051-6.

Правоохранительные органы и организации России: Учебное пособие. [Law Enforcement Agencies and Organisations of Russia]. Ed. A. P. Guliaev. M.: Sobranie, 1999. 144 p. 1250 ptd. ISBN 5-86605-011-0.

Правоохранительные органы Российской Федерации: Сборник нормативных актов. [Law Enforcement Agencies of the Russian Federation: Collection of Normative Acts]. 2nd. rev. ed. M.: Iurait, 1999. 394 p. 6000 ptd. ISBN 5-85294-089-5.

Правоохранительные органы Российской Федерации: Учебник для вузов. [Law Enforcement Agencies of the Russian Federation: Textbook for Institutes of Higher Education]. 2d. rev. ed. Ed. V. P.

Also published:
M.: Spark, 1999. 414 p. 10000 ptd. ISBN 5-88914-127-9. (3rd. rev. ed.)

Правоохранительные органы Российской Федерации: Учебное пособие. [Law Enforcement Agencies of the Russian Federation: Instructional Manual]. Ed. V. K. Bobrov. M.: Shchyt-M, 1999. 212 p. 2000 ptd. ISBN 5-93004-042-7.

Профессиональная этика сотрудников правоохранительных органов: Учебное пособие. [Professional Ethics of Personnel of Law Enforcement Agencies: Instructional Manual]. Eds. G. B. Dubov, A. V. Opalev. 2d. rev. ed. M.: Shchyt-M, 1999. 227 p. 1000 ptd. ISBN 5-93004-027-3.

Shumilov, A. Iu. *Частное детективное и охранное право.* [Private Detective and Protection Law]. M.: NORMA-INFRA-M, 1999. 43 p. 40000 ptd. ISBN 5-89123-368-1, ISBN 5-86225-552-4.

Shumilov, A. Iu. *Новый закон о милиции: Учебно-практическое пособие.* [New Law on the Police: Instructional-Methods Manual]. M.: Izdatel Shumilova I. I., 1999. 56 p. 5000 ptd. ISBN 5-89784-017-2.

Закон Российской Федерации о милиции. [Law of Russian Federation on the Police]. M.: Prospekt, Kodeks, 1999. 40 p. 10000 ptd. ISBN 5-8369-0025-6.

Законодательство России об оружии. Частная охранная и детективная деятельность: Сборник нормативных актов. [Legislation of Russia on Weapons. Private Protection and Detective Activity. Collection of Normative Acts]. Ed. V. L. Mironov. M.: Mir bezopasnosti, 1999. 607 p. 10000 ptd. ISBN 5-89258-020-2.

Criminal Law

Borodin, S. V. *Преступления против жизни.* [Crimes Against Life]. M.: Iurist', 1999. 356 p. 5000 ptd. ISBN 5-7975-0221-6.

Diakov, S. V. *Государственные преступления (против основ конституционного строя и безопасности государства) и государственная преступность.* [State Crimes (Against

Fundamental Principles of Constitutional Structure and State Security) and State Criminality]. M.: NORMA, 1999. 307 p. 3000 ptd. ISBN 5-89123-332-0.

Galiakbarov, R. R. *Уголовное право Российской Федерации: Общая часть. Конспекты и иные материалы.* [Criminal law of the Russian Federation: General Part Notes and Other Materials]. Krasnodar: Kuban. gos. agrarny un-t, 1999. 280 p. 3000 ptd.

Khabarov, A. *Россия ментовская.* [Cop-Shop Russia]. M.: EKSMO-Press, 1999. 480 p. 10000 ptd. ISBN 5-04-001813-4.

Iakubovskie, D. & I. *Что такое арест и как с ним бороться: Практическое пособие.* [What It Is To Be Arrested and How To Fight Against It: Practical Manual]. M.: Politbiuro, 1999. 575 p. 11000 ptd. ISBN 5-89756-016-1.

Ivanov, E. A. *Отмывание денег и правовое регулирование борьбы с ним.* [Money Laundering and Legal Regulation of the Struggle Against It]. M.: Ros. Iurid. Izdat. Dom, 1999. 176 p. ISBN 5-88635-030-6.

Kibalnik, A. G. *Иммунитеты в уголовном праве.* [Immunities in Criminal Law]. Stavropol: Stavropolservisshkola, 1999. 173 p. 1000 ptd. ISBN 5-93078-029-3.

Комментарий к Федеральному закону «Об оружии» (с постатейными материалами и образцами документов). [Commentary to the Federal Law "On Weapons" (with Article by Article Materials and Models of Documents)]. Ed. S. A. Karapetian. M.: Gorodets, 1999. 511 p. 5000 ptd. ISBN 5-89391-040-0.

Комментарий к постановлениям Пленума Верховного Суда Российской Федерации по уголовным делам. [Commentary to the Decrees of the Plenum of the Supreme Soviet of the Russian Federation on Criminal Matters]. Eds. V. M. Lebedev, B. N. Topornin. M.: Iurist', 1999. 412 p. 40000 ptd. ISBN 5-7975-0194-5.

Комментарий к Уголовному кодексу Российской Федерации. [Commentary to the Criminal Code of the Russian Federation]. Ed. A.

V. Naumov. 2nd. rev. ed. M.: Iurist', 1999. 864 p. 50000 ptd. ISBN 5-7975-0190-2.

Also published:

M.: NORMA-INFRA-M, 1999. 815 p. 90000 ptd. ISBN 5-89123-193-X.

Kovalev, M. I. *Соучастие в преступлении.* [Conspiracy in Crime]. Ekaterinburg: Izd-vo UrGIUA, 1999. 203 p. 500 ptd. ISBN 5-7845-0087-2.

Kucherena, A. *Бал беззакония: Диагноз адвоката.* [Lawlessness Ball: An Advocate's Diagnosis]. M.: Politbiuro, 1999. 351 p. 15000 ptd. ISBN 5-89756-017-X.

Kudriavtsev, V. N. *Общая теория квалификации преступлений.* [General Theory of the Qualification of Crimes]. M.: Iurist', 1999. 302 p. 3000 ptd. ISBN 5-7975-0170-8.

Курс уголовного права: Общая часть. Т.1: Учение о преступности. [Criminal Law Course: General Part. Vol.1: Doctrine on Criminality]. Eds. N. F. Kuznetsovaia, I. M. Tiazhkovaia. M.: Zertsalo, 1999. 577 p. 8000 ptd. ISBN 5-8078-0039-7.

Курс уголовного права: Общая часть: Том 2. [Criminal Law Course: General Part: Vol.2]. Eds. N. F. Kuznetsova, I. M. Tiazhkova. M.: Zertsalo, 1999. 400 p. 8000 ptd. ISBN 5-8078-0047-8.

Litvinov, N. D. *Террористические организации: формирование и деятельность: Политико-правовой анализ.* [Terrorist Organisations: Formation and Activity: Political Legal Analysis]. Ed. S. E. Bitsin. M.: Golos, 1999. 219 p. 5000 ptd. ISBN 5-7117-0381-1.

Mikhailov, V. I., Fedorov, A. V. *Таможенные преступления: Уголовно-правовой анализ.* [Customs Crimes: Criminal Law Analysis. Spb.: Iurid. tsentr deiatelnosti. Spb.: Iurid. tsentr Press, 1999. 324 p. 2000 ptd. ISBN 5-93292-006-8.

Надежда в беде: Наркотики и наркоманы. [Hope in Misfortune: Drugs and Drug Addicts]. M.: Samarianin, 1999. 118 p. 2000 ptd.

Nafiev, S. Kh. *Корыстное убийство: понятие, виды, квалификация: Уголовно-правовые и криминологические аспекты.* [Mercenary Homicide: Concepts, Types, Classification: Criminal Legal and Criminological Aspects]. Kazan: Tatar. gazetno-kn. izd-vo, 1999. 117 p. 1000 ptd. ISBN 5-85247-095-3.

Наркотики в России: преступления и расследование. [Narcotics in Russia: Crimes and Investigation]. Ed. V. P. Salnikov. Spb.: Fond podderzhki i obrazovaniia v obl. pravookhranit. deiatelnosti "Universitet", 1999. 425 p. 5000 ptd. ISBN 5-93598-004-5.

Об оружии: Федеральный закон. [On Weapons: Federal Law]. M.: INFRA-M, 1999. 24 p. 3000 ptd. ISBN 5-86225-616-4.

Petrukhin, I. L. *Человек и власть (в сфере борьбы с преступностью).* [Man and Power (in the Sphere of the Struggle Against Criminality]. M.: Iurist', 1999. 391 p. 1500 ptd. ISBN 5-7975-0255-0.

Пособие для следователя. [Manual for the Investigator]. Eds. N. A. Selivanov, A. I. Dvorkin. 2nd. rev. ed. M.: Liga Razum, 1999. 505 p. 3000 ptd. ISBN 5-89795-008-3.

Практикум по уголовному праву. [Practical Work on Criminal Law]. Ed. I. Ia. Kozachenko. M.: NORMA-INFRA-M, 1999. 539 p. 30000 ptd. ISBN 5-89123-250-2, ISBN 5-86225-822-1.

Prokhorov, L. A., Prokhorova, M. L. *Уголовное право: Учебник.* [Criminal Law: Textbook]. M.: Iurist', 1999. 479 p. 10000 ptd. ISBN 5-7975-0203-8.

Rarog, A. I., Stepalin, V. P. *Уголовное право: Общая часть в вопросах и ответах.* [Criminal Law: General Part in Questions and Answers]. M.: Iurist', 1999. 228 p. 10000 ptd. ISBN 5-7975-0144-9.

Romanov, S. *Мошенничество в России: Как уберечься от аферистов.* [Swindling in Russia: How to Protect Oneself from Swindlers]. M.: EKSMO-Press, 1999. 751 p. 5000 ptd. ISBN 5-04-000829-5.

Российское уголовное право: Общая часть. Учебник. [Russian Criminal Law: General Part. Textbook]. Ed. M. P. Zhuravlev. M.: Shchyt-M, 1999. 280 p. 500 ptd. ISBN 5-93004-040-0.

Сборник постановлений Пленумов Верховных Судов СССР и РСФСР(Российской Федерации) по уголовным делам. [Collection of Decrees of Plenums of the USSR and RSFSR (Russian Federation) Supreme Courts on Criminal Cases]. M.: Spark, 1999. 560 p. 6000 ptd. ISBN 5-88914-011-6.

Сборник задач по уголовному праву: Общая часть. Учебное пособие. [Collection of Tasks on Criminal Law: General Part. Instructional Manual]. Ed. V. B. Borovikov. M.: Shchyt-M, 1999. 172 p. 1000 ptd. ISBN 5-93004-037-0.

Shatalov, A., Vaksian, A. *Фальсификация, подделка, подлог ...* [Falsification, Simulation, Forgery ...]. M.: Liga Razum, 1999. 160 p. 6000 ptd. ISBN 5-89795-006-7.

Shumilov, A. Iu., Ivasenko, V. B. *Новый закон о наркотиках и терминология противодействия наркобизнесу.* [New Law on Narcotics and the Terminology of Opposition to the Narcotics' Business]. 2nd. rev. ed. M.: Izdatel Shumilova I. I., 1999. 72 p. 2000 ptd. ISBN 5-89784-021-0.

Smakhtin, E. V. *Расследование контрабанды стратегически важных сырьевых товаров.* [Investigation of Smuggling of Strategically Important Raw Goods]. Tiumen: Izd-vo Iu. Mandriki, 1999. 255 p. 500 ptd. ISBN 5-93020-031-9.

Tarabrin, A. *Беспредел.* [Chaos]. Intro. A. Aleksakhin, I. Riasny. M.: Panorama, 1999. 320 p. 7000 ptd. ISBN 5-85220-556-7.

Tarabrin, A. *Детоторговцы.* [Traders in Children]. M.: Panorama, 1999. 333 p. 7000 ptd. ISBN 5-85220-404-8.

Topilskaia, E. V. *Организованная преступность.* [Organised Criminality]. Spb.: Iurid. tsentr Press, 1999. 233 p. 5000 ptd. ISBN 5-93292-005-X.

Уголовное право: Часть Общая. Часть Особенная. Учебник. [Criminal Law: General Part. Particular Part. Textbook]. Eds. L. D. Gaukhman, L. M. Kolodkin, S. V. Maksimov. M.: Iurisprudentsiia, 1999. 784 p. 15000 ptd. ISBN 5-8401-0003-X.

Уголовное право. Особенная часть: Учебник. [Criminal Law. Particular Part: Textbook]. Ed. V. N. Petrashev. M.: Prior, 1999. 607 p. 4000 ptd. ISBN 5-7990-03-71-3.

Уголовное право: Учебник. [Criminal Law: Textbook]. Ed. V. N. Petrasheva. M.: Prior, 1999. 544 p. 8000 ptd. ISBN 5-7990-0228-8.

Also published:

M.: NORMA-INFRA-M, 1999. 405 p. 40000 ptd. ISBN 5-89123-376-2, ISBN 5-86225-849-3.

Уголовное право России: Часть Общая: Учебник для вузов. [Criminal Law of Russia: General Part. Textbook for Institutes of Higher Education]. Ed. L. L. Kruglikov. M.: BEK, 1999. 558 p. 3000 ptd. ISBN 5-85639-247-7.

Уголовное право России: Часть Особенная: Учебник для вузов. [Criminal Law of Russia: Special Part: Textbook for Institutes of Higher Education]. Ed. L. L. Kruglikov. M.: BEK, 1999. 832 p. 6000 ptd. ISBN 5-85639-249-3.

Уголовное право России и Особенная часть: Для вузов. [Criminal Law of Russia and Particular Part: For Institutes of Higher Education]. Eds. V. N. Kudriavtsev, A. V. Naumov. 2nd. rev. ed. M.:Iurist', 1999. 492 p. 10000 ptd. ISBN 5-7975-0186-4.

Уголовное право Российской Федерации. [Criminal Law of the Russian Federation]. M.: Iurist', 1999. 10000 ptd.

General Part. Ed. L. D. Ermakovaia. 267 p. ISBN 5-7975-0177-5.

Particular Part. Ed. A. V. Gladkov. 251 p. ISBN 5-7975-0178-3.

Уголовное право Российской Федерации: Для вузов. [Criminal Law of the Russian Federation: For Institutes of Higher Education]. 2d. rev. ed. Ed. B. V. Zdravomyslov. M.: Iurist', 1999. 5000 ptd. General Part. 480 p. ISBN 5-7975-0136-8. Special Part. 550 ptd. ISBN 5-7975-0137-6.

Уголовное право Российской Федерации: Учебно-методическое пособие. [Criminal Law of the Russian Federation: Instructional Methods Manual]. Spb.: Lenizdat, 1999. 170 p. 5000 ptd. ISBN 5-289-01862-X.

Уголовный кодекс Российской Федерации. [Criminal Code of the Russian Federation]. Ulianovsk: Knigochei, 1999. 191 p. 5000 ptd. ISBN 5-85525-018-0.

Also published:
M.: Novaia Volna, 1999. 192 p. 5000 ptd. ISBN 5-7864-0040-9.
M.: NIPKTS VOSKHOD, 1999. 147 p. ISBN 5-93055-002-6.
M.: Iurist', 1999. 191 p. 10000 ptd. ISBN 5-7975-02-08-9.
Spb.: Izd. dom "Litera", 1999. 208 p. 10000 ptd. ISBN 5-86617-035-3.
With Changes and additions for 1 April 1999. M.: Prospekt, 1999. 158 p. 7000 ptd. ISBN 5-8369-0006-X.
Official Text for 15 March 1999. M.: NORMA, INFRA-M, 1999. 205 p. 10000 ptd. ISBN 5- 89123-335-5, ISBN 5-86225-981-3.

Уголовный кодекс Российской Федерации: Научно-практический комментарий. [Criminal Code of the Russian Federation: Scientific-Practical Commentary]. M.: NORMA-INFRA-M, 1999. 205 p. 10000 ptd. ISBN 5-89123-335-5; ISBN 5-86225-981-3.

Also published:
M.: Novaia Volna, 1999. 191 p. 5000 ptd. ISBN 5-7864-0040-9.

Уголовный кодекс Российской Федерации: По состоянию на 15 февраля 1999 г. [Criminal Code of the Russian Federation: As of 15 February 1999]. M.: OLMA-Press, Novosibirsk: IUKEA, 1999. 288 p. 11000 ptd. ISBN 5-224-00278-8.

Уголовный кодекс Российской Федерации: С изменениями и дополнениями на 1 февраля 1999 г. [Criminal Code of the Russian Federation: With Changes and Additions for 1 February 1999]. M.: Prospekt, 1999. 158 p. 7000 ptd. ISBN 5-7896-0081-6.

Уголовный кодекс Российской Федерации: С изменениями и дополнениями на 15 августа 1999. [Criminal Code of the Russian Federation: With Changes and Additions for 15 August 1999]. M.:

Prospekt, 1999. 160 p. 7000 ptd. ISBN 5-8369-0006-X.

Уголовный кодекс Российской Федерации: С изменениями и дополнениями на 15 сентября 1999 г. [Criminal Code of the Russian Federation: With Changes and Additions for 15 September 1999]. M.: Prospekt, Kodeks, 1999. 158 p. 10000 ptd. ISBN 5-8369-0006-X.

Usmanov, U. A. *Комментарий к Уголовному кодексу Российской Федерации.* [Commentary to the Criminal Code of the Russian Federation]. M.: PRIOR, 1999. 496 p. 5000 ptd. ISBN 5-7990-0263-0.

Verin, V. P. *Преступления в сфере экономики: Учебное пособие.* [Crimes in the Sphere of the Economy: Instructional Manual]. M.: Delo, 1999. 199 p. 5000 ptd. ISBN 5-7749-0127-0.

Vetrov, N. I. *Уголовное право: Общая часть: Учебник.* [Criminal Law: General Part: Textbook]. M.: IUNITI, 1999. 415 p. 20000 ptd. ISBN 5-238-00121-5.

Vetrov, N. I. *Уголовное право: Общая и Особенная части. Для вузов.* [Criminal Law: General and Particular Parts. For Institutes of Higher Education]. M.: Knizh. mir, 1999. 221 p. 5000 ptd. ISBN 5-8041-0036-X.

Volzhenkin, B. V. *Экономические преступления.* [Economic Crimes]. Spb.: Iurid. tsentr Press, 1999. 299 p. 10000 ptd. ISBN 5-93292-001-7.

Вопросы квалификации и расследования преступлений в сфере экономики. [Questions of Classification and Investigation of Crimes in the Sphere of the Economy]. Eds. N. A. Lopashenko, V. M. Iurin, A. B. Nekhoroshev. Saratov: SIUI MVD Rossii, 1999. 240 p. 1500 ptd. ISBN 5-7485-0033-7.

Criminology

Abeltsev, S. N., Deriabin, S. D., Solodovnikov, S. A. *Побои и истязания: Проблемы криминологии. Учебное пособие.* [Beatings and Torture: Problems of Criminology. Instructional Manual]. Ed. G.

A. Avanesov. M.: Zakon i pravo, IUNITI-DANA, 1999. 127 p. 1000 ptd. ISBN 5-238-00092-8.

Akbarov, N. G. *Состояние и тенденции преступности несовершеннолетних.* [Conditions and Tendencies to Criminality by Minors]. Kazan; Izd-vo Kazan. un-ta, 1999. 165 p. 1000 ptd. ISBN 5-7464-0433-0.

Baimukhametov, S. *Сны золотые: Исповеди наркоманов.* [Golden Dreams: Confessions of Drug Addicts]. M.: PanBinter, 1999. 191 p. ISBN 5-89884-006-0.

Dolgova, A. I. *Криминология: Учебник для вузов.* [Criminology: Textbook for Institutes of Higher Education]. M.: NORMA-INFRA-M, 1999. 272 p. 40000 ptd. ISBN 5-89123-375-4, ISBN 5-86225-847-7.

Dyshev, S. *Россия бандитская.* [Gangster Russia]. M.: EKSMO-Press, 1999. 432 p. 10000 ptd. ISBN 5-04-001619-0.

Eminov, V. E., Matskevich, I. M. *Преступность военнослужащих: Исторический, криминологический, социально-правовой анализ.* [Criminality of Military Servicemen: Historical, Criminological, Socio-Legal Analysis]. M.: Penates-Penaty, 1999. 261 p. 2000 ptd.

Khokhriakov, G. F. *Криминология: Учебник.* [Criminology: Textbook]. Ed. V. N. Kudriavtsev. M.: Iurist', 1999. 511 p. 10000 ptd. ISBN 5-7975-0192-9.

Karyshev, V. *Жизнь бандитская: История группировки. Взгляд изнутри.* [A Gangster's Life: History of the Group. An Opinion from Within the Group]. M.: EKSMO-Press, 1999. 480 p. 5000 ptd. ISBN 5-04-002559-9.

Konstantinov, A. *Бандитский Петербург-98.* [Gangster St Petersburg-98]. 2d. rev. ed. M.: OLMA-Press, 1999. 559 p. 15000 ptd. ISBN 5-224-00161-7.

Konstantinov, A. & K. *Коррумпированный Петербург-98.* [Corrupt St Petersburg-98]. M.: OLMA-Press, 1999. 543 p. 15000 ptd. ISBN 5-

224-00162-5.

Криминология: Для вузов. [Criminology: For Institutes of Higher Education]. Eds. V. N. Kudriavtsev, V. E. Eminov. 2nd. rev. ed. M.: Iurist', 1999. 678 p. 10000 ptd. ISBN 5-7975-0193-7.

Also published:

Spb.: Spb. un-t MVD Rossii, Lan, 1999. 608 p. 10000 ptd. ISBN 5-8114-0059-4.

Криминология: Словарь. [Criminology: Dictionary]. Comp. V. N. Burlakov et al. Spb.: Lan, Izd-vo Spb. un-ta MVD Rossii, 1999. 254 p. 5000 ptd. ISBN 5-8114-0164-7.

Maksimov, A. *Бандиты в белых воротничках: Как разворовывали Россию.* [Bandits in White Collars: How They Plundered Russia]. M.: EKSMO-Press, 1999. 480 p. 20000 ptd. ISBN 5-04-002634-X.

Pavlov, V. G. *Субъект преступления в уголовном праве: Ист.-правовое исследование.* [Subject of Crime in Criminal Law: Historical-Legal Investigation]. M.: Spb.: Spb, iurid. akad. Gerda, 1999. 118 p. 4000 ptd. ISBN 5-7978-0049-7.

Преступность и культура. [Criminality and Culture]. Ed. A. I. Dolgovaia. M.: Kriminol. Assots., 1999. 159 p. 1000 ptd. ISBN 5-87817-019-1.

Repetskaia, A. L., Rybalskaia, V. Ia. *Криминология: Общая часть: Учебное пособие.* [Criminology: General Part: Instructional Manual]. Irkutsk: Izd-vo IGEA, 1999. 237 p. 700 ptd. ISBN 5-7253-0303-9.

Soldatenko, B. *Москва криминальная.* [Criminal Moscow]. M.: Tsentrpoligraf, 1999. 409. 15000 ptd. ISBN 5-227-00256-8.

Criminalistics

Antonian, Iu. M., Tkachenko, A. A., Shostakovich, B. V. *Криминальная сексология.* [Criminal Sexology]. M.: Spark, 1999. 464 p. 4000 ptd. ISBN 5-88914-109-0.

Belkin, R. T. *Криминалистика.* [Criminalistics]. M.: Iurist', 1999. 266 p. 5000 ptd. ISBN 5-7975-0230-5.

Chuvilev, A. A. *Оперативно-розыскное право.* [Operational Search Law]. M.: NORMA-INFRA-M, 1999. 75 p. 40000 ptd. ISBN 5-89123-369-X, ISBN 5-86225-603-2.

Dmitrienko, T. M., Chaadaev, S. G. *Судебная (правовая) бухгалтерия: Учебник.* [Forensic (Legal) Accountancy: Textbook]. M.: Prospekt, 1999. 335 p. 5000 ptd. ISBN 5-7896-0049-2.

Eremin, S. G., Rezvan, A. P. *Раскрытие и расследование хищений на предприятиях рыбного хозяйства: Учебное пособие.* [Uncovering and Investigation of Stealing at Fish Farming Enterprises: Instructional Manual]. Volgograd: VIUI MVD Rossii, 1999. 104 p. 300 ptd. ISBN 5-7899-0053-4.

Ishchenko, E. P., Ishchenko, P. P., Zotchev, V. A. *Криминиалистическая фотография и видеозапись: Учебно-практическое пособие.* [Criminalistics Photography and Video Recording: Instructional Practical Manual]. Ed. E. P. Ishchenko. M.: Iurist', 1999. 436 p. 5000 ptd. ISBN 5-7975-0202-X.

Комментарий к Федеральному закону «Об оперативно-розыскной деятельности». [Commentary to the Federal Law "On Operational Search Activity"]. M.: Izdatel Shumilova I. I., 1999. 263 p. 3000 ptd. ISBN 5-89784-016-4.

Криминалистика: Для вузов. [Criminalistics: For Institutes of Higher Education]. Ed. A. F. Vorlinskii. M.: Zakon i pravo, IUNITI-DANA, 1999. 615 p. 20000 ptd. ISBN 5-238-00083-9.
Also published:
M.: Iurist', 1999. 718 p. 10000 ptd. ISBN 5-7975-0167-8.

Криминалистика: Схемы и комментарий. [Criminalistics: Diagrams and Commentary]. Ed. A. G. Filippov. M.: Iurisprudentsiia, 1999. 240 p. 8000 ptd. ISBN 5-86532-05-6.

Криминалистика: Учебник. [Criminalistic: Textbook]. Ed. V. A. Obraztsov. 2d. rev. ed. M.: Iurist', 1999. 734 p. 10000 ptd. ISBN 5-

7975-0187-2.

Криминалистика: Учебник для вузов. [Criminalistics: Textbook for Institutes of Higher Education]. Ed. R. S. Belkin. M.: NORMA-INFRA-M, 1999. 971 p. 60000 ptd. ISBN 5-89123-302-9, ISBN 5-86225-949-X.

Also published:

M.: Spark, 1999. 543 p. 8000 ptd. ISBN 5-88914-084-1.

Meshkov, V. M., Popov, V. L. *Оперативно-розыскная тактика и особенности легализации полученной информации в ходе предварительного следствия: Учебно-практическое пособие.* [Operational Search Tactics and Peculiarities of the Legalisation of Received Information During the Course of Preliminary Investigation: Instructional Methods Manual]. M.: Shchyt-M, 1999. 79 p. 1000 ptd. ISBN 5-93004-028-1.

Mitrichev, V. C., Khrustalev, V. N. *Криминалистическое исследование лакокрасочных материалов, покрытий и окрашенных предметов: Учебно-методическое пособие для образоват. учерждений МВД России.* [Criminalistics Research of Lacquer and Paint Materials, Coverings and Painted Objects: Instructional Methods Manual for the Educational Institutions of the Russian Ministry for Internal Affairs]. Saratov: Sarat. iurid. in-t, 1999. 148 p. 250 ptd. ISBN 5-7485-0012-4.

Motorny, I. D. *Теоретико-прикладные основы применения средств и методов криминалистической взрывотехники в борьбе с терроризмом.* [Theoretical and Practical Fundamental Principles of the Application of Means and Methods of Criminalistics Explosives Technology in the Struggle Against Terrorism]. M.: Izdatel Shumilova I. I., 1999. 199 p. 1000 ptd. ISBN 5-89784-019-9.

Новый оперативно-розыскной закон России: Учебно-практическое пособие. [New Operational Search Law of Russia: Instructional Practical Manual]. Comp. A. Iu. Shumilov. 5th rev. ed. M.: Izdatel Shumilova I. I., 1999. 48 p. 3000 ptd. ISBN 5-89784-014-8.

Новые правила документирования результатов оперативно-розыскной деятельности. [New Rules for Documenting the Results of Operational-Search Activity]. Comp. A. Iu. Shumilov. M.: Izdatel Shumilova I. I., 1999. 16 p. 3000 ptd. ISBN 5-89784-015-6.

Организация и производство расследования преступлений. [Organisation and Conducting of Investigation of Crimes]. Eds. I. A. Kopylov, V. F. Shcherbatov. Volgograd: VIUI MVD RF, 1999. 208 p. 400 ptd. ISBN 5-7899-0069-0.

Основы оперативно-розыскной деятельности: Учебник. [Fundamental Principles of Operational Search Activity: Textbook]. Ed. S. V. Stepashin. Spb.: Lan, 1999. 704 p. 5000 ptd. ISBN 5-8114-0153-1.

Pleskachevskii, V. M. *Оружие в криминалистике. Понятие и классификация.* [Weapons in Criminalistics. Concept and Classification]. M.: NIPKTS VOSKHOD, 1999. 383 p. ISBN 5-93055-011-5.

Расследование контрабанды: Практическое пособие. [Investigation into Smuggling: Practical Manual]. Ed. K. F. Skvortsov. M.: Iurist', 1999. 206 p. 7500 ptd. ISBN 5-7975-0116-3.

Расследование преступлений в сфере экономики: Руководство для следователей. [Investigation of Crimes in the Sphere of the Economy: Guide for the Investigator]. Ed. I. N. Kozhevnikov. M.: Spark, 1999. 415 p. 12000 ptd. ISBN 5-88914-118-X.

Расследование преступлений, связанных с незаконным оборотом наркотических средств и психотропных веществ: В 2 ч. Учебное пособие. [Investigation of Crimes Connected with the Illegal Turnover of Narcotics and Psychotropic Substances: In 2 Parts. Instructional Manual].

Часть 1. Уголовно-правовая и криминалистическая характеристика преступлений. [Part 1. Criminal-Legal and Criminalistics Characteristics of Crimes]. V. P. Prikazchikov et al. 76 p. ISBN 5-7899-0056-9.

Часть 2. В. П. Приказчиков, А. П. Резван, В. Н. Косарев. Организация расследования и особенности производства отдельных следственных действий. [Part 2. V. P. Prikazchikov, A. P. Rezvan, V. N. Kosarev. Organisation of

Investigation and Peculiarities of Conducting Separate Investigative Actions]. 68 p. ISBN 5-7899-0059-3.

Rossinskaia, E. R. *Криминалистика: Вопросы и ответы: Учебное пособие для вузов.* [Criminalistics: Questions and Answers: Instructional Manual for Institutes of Higher Education]. M.: IUNITI-DANA, 1999. 351 p. 10000 ptd. ISBN 5-238-00116-9.

Ручное огнестрельное оружие и патроны к нему. [Manual Firearms and Their Cartridges]. M.: Mozhaisk-Terra, 1999. 301 p. 1200 ptd. ISBN 5-7542-0050-1.

Shumilov, A. Iu. *Юридические основы оперативно-розыскных мероприятий: Учебное пособие.* [Legal Fundamental Principles of Operational Search Measures: Instructional Manual]. M.: Izdatel Shumilova I. I., 1999. 128 p. 2000 ptd. ISBN 5-89784-018-0.

Shumilov, A. Iu. *Новый оперативно-розыскной закон России: Учебно-практическое пособие.* [New Operational Search Law of Russia: Instructional Practical Manual]. 6th rev. ed. M.: Izd. Shumilova I. I., 1999. 48 p. 3000 ptd. ISBN 5-89784-020-2.

Shurukhnov, N. G. *Расследование краж: Практическое пособие.* [Investigation of Thefts: Practical Manual]. M.: Iurist', 1999. 111 p. 5000 ptd. ISBN 5-7975-0114-7.

Skorchenko, P. T. *Криминалистика: Учебное пособие.* [Criminalistics: Instructional Manual]. M.: Bylina, 1999. 270 p. 3000 ptd. ISBN 5-93384-002-5.

Современные проблемы криминалистики. [Contemporary Criminalistics Problems]. Ed. B. P. Smagorinskii. Volgograd: VIUI MVD Rossii, 1999. 224 p. 200 ptd. ISBN 5-7899-0043-7.

Topilskaia, E. V. *Записки сумасшедшего следователя.* [Notes of a Mad Investigator]. Spb.: Izd-vo Spb. un-ta, 1999. 151 p. 1000 ptd. ISBN 5-288-02253-4.

Toporkov, A. A. *Словесный портрет: Практическое пособие.* [Description: Practical Manual]. M.: Iurist', 1999. 111 p. 5000 ptd.

ISBN 5-7975-0149-X.

Forensic Medicine, Psychology and Psychiatry

Sakhnova, T. V. *Судебная экспертиза.* [Forensic Expert Examination]. M.: Gorodets, Formula prava, 1999. 367 p. 1500 ptd. ISBN 5-89391-052-4.

Segela, J. *Национальные особенности охоты за голосами.* [National Peculiarities of the Hunt for Votes]. Trans. from French. M.: VAGRIUS, 1999. 263 p. 5000 ptd. ISBN 5-264-00109-X.

Sitkovskaia, O. D. *Психологический комментарий к Уголовному кодексу Российской Федерации.* [Psychological Commentary to the Criminal Code of the Russian Federation]. M.: Zertsalo, 1999. 89 p. 3000 ptd. ISBN 5-8078-0048-6.

Military Justice

Комментарий Федерального закона «О статусе военнослужащих». [Commentary to the Federal Law "On the Status of Military Servicemen"]. Ed. V. G. Strekozov. M.: Spark, 1999. 576 p. 10000 ptd. ISBN 5-88914-098-1.

О призыве на военную службу: Сборник нормативных актов. [On the Call-Up for Military Service: Collection of Normative Acts]. 3rd. rev. ed. M.: Iurait, 1999. 294 p. 3000 ptd. ISBN 5-85294-070-4.

О ветеранах: Федеральный закон. [On Veterans: Federal Law]. M.: INFRA-M, 1999. 33 p. 3000 ptd. ISBN 5-86225-740-3.

О воинской обязанности и военной службе: Федеральный закон. [On Military Duty and Military Service: Federal Law]. M.: INFRA-M, 1999. 51 p. 3000 ptd. ISBN 5-86225-783-7.

О воинской обязанности и военной службе: Федеральный закон от 28 марта 1998 г. No.53-F3. Вопросы прохождения военной службы: Указ Президента РФ от 4 января 1999 г. No.4. [On Military Duty and Military Service: Federal Law of 28 March 1998. No.53-F3. Questions on the Origin of Military Service: Russian

Federation Presidential Edict of 4 January 1999. No.4.]. M.: Iurisprudentsiia, 1999. 55 p. 5000 ptd. ISBN 5-86532-048-3.

Popenko, V. N. *Война без правил.* [War Without Rules]. M.: Boguchar, 1999. 128 p. 6000 ptd. ISBN 5-88276-029-X.

Correctional-Labour Law

Aleksandrov, Iu. K. *Тюремный закон.* [Prison Law]. M.: Pravovoe prosveshchenie, 1999. 278 p. 5000 ptd. ISBN 5-89-661-008-4.

Aleksandrov, Iu. K., Vezhnina, N. N., Klimenko, S. K. *Туберкулез в тюрьме: Пособие для заключенных.* [Tuberculosis in Prison: Manual for Prisoners]. M.: Prava cheloveka, 1999. 70 p. 5000 ptd. ISBN 5-7712-0105-7.

Alikperov, Kh. D. *Освобождение от уголовной ответственности: Уголовно-правовые аспекты.* [Release from Criminal Responsibility: Criminal Legal Aspects]. M.: IPK RK Gen. prokuratury RF, 1999. 127 p. 200 ptd.

Detkov, M. G. *Тюрьмы, лагеря и колонии России.* [Russian Prisons, Camps and Colonies]. M.: Verdykt-1M, 1999. 447 p. 1000 ptd. ISBN 5-87143-013-9.

Dugin, A. N. *Неизвестный ГУЛАГ: Документы и факты.* [The Unknown GULAG: Documents and Facts]. M.: Nauka, 1999. 103 p. 1000 ptd. ISBN 5-02-008352-6.

Комментарий к Уголовно-исполнительному кодексу Российской Федерации. [Commentary to the Criminal Executory Code of the Russian Federation]. Ed. S. V. Stepashin. 2nd. rev. ed. M.: Iurist', 1999. 622 p. 10000 ptd. ISBN 5-7975-0227-5.

Mikhlin, A. S., Seliverstov, V. I., Shmarov, I. V. *Уголовно-исполнительное право: Вопросы и ответы.* [Criminal Executory Law: Questions and Answers]. M.: Iurisprudentsiia, 1999. 160 p. 8000 ptd. ISBN 5-5-8401-0001-31.

Perminov, O. G. *Уголовно-исполнительное право: Для вузов.*

[Criminal-Executory Law: For Institutes of Higher Education]. M.: Bylina, 1999. 238 p. 3000 ptd. ISBN 5-88528-238-2.

Проблемы формирования уголовно-розыскного права: Выпуск 2. [Problems of the Formation of Criminal Executory Law: Issue 2]. Ed. A. Iu. Shumilov. M.: Izdatel Shumilova I. I., 1999. 136 p. 500 ptd. ISBN 5-89784-023-7.

Stanovskii, M. N. *Назначение наказания.* [Assignment of Punishment]. Spb.: Iurid. tsentr Press, 1999. 480 p. 2000 ptd. ISBN 5-93292-004-1.

Уголовная ответственность несовершеннолетних: Научно-практическое пособие. [Criminal Responsibility of Minors: Scientific-Practical Manual]. Ed. V. P. Kashepov. M.: Iurid, lit., 1999. 159 p. 3000 ptd. ISBN 5-7260-0924-X.

Уголовно-исполнительное право России: Учебник для вузов. [Criminal Executory Law of Russia: Textbook]. M. G. Detkov et al. M.: NORMA-INFRA-M, 1999. 599 p. 6000 ptd. ISBN 5-89123-135-2, ISBN 5-86225-548-6.

Уголовно-исполнительный кодекс Российской Федерации: Официальный текст по состоянию на 1 февраля 1999 г. [Criminal Executory Code of the Russian Federation: Official Text for 1 February 1999]. M.: NORMA-INFRA-M, 1999. 144 p. 3000 ptd. ISBN 5-89123-295-2, ISBN 5-86225-937-6.

Уголовно-исполнительный кодекс Российской Федерации: Официальный текст по состоянию на 15 марта 1999 г. [Criminal Executory Code of the Russian Federation: Official Text for 15 March 1999]. M.: NORMA, INFRA-M, 1999. 139 p. 3000 ptd. ISBN 5-89123-295-2, ISBN 5-86225-937-6.

Уголовно-исполнительный кодекс Российской Федерации: С изменениями и дополнениями на 15 августа 1999 г. [Criminal Executory Code of the Russian Federation: With Changes and Additions for 15 August 1999]. M.: Prospekt, 1999. 108 p. 5000 ptd. ISBN 5-8369-0030-2.

Уголовно-исполнительный кодекс Российской Федерации: С изменениями и дополнениями на 15 октября 1999 г. [Criminal Executory Code of the Russian Federation: With Changes and Additions for 15 October 1999]. M.: Kodeks, Prospekt, 1999. 108 p. 7000 ptd. ISBN 5-8369-0030-2.

Law of Procedure

Lifanova, M. V. *Выявление и разоблачение ложных показаний на предварительном следствии: Учебное пособие.* [Disclosure and Unmasking of False Testimony During Preliminary Investigation: Instructional Manual]. Ufa: Vost. un-t, 1999. 43 p. 200 ptd.

Tikhomirov, M. Iu. *Исковые заявления в суд общей юрисдикции.* [Petition to Sue in the Court of General Jurisdiction]. M.: Izd. g-na Tikhomirova M. Iu., 1999. 89 p. 3000 ptd. ISBN 5-89194-029-9.

Treushnikov, M. K. *Судебные доказательства.* [Judicial Evidence]. 2nd. rev. ed. M.: Gorodets, 1999. 288 p. ISBN 5-89391-014-1.

Arbitrazh Procedure

Anokhin, V. S. *Арбитражное процессуальное право России: Учебник.* [Arbitrazh Procedure Law of Russia: Textbook]. M.: VLADOS, 1999. 495 p. 10000 ptd. ISBN 5-691-00352-6.

Арбитражная практика за 1998 г. [Arbitrazh Practice for 1998]. Comp. M. G. Rozenberg. M.: Statut, 1999. 269 p. 7000 ptd. ISBN 5-8354-0013-6.

Арбитражный процесс: Практикум. [Arbitrazh Procedure: Practical Work]. Ed. V. V. Iarkov. M.: Iurist', 1999. 186 p. 10000 ptd. ISBN 5-5-7975-0222-4.

Арбитражный процессуальный кодекс Российской Федерации. Федеральный конституционный закон «Об арбитражных судах в Российской Федерации»: Официальные тексты по состоянию на 15 января 1999г. [Code of Arbitrazh Procedure of the Russian Federation. Federal Constitutional Law "On Arbitrazh Courts in the Russian Federation": Official Texts as of 15 January

1999]. M.: EKMOS, 1999. 96 p. 3000 ptd. ISBN 5-88124-036-7.

Арбитражный процессуальный кодекс Российской Федерации. Федеральный конституционный закон «Об арбитражных судах в Российской Федерации»: Официальные тексты по состоянию на 1 февраля 1999 г. [Code of Arbitrazh Procedure of the Russian Federation. Federal Constitutional Law "On Arbitrazh Courts in the Russian Federation": Official Texts from 1 February 1999]. M.: NORMA-INFRA-M, 1999. 156 p. 4000 ptd. ISBN 5-89123-318-5, ISBN 5-86225-972-4.

Арбитражный процессуальный кодекс Российской Федерации: С изменениями и дополнениями на 1 февраля 1999 г. [Code of Arbitrazh Procedure of the Russian Federation: With Changes and Additions for 1 February 1999]. M.: Prospekt, 1999. 96 p. 5000 ptd. ISBN 5-7896-0072-7.

Арбитражный процессуальный кодекс Российской Федерации: С изменениями и дополнениями на 5 апреля 1999 г. [Code of Arbitrazh Procedure of the Russian Federation: With Changes and Additions for 5 April 1999]. M.: Prospekt, 1999. 96 p. 5000 ptd. ISBN 5-8369-0008-6.

Арбитражный процессуальный кодекс Российской Федерации: С изменениями и дополнениями на 1 сентября 1999 г. [Code of Arbitrazh Procedure of the Russian Federation: With Changes and Additions for 1 September 1999]. M.: Prospekt, 1999. 96 p. 5000 ptd. ISBN 5-8369-0043-4.

Арбитражный процессуальный кодекс Российской Федерации: с изменениями и дополнениями на 15 октября 1999 г. [Code of Arbitrazh Procedure of the Russian Federation: With Changes and Additions for 15 October 1999]. M.: Prospekt, Kodeks, 1999. 96 p. 10000 ptd. ISBN 5-8369-0043-4.

Fursov, D. A. *Предмет, система и основные принципы арбитражного процессуального права: Проблемы теории и практики.* [Subject, System and Fundamental Principles of Arbitrazh Procedure Law: Problems of Theory and Practice]. M.: INFRA-M, 1999. 452 p. 3000 ptd. ISBN 5-86225-970-8.

Ivanova, N. R. *Защита права собственности в арбитражном суде: Комментарий арбитраж. практики.* [Defence of the Rights of Ownership in an Arbitrazh Court: Commentary to Arbitrazh Practice]. M.: Kontrakt, INFRA-M, 1999. 295 p. 3000 ptd. ISBN 5-86225-921-X.

Kananovich, I. V. *Арбитражный процесс: Вопросы и ответы.* [Arbitrazh Procedure: Questions and Answers]. M.: Iurisprudentsiia, 1999. 141 p. 7000 ptd. ISBN 5-8401-0008-0.

Комментарий арбитражно-судебной практики по делам, связанным с малым предпринимательством и законодательством о применении контрольно-кассовых машин. [Commentary of Arbitrazh and Judicial Practice on Matters Connected with Small Entrepreneurship and Legislation on the Application of Cash Checking Machines]. Mytishchi: IITS "Alfa-Kompozit", 1999. 48 p. 1000 ptd.

Комментарий к Арбитражному процессуальному кодексу Российской Федерации. [Commentary to the Code of Arbitrazh Procedure of the Russian Federation]. Intro. V. F. Iakovlev. 2nd. rev. ed. M.: Kontrakt, INFRA-M, 1999. 516 p. 40000 ptd. ISBN 5-90785-013-2, ISBN 5-86225-676-8.

Комментарий судебно-арбитражной практики: Выпуск 6. [Commentary to Judicial Arbitrazh Practice: Issue 6]. Ed. V. F. Iakovlev. M.: Iurid. lit., 1999. 295 p. 5000 ptd. ISBN 5-7260-0935-5.

Практическое пособие по арбитражному управлению предприятием. [Practical Manual on the Arbitration Management of Enterprises]. G. K. Tal et al. M.: Statut, 1999. 379 p. 300 ptd.

Справочник по арбитражному процессу. [Manual on Arbitrazh Procedure]. 3rd. rev. ed. Intro. V. F. Iakovlev. Ed. V. V. Antonov. M.: DiS, IUKEA, 1999. 761 p. 7000 ptd. ISBN 5-86750-124-8.

Vandyshev, V. V., Dernova, D. V. *Арбитражный процесс: Сборник схем с комментарий: Учебное пособие.* [Arbitrazh Procedure: Collection of Models with Commentary: Instructional Manual]. Spb.: Paritet, 1999. 223 p. 5000 ptd. ISBN 5-89715-005-2.

Civil Procedure

Гражданский процесс: Учебник. [Civil Procedure: Textbook]. 2d. rev. ed. Eds. V. A. Musin, N. A. Chechinaia, D. M. Chechota. M.: Prospekt, 1999. 472 p. 10000 ptd. ISBN 5-7896-0069-7.

Also published:
M.: Spark, Gorodets, 1999. 544 p. 8000 ptd. ISBN 5-88914-107-4.
M.: Novy Iurist, 1999. 400 p. 2000 ptd. ISBN 5-7969-0076-5.
M.: BEK, 1999. 593 p. 20000 ptd. ISBN 5-85639-264-7.
M.: Prospekt, 1999. 472 p. 10000 ptd. ISBN 5-8369-0049-3. (2nd. rev. ed).

Гражданский процессуальный кодекс РСФСР. [RSFSR Code of Civil Procedure]. M.: NORMA-INFRA-M, 1999.

Официальный текст по состоянию на 15 декабря 1998 г. [Official Text as of 15 December 1998]. 219 p. 8000 ptd. ISBN 5-89123-325-8.

Официальный текст по состоянию на 15 февраля 1999 г. [Official Text as of 15 February 1999]. 219 p. 10000 ptd. ISBN 5-89123-325-8.

Also published:
M.: Iurist', 1999. 176 p. 10000 ptd. ISBN 5-7975-0188-0.

Гражданский процессуальный кодекс РСФСР: Официальный текст с изменениями и дополнениями по состоянию на 1 сентября 1999 г. [RSFSR Code of Civil Procedure: Official Text with Changes and Additions for 1 September 1999]. M.: TANDEM, EKMOS, 1999. 128 p. 3000 ptd. ISBN 5-88124-050-2.

Гражданский процессуальный кодекс РСФСР: С изменениями и дополнениями на 15 мая 1999 г. [RSFSR Code of Civil Procedure: With Changes and Additions for 15 May 1999]. M.: Prospekt, Kodeks, 1999. 166 p. 10000 ptd. ISBN 5-8369-0010-8.

Гражданский процессуальный кодекс РСФСР: С изменениями и дополнениями на 15 сентября 1999 г. [RSFSR Code of Civil Procedure: With Changes and Additions for 15 September 1999]. M.: Prospekt, 1999. 168 p. 10000 ptd. ISBN 5-8369-0010-8.

Гражданский процессуальный кодекс РСФСР с постатейным приложением судебных документов и комментариями. [RSFSR Code of Civil Procedure with Article by Article Annex of Judicial Documents and Commentaries]. Comp. N. R. Vilchur et al. M.: Prospekt, Kodeks, 1999. 416 p. 5000 ptd. ISBN 5-8369-0036-1.

Гражданский процессуальный кодекс РСФСР с судебными документами. [RSFSR Code of Civil Procedure with Judicial Documents]. N. R. Vilchur et al. M.: Kodeks, Prospekt, 1999. 416 p. 5000 ptd. ISBN 5-8369-0068-X.

Гражданское процессуальное право России: Учебник для вузов. [Law of Civil Procedure of Russia: Textbook for Institutes of Higher Education]. 2d. rev. ed. Ed. M. S. Shakarian. M.: Bylina, 1999. 500 p. 5000 ptd.

Комментарий к Гражданскому процессуальному кодексу РСФСР. [Commentary to the RSFSR Code of Civil Procedure]. 2d. rev. ed. Ed. M. K. Treushnikov. M.: Spark, Gorodets, 1999. 588 p. 10000 ptd. ISBN 5-88914-080-9, ISBN 5-89391-021-4.

Комментарий к постановлениям Пленума Верховного Суда Российской Федерации по гражданским делам. [Commentary to the Decrees of the Plenum of the Supreme Court of the Russian Federation on Civil Cases]. Comps. E. A. Borisova, V. M. Zhuykov. Ed. V. M. Zhuykov. M.: Iurist', 1999. 582 p. 50000 ptd. ISBN 5-7975-0260-7.

Научно-практический комментарий к Гражданскому процессуальному кодексу РСФСР. [Scientific Practical Commentary to the RSFSR Code of Civil Procedure]. Ed. M. K. Treushnikov. M.: Gorodets, 1999. 672 p. 10000 ptd. ISBN 5-89391-051-6.

Практикум по гражданскому процессуальному праву: Учебное пособие. [Practical Work on the Law of Civil Procedure: Instructional Manual]. Ed. M. K. Treushnikov. M.: Gorodets, Formula prava, 1999. 288 p. 5000 ptd. ISBN 5-89393-003-6.

Ryzhakov, A. P., Sergeev, D. A. *Постатейный комментарий к Гражданскому процессуальному кодексу РСФСР.* [Article by

Article Commentary to the RSFSR Code of Civil Procedure]. M.: Statut, 1999. 718 p. 10000 ptd. ISBN 5-8354-0011-X.

Сборник постановлений Пленумов Верховного Суда и Высшего Арбитражного Суда Российской Федерации по гражданским делам. [Collection of Decrees of the Plenums of the Supreme Court and the Supreme Arbitrazh Court of the Russian Federation on Civil Cases]. Comp. A. P. Sergeev. M.: Prospekt, Kodeks, 1999. 829 p. 10000 ptd. ISBN 5-8369-0033-7.

Сборник постановлений Пленумов Верховных Судов СССР и РСФСР (Российской Федерации) по гражданским делам. [Collection of Decrees of the Plenums of the USSR and RSFSR (Russian Federation) Supreme Courts on Civil Cases]. Comps. A. Ia. Kachanov, S. N. Zabarin, A. L. Soloviev. M.: Spark, 1999. 399 p. 10000 ptd. ISBN 5-88914-018-3.

Сборник задач по гражданскому процессуальному праву. [Collection of Tasks on the Law of Civil Procedure]. Ed. M. S. Shakarian. M.: Iurist', 1999. 144 p. 10000 ptd. ISBN 5-7975-0021-3.

Taranina, I. V. *Краткий справочник по гражданскому процессу.* [A Short Manual on Civil Procedure]. Novosibirsk: IUKEA, 1999. 159 p. 3000 ptd. ISBN 5-93376-016-1.

Turusov, A. A. *Осторожно: ГПК - защищайтесь! Защита прав граждан в процессе применения Гражданского процессуального кодекса.* [Be Careful: The Code of Civil Procedure - Defend Yourselves! Defence of the Rights of Citizens During the Process of the Application of the Code of Civil Procedure]. Rostov n/D: Feniks, 1999. 318 p. 10000 ptd. ISBN 5-222-00766-9.

Vikut, M. A., Zaitsev, I. M. *Гражданский процесс России: Учебник для вузов.* [The Civil Procedure of Russia: Textbook for Institutes of Higher Education]. M.: Iurist', 1999. 383 p. 10000 ptd. ISBN 5-7975-0238-0.

Zviagintsev, L. M., Pliukhina, M. A., Reshetnikova, I. V. *Доказывание в судебной практике по гражданским делам: Учебно-практическое пособие.* [Proof in Judicial Practice in Civil Cases:

Instructional Practical Manual]. M.: NORMA-INFRA-M, 1999. 283 p. 3000 ptd. ISBN 5-89123-377-0.

Criminal Procedure

Aleksandrov, A., Kovtun, N. *Апелляция в русском уголовном судопроизводстве.* [Appeal in Russian Criminal Court Proceeding]. N. Novgorod: Izd-vo Volgo-Viat. akad. gos. sluzhby, 1999. 108 p. 250 ptd. ISBN 5-85152-177-5.

Aleksandrov, Iu. K. *Если вас арестовали ...: Справочник для лиц, содержащихся под стражей в следственных изоляторах.* [If They Have Arrested You ...: Manual for Persons Detained Under Guard in Solitary Confinement]. M.: Prava cheloveka, 1999. 279 p. 2000 ptd. ISBN 5-7712-0107-3.

Brusnitsyn, L. V. *Правовое обеспечение безопасности лиц, содействующих уголовному правосудию.* [Legal Ensuring of the Safety of Persons Assisting Criminal Justice]. M.: Spark, 1999. 108 p. 2000 ptd. ISBN 5-88914-110-4.

Дознание и предварительное следствие в органах Федеральной службы налоговой полиции России: Сборник нормативных актов. [Inquiry and Preliminary Investigation in the Agencies of the Federal Service of the Tax Police of Russia: Collection of Normative Acts]. Ed. V. E. Manuylov. Comps. V. N. Galuzo, M. P. Smirnov. M.: Iurait, 1999. 493 p. 5000 ptd. ISBN 5-85294-075-5.

Gelmanov, A. G., Gontar, S. A. *Как установить участие лица в правонарушении.* [How to Establish the Participation of a Person in the Violation of Law]. M.: Mozhaisk. poligraf. komb., 1999. 160 p. 5000 ptd. ISBN 5-8493-0063-5.

Grigoriev, V. N. *Задержание подозреваемого.* [Detention of Suspect]. M.: IurInfoR, 1999. 541 p. 5000 ptd. ISBN 5-89158-029-2.

Gromov, N. A. *Вновь открывшиеся обстоятельства в уголовном процессе.* [Newly Discovered Circumstances in Criminal Procedure]. M.: Spark, 1999. 220 p. 1500 ptd.

Хрестоматия по уголовному процессу России. [Anthology on Russian Criminal Procedure]. Comp. E. F. Kutsov. M.: Gorodets, 1999. 269 p. 4000 ptd. ISBN 5-89391-033-8.

Iakupov, R. Kh. *Уголовный процесс: Учебник для вузов.* [Criminal Procedure: Textbook for Institutes of Higher Education]. Ed. V. N. Galuzo. M.: Zertsalo, 1999. 464 p. 8000 ptd. ISBN 5-8078-0037-0.

Комментарий к Федеральному закону «О содержании под стражей подозреваемых и обвиняемых в совершении преступлений». [Commentary to the Federal Law "On the Keeping Under Guard of Suspects and Those Accused of the Commission of a Crime"]. Eds. A. S. Mikhlin, V. I. Seliverstov. M.: Spark, 1999. 191 p. 8000 ptd. ISBN 5-88914-125-2.

Комментарий к Уголовно-процессуальному кодексу РСФСР. [Commentary to the RSFSR Code of Criminal Procedure]. Ed. V. M. Savitskii et al. M.: Prospekt, 1999. 576 p. 15000 ptd. ISBN 5-8369-0048-5.

Also published:
M.: Iurait, 1999. 742 p. 10000 ptd. ISBN 5-85294-087-9.
M.: Iurait, 1999. 729 p. 10000 ptd. ISBN 5-85294-058-5. (2d. rev. ed.)

Medvedev, M. Iu. *Уголовный процесс: Консультации. Образцы документов. Судебная практика.* [Criminal Procedure: Consultations. Samples of Documents. Judicial Practice]. M.: Iurisprudentsiia, 1999. 394 p. 10000 ptd. ISBN 5-8401-0009-9.

Образцы уголовно-процессуальных документов. [Models of Criminal Procedure Documents]. Eds. E. F. Kutsovaia, Iu. K. Orlov. M.: Iurist', 1999. 426 p. 7500 ptd. ISBN 5-7975-0173-2.

Riapisov, S. V., Ryzhakov, A. P. *Уголовно-процессуальный кодекс РСФСР с постатейными материалами.* [RSFSR Code of Criminal Procedure with Article by Article Materials]. M.: PRIOR, 1999. 750 p. 5000 ptd. ISBN 5-7990-0366-7.

Ryzhakov, A. P. *Окончание предварительного расследования: Учебное пособие.* [Completion of Preliminary Investigation:

Instructional Manual]. M.: Gorodets, Formula prava, 1999. 255 p. ISBN 5-89391-049-4.

Ryzhakov, A. P. *Органы дознания в уголовном процессе.* [Agencies of Inquiry in the Criminal Procedure]. M.: Gorodets, Formula prava, 1999. 356 p. 2000 ptd. ISBN 5-89391-042-7.

Ryzhakov, A. P. *Уголовный процесс: Учебник для вузов.* [Criminal Procedure: Textbook for Institutes of Higher Education]. M.: PRIOR, 1999. 592 p. 8000 ptd. ISBN 5-7990-0284-9.

Savitskii, V. M., Larin, A. M. *Уголовный процесс: Словарь-справочник.* [Criminal Procedure: Dictionary-Manual]. Ed. V. M. Savitskii. M.: Kontrakt, INFRA-M, 1999. 271 p. 6000 ptd. ISBN 5-900785-31-9, ISBN 5-16-000020-8.

Сборник постановлений Пленумов Верховных Судов СССР и РСФСР(Российской Федерации) по уголовным делам. [Collection of Decrees of the Plenums of the USSR and RSFSR (Russian Federation) Supreme Soviets on Criminal Cases]. M.: Spark, 1999. 560 p. 100000 ptd. ISBN 5-88914-011-6.

Serebriakov, D. *Особенности национального следствия: Лучшие комментарии к Уголовно-процессуальному кодексу Российской Федерации.* [Peculiarities of National Investigation: Best Commentaries to the Code of Criminal Procedure of the Russian Federation]. Spb.: Izd: dom "Neva". M.: OLMA-Press, 1999. 15000 ptd.

Chapter 1. 352 p. ISBN 5-5-7654-0256-9, ISBN 5-224-00204-4.
Chapter 2. 400 p. ISBN 5-7654-0257-7, ISBN 5-5-224-00205-2.

Следственные действия. [Investigative Actions]. Ed. V. A. Obraztsov. M.: Iurist', 1999. 499 p. 5000 ptd. ISBN 5-7975-0115-5.

Уголовно-процессуальный кодекс: По состоянию на 15 февраля 1999 г. [Code of Criminal Procedure: As of 15 February 1999]. M.: Biznes-Inform, 1999. 177 p. 4000 ptd. ISBN 5-89563-005-4.

Уголовно-процессуальный кодекс РСФСР. [RSFSR Code of Criminal Procedure]. M.: Iurist', 1999. 229 p. 10000 ptd. ISBN 5-7975-0207-0.

Уголовно-процессуальный кодекс РСФСР: Официальный текст с изменениями и дополнениями по состоянию на 1 марта 1999 г. [RSFSR Code of Criminal Procedure: Official Text with Changes and Additions as of 1 March 1999]. M.: Tandem, EKSMOS, 1999. 176 p. 3000 ptd. ISBN 5-88124-049-9.

Уголовно-процессуальный кодекс РСФСР: С изменениями и дополнениями на 15 февраля 1999 г. [RSFSR Code of Criminal Procedure: With Changes and Additions for 15 February 1999]. M.: Prospekt, 1999. 208 p. 10000 ptd. ISBN 5-7896-0077-8.

Уголовно-процессуальный кодекс РСФСР: С изменениями и дополнениями на 15 августа 1999 г. [RSFSR Code of Criminal Procedure: With Changes and Additions for 15 August 1999]. M.: Prospekt, 1999. 208 p. 10000 ptd. ISBN 5-8369-0029-9.

Уголовно-процессуальный кодекс РСФСР: С изменениями и дополнениями на 1 октября 1999 г. [RSFSR Code of Criminal Procedure: With Changes and Additions for 1 October 1999]. M.: Prospekt, 1999. 208 p. 10000 ptd. ISBN 5-8369-0029-9.

Уголовный процесс: Сборник задач. [Criminal Procedure: Collection of Tasks]. Ed. V. S. Shadrin. Volgograd: VIUI MVD Rossii, 1999. 156 p. 500 ptd. ISBN 5-7899-0070-4.

Уголовный процесс: Учебник для вузов. [Criminal Procedure: Textbook for Institutes of Higher Education]. Ed. K. F. Gutsenko. 3rd. rev. ed. M.: Zertsalo, 1999. 608 p. 8000 ptd. ISBN 5-8078-0030-3.
Also published:
M.: NORMA-INFRA-M, 1999. 384 p. 60000 ptd. ISBN 5-89123-344-4, ISBN 5-86225-951-1.

Court Organisation

Barak, A. *Судейское усмотрение.* [Judicial Discretion]. Trans. from English. M.: NORMA, 1999. 364 p. 3000 ptd. ISBN 5-89123-370-3.

Iarkov, V. V. *Комментарий к Федеральному закону «Об исполнительном производстве» (постатейный) и к Федеральному закону «О судебных приставах».* [Commentary to the Federal Law "On Execution Proceeding" (Article by Article) and to the Federal Law "On Bailiffs"]. M.: Iurist', 1999. 384 p. 10000 ptd. ISBN 5-7975-0206-2.

Kleandrov, M. I. *Судья - центральное звено судебной системы: Учебное пособие.* [The Judge - The Central Link of the Judicial System: Instructional Manual]. Tiumen: Izd-vo TiumGU, 1999. 232 p. 500 ptd. ISBN 5-5-88081-168-9.

Комментарий судебной практики: Выпуск 5. [Commentary to Judicial Practice: Issue 5]. Ed. K. B. Iaroshenko. M.: Iurid. lit., 1999. 256 p. 5000 ptd. ISBN 5-7260-0934-7.

Kunitsyn, A. R. *Образцы судебных документов: С коммент. законодательства и судебной практики. Практическое пособие.* [Models of Judicial Documents: With a Commentary of the Legislation and Judicial Practice. Practical Manual]. 2d. rev. ed. M.: Soleks, 1999. 370 p. 10000 ptd. ISBN 5-900216-08-X.

Marshunov, M. N. *Федеральный Закон о судебных приставах в схемах: Постатейный комментарий.* [Federal Law on Bailiffs in Diagrams: Article by Article Commentary]. M.: Spb.: Gerda, 1999. 350 p. 5000 ptd. ISBN 5-7978-0047-0.

Piskarev, I. K. *Образцы судебных документов: Практическое пособие.* [Models of Judicial Documents: Practical Manual]. 2d. rev. ed. M.: Gorodets, 1999. 248 p. 5000 ptd. ISBN 5-89391-015-X.

Постатейный комментарий к Федеральному закону «О судебных приставах». [Article by Article Commentary to the Federal Law "On Bailiffs"]. Ed. E. N. Sidorenko. M.: Statut, 1999. 127 p. 5000 ptd. ISBN 5-8354-0019-5.

Сборник судебных документов с дискетой. [Collection of Judicial Documents with Diskette]. N. R. Vilchur et al. M.: Prospekt, 1999. 376 p. 10000 ptd. ISBN 5-8369-0058-2.

Serebriakov, D. *Особенности национального суда. 1: Лучшие комментарии к Уголовно-процессуальному Кодексу Российской Федерации.* [Peculiarities of the National Court. 1: Best Commentaries to the Code of Criminal Procedure of the Russian Federation]. Spb.: Izd. Dom "Neva", OLMA-Press, 1999. 320 p. 15000 ptd. ISBN 5-7654-0258-5, ISBN 5-224-00206-0.

Stetstovskii, Iu. I. *Судебная власть: Учебное пособие.* [Judicial Power: Instructional Manual]. M.: Delo, 1999. 399 p. 3000 ptd. ISBN 5-7749-0121-1.

Суд и правоохранительные органы: Хрестоматия. [The Court and Law Enforcement Agencies: Anthology]. Comps. Iu. K. Orlov, G. V. Kruchinina. M.: Iurist', 1999. 476 p. 10000 ptd. ISBN 5-7975-0169-4.

Судебная практика по гражданским делам. [Judicial Practice in Civil Affairs]. Ed. V. M. Zhuykov. M.: Gorodets - Formula prava, 1999. 445 p. 7000 ptd. ISBN 5-89391-042-7.

Судебные документы: Сборник образцов более 450 документов. [Judicial Documents: Collection of Models of Over 450 Documents]. N. R. Vilchur et al. M.: Prospekt, 1999. 569 p. 10000 ptd. ISBN 5-8369-0074-4.

Судебные приставы. Исполнительное производство. [Bailiffs. Execution Proceeding]. 2d. rev. ed. Intro. Iu. N. Vlasov. Comps. Iu. N. Vlasov, A. P. Dolina. M.: Iurait, Propaganda Biznes Media, 1999. 174 p. (Ros. pravovaia biblioteka). 2000 ptd. ISBN 5-85294-055-0.

Судебные приставы и исполнительное производство в законодательстве Российской Федерации: Сборник нормативных актов и документов. Том 1. [Bailiffs and Execution Proceeding in the Legislation of the Russian Federation: Collection of Normative Acts and Documents. Vol.1]. Ed. B. P. Kondrashov. M.: Mir bezopasnosti, 1999. 800 p. 10000 ptd. ISBN 5-89258-018-0.

Судебные приставы и исполнительное производство в законодательстве Российской Федерации: Сборник нормативных актов и документов. Том 2. [Bailiffs and Execution Proceeding in the Legislation of the Russian Federation: Collection of Normative Acts and Documents. Vol.2]. Ed. B. P. Kondrashov. M.: Mir bezopasnosti, 1999. 904 p. 10000 ptd. ISBN 5-89258-019-9.

Trubnikova, T. V., Iakimovich, Iu. K. *Организация и деятельность мировых судей в России.* [Organisation and Activity of Justices of the Peace in Russia]. Tomsk: Izd-vo Tom. un-ta, 1999. 82 p. 500 ptd. ISBN 5-7511-1111-7.

Закон Российской Федерации «О статусе судей в Российской Федерации». Федеральный конституционный закон «О судебной системе Российской Федерации». Федеральный закон «Об исполнительном производстве». [Law of Russian Federation "On the Status of Judges in the Russian Federation". Federal Constitutional Law "On the Judicial System of the Russian Federation". Federal Law "On Execution Proceeding"]. M.: Iurlit, 1999. 96 p. 3500 ptd. ISBN 5-93342-001-8.

Procuracy

Baskov, V. I. *Курс прокурорского надзора: Учебник для вузов.* [Procuracy Supervision Course: Textbook for Institutes of Higher Education]. M.: Zertsalo, 1999. 468 p. 8000 ptd. ISBN 5-8078-0004-4.

Berlin, N. *Записки прокурора.* [A Procurator's Notes]. Perm: Pushka, 1999. 156 p. 3000 ptd.

Chuvilev, A. A. *Прокурорский надзор за исполнением законов при задержании подозреваемых: Учебное пособие.* [Procuracy Supervision over the Execution of Laws During the Detention of Suspects: Instructional Manual]. Eds. R. Z. Livshitz, Iu. P. Orlovskii. M.: NORMA-INFRA-M, 1999. 473 p. 60000 ptd. ISBN 5-89123-175-1, ISBN 5-86225-672-5.

Chuvilev, A. A., Chuvilev, An. A. *Прокурорский надзор: Вопросы и ответы.* [Procuracy Supervision: Questions and Answers]. M.: Novy Iurist, 1999. 136 p. 7000 ptd. ISBN 5-7969-0064-1.

Комментарии и разъяснения к Федеральному закону «О прокуратуре Российской Федерации». [Commentaries and Explanations to the Federal Law "On the Procuracy of the Russian Federation"]. N. P. Kirillova et al. Spb.: Izd-vo Mikhailova V. A., 1999. 175 p. 2000 ptd. ISBN 5-8016-0155-4.

Очерки истории кубанской прокуратуры: Материалы и документы. [Essays on the History of the Kuban Procuracy: Materials and Documents]. Ed. & Comp. N. N. Grigorieva et al. Krasnodar: Sov. Kuban, 1999. 336 p. 3000 ptd. ISBN 5-7221-0228-8.

Прокурорский надзор в Российской Федерации: Учебное пособие для вузов. [Procuracy Supervision in the Russian Federation: Instructional Manual for Institutes of Higher Education]. Ed. A. A. Chuvileva. M.: Iurist', 1999. 398 p. 10000 ptd. ISBN 5-7975-0189-9.

Сборник основных приказов и указаний Генерального прокурора Российской Федерации. [Collection of Basic Orders and Instructions of the Procurator General of the Russian Federation]. M.: NORMA, 1999. 632 p. 10000 ptd. ISBN 5-89123-327-4.

Shulzhenko, Iu. L. *Конституционный статус прокуратуры Российской Федерации.* [Constitutional Status of the Procuracy of the Russian Federation]. In-t gosudarstva i prava RAN. M., 1999. 42 p. 1600 ptd. ISBN 5-88720-057-X.

Zhapparov, Sh. *За закрытой дверью: Записки прокурора-журналиста.* [Behind Closed Doors: Notes of a Procurator-Journalist]. Orenburg: Kn. izd-vo, 1999. 188 p. 2000 ptd. ISBN 5-88788-061-9.

Zviagintsev, A. G., Orlov, Iu. G. *Российские прокуроры.* [Russian Procurators]. M.: Mol. gvardiia, 1999. 570 p. 5000 ptd. ISBN 5-235-02343-9.

Notariat

Glushchenko, P. P., Sedov, A. M. *Основы нотариальной деятельности: Учебное пособие.* [Fundamental Principles of Notarial Activity: Instructional Manual]. Spb.: Izd-vo Mikhailova V. A., 1999. 367 p. 5000 ptd. ISBN 5-8016-0036-1.

Ianushkevich, I. P. *Нотариат в России: Учебное пособие.* [The Notariat in Russia: Instructional Manual]. M.: INITS Rospatenta, 1999. 83 p. 150 ptd.

Lustov, A. V. *Образцы нотариальных документов.* [Models of

Notarial Documents]. 3rd. rev. ed. M.: Iurait, 1999. 336 p. 3000 ptd. ISBN 5-85294-053-4.

Mikhailova, E. P., Taranina, I. V. *Краткий справочник по нотариату.* [A Short Manual About the Notariat]. Novosibirsk: IUKEA, 1999. 128 p. 3000 ptd. ISBN 5-93376-012-9.

Образцы нотариальных документов. [Models of Notarial Documents]. Comp. A. P. Ryzhakov. M.: Gorodets, Formula prava, 1999. 381 p. ISBN 5-89391-050-8.

Also published:

M.: Iurait, 1999. 336 p. 5000 ptd. ISBN 5-85294-053-4.

Repin, V. S. *Комментарий к Основам законодательства Российской Федерации о нотариате.* [Commentary to the Fundamental Principles of Russian Federation Legislation on the Notariat]. M.: NORMA-INFRA-M, 1999. 291 p. 30000 ptd. ISBN 5-89123-207-3, ISBN 5-86225-681-4.

Private International Law

Reference Works

Dmitrieva, G. K., Filimonova, M. V. *Международное частное право: Действующие нормативные акты: Учебное пособие.* [International Private Law: Prevailing Normative Acts: Instructional Manual]. M.: In-t mezhdunar. prava i ekonomiki im. A. S. Griboekova, 1999. 624 p. 5000 ptd. ISBN 5-86344-100-3.

General Studies

Boguslavskii, M. M. *Международное частное право: Практикум.* [International Private Law: Practical Work]. M.: Iurist', 1999. 300 p. 10000 ptd. ISBN 5-7975-0240-2.

Ermolaev, V. G., Sivakov, O. V. *Международное частное право: Курс лекций.* [International Private Law: Course of Lectures]. M.: Bylina, 1999. 176 p. 5000 ptd. ISBN 5-88528-238-2.

Fedoseeva, G. Iu. *Международное частное право.* [International Private Law]. M.: Ostozhie, 1999. 295 p. 3000 ptd. ISBN 5-86-095-195-7.

Rovny, V. V. *Проблемы единства российского частного права.* [Problems of the Unity of Russian Private Law]. Irkutsk: Izd-vo Irkut. un-ta, 1999. 310 p. 1000 ptd. ISBN 5-7430-0592-3.

Zvekov, V. P. *Международное частное право: Курс лекций.* [Private International Law: Course of Lectures]. M.: NORMA-INFRA-M, 1999. 667 p. 30000 ptd. ISBN 5-89123-269-3, ISBN 5-86225-974-0.

International Trade and Finance

Borisov, K. G. *Международный туризм и право: Для вузов.* [International Tourism and Law: For Institutes of Higher Education]. M.: NIMP, 1999. 352 p. 3000 ptd. ISBN 5-88720-024-3.

Право Европейского Союза: правовое регулирование торгового оборота: Учебное пособие. [Law of the European Union: Legal Regulation of Trade Turnover: Instructional Manual]. Eds. V. V. Bezbakh, A. Ia. Kapustin, V. K. Puchinskii. M.: Zerstalo, 1999. 389 p. 3000 ptd. ISBN 5-8078-0035-8.

Rozenberg, M. G. *Исковая давность в международном коммерческом обороте: практика применения.* [Limitation of Action in International Commercial Turnover: Practice of Application]. M.: Statut, 1999. 142 p. 5000 ptd. ISBN 5-8354-0022-5.

Intellectual Property

Международное авторское право. [International Copyright Law]. Comp. E. M. Buriak. 2nd. ed. M.: INITS Rospatenta, 1999. 95 p. 150 ptd.

Public International Law

Reference Works

Действующее международное право: В 3 томах. Учебное пособие для вузов. [Prevailing International Law: In 3 Volumes. Instructional Manual for Institutes of Higher Education]. Comps. Iu. M. Kolosov, E. S. Krivchikova. M.: Izd-vo Mosk. nezavisimogo in-ta mezhdunar. prava, 1999. 3000 ptd.

Vol.1. 864 p. ISBN 5-88720-008-1.
Vol.2. 832 p. ISBN 5-88720-009-X.
Vol.3. 825 p. ISBN 5-88720-012-X.

General Studies

Biriukov, P. N. *Международное право: Учебное пособие.* [International Law: Instructional Manual]. 2d. rev. ed. M.: Iurist', 1999. 415 p. 10000 ptd. ISBN 5-7975-0191-0.

Blishchenko, I. P., Doria, Zh. *Прецеденты в международном публичном и частном праве.* [Precedents in International Public and Private Law]. 2d. rev. ed. M.: Izd-vo MNIMP, 1999. 472 p. 1000 ptd. ISBN 5-88720-020-0.

Chernichenko, S. V. *Теория международного права: В 2 томах.* [Theory of International Law: In 2 Volumes]. M.: NIMP, 1999. 3000 ptd.

Vol.1. *Современные теоретические проблемы.* [Contemporary Theoretical Problems]. 335 p. ISBN 5-88720-021-9.
Vol.2. *Старые и новые теоретические проблемы.* [Old and New Theoretical Problems]. 526 p. ISBN 5-88720-022-7.

Международное право: Учебник для вузов. [International Law: Textbook for Institutes of Higher Education]. Eds. Iu. M. Kolosov, V. I. Kuznetsov. M.: Mezhdunar. otnosheniia, 1999. 619 p. ISBN 5-7133-0991-6.

Also published:
M.: NORMA-INFRA-M, 1999. 584 p. 50000 ptd. ISBN 5-89123-271-5, ISBN 5-86225-875-2.

M.: Iurid. lit., 1999. 559 p. 5000 ptd. ISBN 5-7260-0933-9.

Международное право: Учебно-метод. комплекс. [International Law: Instructional Methods System]. Comps. S. A. Grigorian, T. I. Strokova. Rostov na Donu, Izd-vo RGEA, 1999. 300 p. 100 ptd.

Международное публичное право: Учебник. [Public International Law: Textbook]. Ed. K. A. Bekiashev. M.: Prospekt, 1999. 608 p. 10000 ptd. ISBN 5-7896-0055-7.

Shumilov, V. M. *Международное экономическое право: Учебно-методическое пособие.* [International Economic Law: Instructional-Methods Manual]. M.: DeKA, 1999. 399 p. 1000 ptd. ISBN 5-89645-011-7.

Shutak, I. D. *Правовые оговорки в доктрине международного права.* [Legal Clauses in the Doctrine of International Law]. Spb.: Aleteia, 1999. 251 p. 2200 ptd. ISBN
5-89329-186-7.

States

Kalamkarian, R. A. *Поведение государств в международном суде ООН.* [Conduct of States in the International Court of the United Nations]. M.: Nauka, 1999. 160 p. 420 ptd. ISBN 5-02-008276-7.

Вторая международная конференция по федерализму: Москва, 16-17 декабря 1997 г. [Second International Conference on Federalism: Moscow, 16-17 December 1997]. Trans. from English. Eds. S. S. Artobolevskii, V. V. Klimanov. M.: Editorial URSS, 1999. 316 p. 1500 ptd. ISBN 5-8360-0019-0.

Space Law

Iakovenko, A. V. *Прогрессивное развитие международного космического права: Актуальные проблемы.* [Progressive Development of International Space Law: Urgent Problems]. M.: Mezhundar. otnosheniia, 1999. 166 p. 1000 ptd. ISBN 5-7133-1022-1.

Международное космическое право: Учебник для вузов.

[International Space Law: Textbook for Institutes of Higher Education]. Eds. G. P. Zhukov, Iu. M. Kolosov. M.: Mezhdunar. otnosheniia, 1999. 358 p. 5000 ptd. ISBN 5-7133-0994-0.

Human Rights

Актуальные проблемы миграции. Международные механизмы защиты прав беженцев. [Urgent Problems of Migration. International Mechanisms for the Defence of the Rights of Refugees]. Comps. S. A. Gannushkina, I. A. Zolotarevskaia. M.: Zvenia, 1999. 207 p. 2300 ptd. ISBN 5-7870-0029-3.

Erdelevskii, A. M. *Обращение в Европейский Суд.* [Appeal to the European Court]. M.: Iurist', 1999. 156 p. 5000 ptd. ISBN 5-7975-0171-6.

Kartashkin, V. A. *Как подать жалобу в Европейский Суд по правам человека. Комментарий к правилам обращения в органы Совета Европы по защите прав человека.* [How to Lodge an Appeal with the European Court of Human Rights. Commentary to the Rules for Appeal to the Agencies of the Council of Europe for the Defence of Human Rights]. M.: NORMA-INFRA-M, 1999. 96 p. 50000 ptd. ISBN 5-89123-219-7, ISBN 5-86225-718-7.

Tiunov, O. I. *Международное гуманитарное право: Учебник для вузов.* [International Humanitarian Law: Textbook for Institutes of Higher Education]. M.: NORMA-INFRA-M, 1999. 315 p. 30000 ptd. ISBN 5-89123-270-7, ISBN 5-86225-873-6.

Защита прав человека и соблюдение законности органами внутренних дел: Материалы международной научно-практической конференции (10 декабря 1998 г.). [Defence of Human Rights and Compliance with the Legality of Internal Affairs Agencies: Materials from an International Scientific-Practical Conference (10 December 1998)]. Eds. L.Sh. Berekashvili, V. P. Ignatov. M.: Shchyt-M, 1999. 207 p. 5000 ptd. ISBN 5-93004-046-X.

International Criminal Law

Illarionov, V. P., Putova, I. V. *Правовые и организационно-*

методические аспекты международного розыска преступников: Для вузов. [Legal and Organisational-Methods Aspects of the International Search for Criminals: For Institutes of Higher Education]. M.: Knizh. mir, 1999. 94 p. 2000 ptd. ISBN 5-8041-0040-8.

Liakhov, E. G., Popov, A. V. *Терроризм: национальный: региональный и международный контроль.* [Terrorism: National, Regional and International Control]. M.: Rostov n/D: RIUI MVD Rossii, 1999. 435 p. 2200 ptd.

Lukashuk, I. I., Naumov, A. V. *Международное уголовное право: Учебник для вузов.* [International Criminal Law: Textbook for Institutes of Higher Education]. M.: Spark, 1999. 287 p. 5000 ptd. ISBN 5-88914-129-5.

Luneev, V. V. *Преступность XX века: Мировые, регион. и рос. тенденции. Мировой криминологический анализ.* [Criminality in the 20th Century: World, Regional and Russian Trends. World Criminological Analysis]. M.: NORMA, 1999. 516 p. 1500 ptd. ISBN 5-89123-393-2.

Международное уголовное право: Для вузов. [International Criminal Law: For Institutes of Higher Education]. Ed. V. N. Kudriavtsev. M.: Nauka, 1999. 264 p. 3000 ptd. ISBN 5-02-008292-9.

Osmaev, I. B. *Международные и национальные правовые средства борьбы с отмыванием преступных доходов.* [International and National Legal Means for the Struggle Against the Laundering of Criminal Revenues]. M.: Izd-vo RUDN, 1999. 296 p. 1000 ptd. ISBN 5-209-973-4.

International Organisations

Glotov, S. A. *Совет Европы как политико-правовой институт.* [The Council of Europe as a Political-Legal Institute]. Krasnodar: Sov. Kuban, 1999. 192 p. 2000 ptd. ISBN 5-7221-0240-7.

Neshataeva, T. N. *Международные организации и право: Новые тенденции в международно-правовом регулировании.* [International Organisations and Law: New Trends and International Law Regulation]. M.: Delo, 1999. 271 p. 2000 ptd. ISBN 5-7749-0058-4.

Foreign and Comparative Law

General Works

Anners, E. *История европейского права.* [History of European Law]. Trans. from Swedish. M.: Nauka, 1999. 395 p. 700 ptd. ISBN 5-02-008330-5.

Антология мировой правовой мысли: В 5 томах. [Anthology of World Legal Thought: In 5 Volumes]. Comp. G. Iu. Semigin. M.: Mysl, 1999. 3000 ptd. ISBN 5-244-00935-4.

Vol.1. *Античность. Восточные цивилизации.* [Antiquity. Eastern Civilisations]. Ed. L. R. Siukiianen. 150 p. ISBN 5-244-00936-2.

Vol.2. *Европа: V-XVII вв.* [Europe: 5th-17th Centuries]. 830 p. ISBN 5-244-00937-0.

Vol.3. *Европа. Америка: XVII-XX вв.* [Europe. America: 17th-20th Centuries]. 830 p. ISBN 5-244-00938-9.

Vol.4. *Россия. XI-XIX вв.* [Russia. 11th-19th Centuries]. Ed. E. A. Skrypilev. 813 p. ISBN 5-244-00939-7.

Vol.5. *Россия. Конец XIX-XX в.* [Russia. End 19th-20th Centuries]. Ed. I. A. Isaev. 829 p. ISBN 5-244-00940-0.

Chirkin, V. E. *Конституционное право зарубежных стран: Практикум.* [Constitutional Law of Foreign Countries: Practical Work]. M.: Iurist', 1999. 429 p. 5000 ptd. ISBN 5-7975-0151-1.

Chirkin, V. E. *Конституционное право зарубежных стран: Учебник.* [Constitutional Law of Foreign Countries: Textbook]. 2nd. rev. ed. M.: Iurist', 1999. 599 p. 10000 ptd. ISBN 5-7975-0267-4.

Danilov, S. Iu. *Правовые демократические государства: очерки истории: Выпуск 1.* [Rule-of-Law Democratic States: History Essays: Issue 1]. M., 1999. 291 p. 3000 ptd. ISBN 5-7856-0117-6.

David, R., Joffre-Spinozi, K. *Основные правовые системы*

современности. [Fundamental Contemporary Legal Systems]. Trans. from French. M.: Mezhdunar. otnosheniia, 1999. 399 p. 2000 ptd. ISBN 5-7133-0997-5.

Хрестоматия по истории государства и права зарубежных стран: Древность и сред. века. [Anthology on the History of State and Law of Foreign Countries: Antiquity and the Middle Ages]. Comp. V. A. Tomsinov. M.: Zertsalo, 1999. 467 p. 8000 ptd. ISBN 5-8078-0041-9.

Хрестоматия по истории государства и права зарубежных стран: Новое и Новейшее время. [Anthology on the History of the State and Law of Foreign Countries]. Comp. N. A. Krasheninnikov. M.: Zertsalo, 1999. 563 p. 8000 ptd. ISBN 5-8078-0042-7.

Иностранные юридические лица: Налогообложение, учет, отчетность. [Foreign Juridical Persons: Taxation, Settlement of Accounts, Accountability]. M.: Ucheb.-inform. tsentr pri Gos. nalogovoi inspektsii po g. Moskve, 1999. 352 p. 3000 ptd. ISBN 5-86297-107-6.

История государства и права зарубежных стран: Учебник для вузов. [History of State and Law of Foreign Countries: Textbook for Institutes of Higher Education]. Eds. O. A. Zhidkov, N. A. Krasheninnikova. 2nd. ed. M.: NORMA-INFRA-M, 1999.

Part 1. 609 p. 30000 ptd. ISBN 5-89123-341-X, ISBN 5-86225-950-3.

Part 2. 703 p. 30000 ptd. ISBN 5-89123-380-0, ISBN 5-16-000081-X.

Kiselev, I. Ia. *Сравнительное и международное трудовое право: Учебник.* [Comparative and International Labour Law: Textbook]. M.: Delo, 1999. 728 p. 5000 ptd. ISBN 5-7749-0158-0.

Конституции государств-участников СНГ. [Constitutions of the Member States of the CIS]. Ed. L. A. Okunkov et al. M.: NORMA-INFRA-M, 1999. 736 p. 3000 ptd. ISBN 5-89123-355-X, ISBN 5-16-000046-1.

Конституции стран СНГ и Балтии. [Constitutions of the Countries of the CIS and the Baltics]. Comp. & Intro. G. N. Andreev.

M.: Iurist', 1999. 639 p. 5000 ptd. ISBN 5-7975-0157-0.

Конституционное (государственное) право зарубежных стран: Часть общая. [Constitutional (State) Law of Foreign Countries: General Part]. 3rd. rev. ed. Ed. B. A. Strashun. M.: BEK, 1999. 784 p. 30000 ptd. ISBN 5-85639-276-0.

Конституционное право зарубежных стран: Учебник. [Constitutional Law of Foreign Countries: Textbook]. Eds. M. V. Baglai, Iu. I. Leibo, L. M. Entin. M.: NORMA-INFRA-M, 1999. 819 p. 60000 ptd. ISBN 5-89123-342-8, ISBN 5-86225-905-8.

Koveshnikov, E. M., Marchenko, M. N., Steshenko, L. A. *Конституционное право стран Содружества Независимых Государств: Учебник.* [Constitutional Law of the Countries of the Commonwealth of Independent States: Textbook]. M.: NORMA-INFRA-M, 1999. 446 p. 30000 ptd. ISBN 5-89123-367-3.

Kuri, Kh. *Развитие преступности на Востоке и Западе.* [Development of Criminality in the East and the West]. M.: Ros. Iurid. izd. Dom, 1999. 80 p. 1000 ptd. ISBN 5-88635-031-4.

Liubimov, A. P. *Правовые институты демократии России и стран Европы, выборы, лоббизм и парламентаризм: Сравнительный анализ.* [Legal Institutes of Democracy of Russia and the Countries of Europe, Elections, Lobbying and Parliamentarism: Comparative Analysis]. M.: In-t Evropy RAN, 1999. 57 p. 500 ptd.

Mishin, A. A. *Конституционное право зарубежных стран: Учебник для вузов.* [Constitutional Law of Foreign Countries: Textbook for Institutes of Higher Education]. 6th rev. ed. M.: Belyt alvy, 1999. 447 p. 3000 ptd. ISBN 5-7619-0067-X.

Обеспечение прав человека в Содружестве Независимых Государств: Выпуск 1. Основополагающие документы Содружества, договоры России о дружбе и сотрудничестве с государствами СНГ. [Ensuring Human Rights in the Commonwealth of Independent States: Issue 1. Basic Documents of the Commonwealth, Treaties of Russia on Friendship and Cooperation with CIS States]. Ed. O. O. Mironov. M.: Nalogovy vestnik, 1999. 143 p. 10000 ptd. ISBN 5-93094-010-X.

Очерки конституционного права иностранных государств: Учебник. [Essays on the Constitutional Law of Foreign States: Textbook]. Ed. D. A. Kovachev. M.: Spark, 1999. 303 p. 2000 ptd. ISBN 5-88914-116-3.

Основные институты гражданского права зарубежных стран. [Principal Institutes of Civil Law of Foreign Countries]. Author V. V. Zaleskii. M.: NORMA, 1999. 645 p. 3000 ptd. ISBN 5-89123-245-6.

Проблемы общей теории права и государства: Учебник. [Problems of the Universal Theory of Law and State: Textbook]. Ed. V. S. Nersesiants. M.: NORMA-INFRA-M, 1999. 813 p. 60000 ptd. ISBN 5-89123-361-4, ISBN 5-86225-910-4.

Stepanov, V. V. *Несостоятельность (банкротство) в России, Франции, Англии, Германии.* [Insolvency (Bankruptcy) in Russia, France, England, Germany]. M.: Statut, 1999. 204 p. 10000 ptd. ISBN 5-8354-0004-7.

Судебная и административная защита прав интеллектуальной собственности в странах-членах Европейского Сообщества. [Judicial and Administrative Defence of Intellectual Ownership Rights in the Member Countries of the European Community]. Trans. M.: Ros. agentstvo po patentam i tovarnym znakam, FIPS, 1999. 460 p. 300 ptd.

Уголовное законодательство зарубежных стран: Англии, США, Франции, Германии, Японии: Сборник законодательных материалов. [Criminal Legislation of Foreign Countries: England, USA, France, Germany, Japan: Collection of Legislative Materials]. Ed. I. D. Kozochkin. M.: Zertsalo, 1999. 346 p. 3000 ptd. ISBN 5-8078-0031-1.

Velichko, A. M. *Государственные идеалы России и Запада. Параллели правовых культур.* [State Ideals of Russia and the West. Parallels of Legal Cultures]. Spb.: Izd-vo iurid. in-ta, 1999. 235 p. 1500 ptd. ISBN 5-86247-024-7.

Visson, L. *Чужие и близкие в русско-американских браках.* [Disparities and Similarities in Russian-American Marriages]. Trans. from English by S. N. Anisimova. M.: Valent, 1999. 206 p. 3000 ptd.

ISBN 5-85677-147-8.

Всеобщая история государства и права: Учебник для вузов. [Universal History of State and Law: Textbook for Institutes of Higher Education]. Ed. K. I. Batyr. M.: Bylina, 1999. 495 p. 10000 ptd. ISBN 5-93384-004-1.

Ziber, U. *Организованная преступность Японии и Германии: Сравнительный анализ на основе работ Коиши Миядзавы.* [Organised Criminality in Japan and Germany: Comparative Analysis on the Basis of the Work of Koishi Miyadzava]. M.: Ros. iurid. izd. dom, 1999. 32 p. 1500 ptd. ISBN 5-88635-030-6.

Zlatopolskii, D. L. *Государственное право зарубежных стран: Восточной Европы и Азии: Учебник.* [State Law of Foreign Countries: Eastern Europe and Asia: Textbook]. M.: Zertsalo, 1999. 306 p. 10000 ptd. ISBN 5-8078-0050-8.

Individual Countries

Belorussia

Модельный закон о порядке выборов депутатов Палаты Представителей Парламента Союза Беларуси и России первого созыва: Одобрен на заседании секции Науч.-метод. совета по общ. пробл. развития федерал. и регион. законодательства о выборах и референдумах в Российской Федерации 28 июля 1999 г. [Model Law on the Procedure for Elections of Deputies of the Chamber of Representatives of the Parliament of the Union of Belorussia and Russia of the first Convocation: Approved at the Session of the Section of the Instructional Methods Council for General Problems of the Development of Federal and Regional Legislation on Elections and Referenda in the Russian Federation on 28 July 1999]. M., 1999. 191 p. 500 ptd.

Canada

Гражданский кодекс Квебека. [Civil Code of Quebec]. Trans. Eds. O. M. Kozyr, A. A. Makovskaia. M.: Statut, 1999. 471 p. 1000 ptd.

ISBN 5-8354-0009-8.

Канада: Справочник иммигранта. [Canada: The Immigrant's Manual]. Comp. L. Mikhailova. M.: Linor, 1999. 352 p. 5000 ptd. ISBN 5-900889-67-X.

China

Уголовные установления Тан с разьяснениями («Тан люй шу и»). [Criminal Enactments of Tan with Explanations ("Tan Liu shu i"). Trans. from Chinese, intro. & commentary: V. M. Rybakov. Spb.: Peterburg. Vostokovedenie, 1999. 376 p. 1000 ptd. ISBN 5-85803-113-7.

Czechoslovakia

Как получить вид на жительство в Чехии. [How to Obtain a Residence Permit in Czechoslovakia]. Ed. D. B. Tolkachev. M.: Kampana, 1999. 153 p. 5000 ptd. ISBN 5-7941-0038-9.

England

Reshetnikova, I. V. *Доказательственное право Англии и США.* [Law of Evidence of England and the USA]. 2d. rev. ed. M.: Gorodets, 1999. 283 p. 1500 ptd. ISBN 5-89391-039-7.

Germany

Деловая переписка: правила написания немецких деловых писем: типовые фразы: образцы писем и документов. [Business Correspondence: Rules for Writing German Business Correspondence: Typical Phrases: Samples of Letters and Documents]. 2d. rev. ed. M.: ETS, 1999. 237 p. 1000 ptd. ISBN 5-86455-045-0.

Соглашение между Федеративной Республикой Германия и Российской Федерацией об избежании двойного налогообложения в отношении налогов на доходы и имущество. [Agreement Between the Federal Republic of Germany and the Russian Federation on the Avoidance of Dual Taxation in Relation to Taxes on Revenues and Property]. Comment. P. Bazedov.

M.: ETS, 1999. 95 p. 1000 ptd. In Russian and German. ISBN 5-86455-002-9.

Kazakhstan

Novikova, E. V. *Теоретические проблемы развития экологического законодательства в Республике Казахстан.* [Theoretical Problems of the Development of Ecological Legislation in the Republic of Kazakhstan]. M.: Iurist', 1999. 199 p. 1000 ptd. ISBN 5-7975-0287-9.

Norway

Законодательство Норвегии по нефти и газу. [Legislation of Norway on Oil and Gas]. Unofficial trans. M.: EPItsentr, 1999. 379 p. 1000 ptd. ISBN 5-89069-016-7.

Roman Law

Dozhdev, D. V. *Римское частное право: Учебник.* [Roman Private Law: Textbook]. Ed. V. S. Nersesiants. 2nd. rev. ed. M.: NORMA-INFRA-M, 1999. 784 p. 40000 ptd. ISBN 5-89123-382-7, ISBN 5-16-000083-6.

Pokrovskii, I. A. *История римского права.* [History of Roman Law]. Spb.: Letnii sad, Zhurn. "Neva", 1999. 532 p. 2500 ptd. ISBN 5-89740-023-7, ISBN 5-89740-123-X.

Pukhan, I., Polenak-Akimovskaia, M. *Римское право: Базовый учебник.* [Roman Law: Standard Textbook]. Trans. from Macedonian. M.: Zertsalo, 1999. 411 p. 5000 ptd.
ISBN 5-8078-0040-0.

Римское частное право: Учебник. [Roman Private Law: Textbook]. Eds. I. B, Novitskii, I. S. Pereterskii. M.: Iurisprudentsiia, 1999. 509 p. 6000 ptd. ISBN 5-86532-045-9.

Also published:
M.: Iurist', 1999. 544 p. 10000 ptd. ISBN 5-7975-0154-6.

Alphabetical By Author or Title

Abeltsev, S. N., Deriabin, S. D., Solodovnikov, S. A. *Побои и истязания: Проблемы криминологии. Учебное пособие.* [Beatings and Torture: Problems of Criminology. Instructional Manual]. Ed. G. A. Avanesov. M.: Zakon i pravo, IUNITI-DANA, 1999. 127 p. 1000 ptd. ISBN 5-238-00092-8.

Административная деятельность органов внутренних дел. [Administrative Activity of Internal Affairs Agencies]. Ed. A. P. Korenev. 3rd. rev. ed. M.: Shchyt-M, 1999. 281 p. 1500 ptd. ISBN 5-93004-047-8.

Административная ответственность: Сборник нормативных правовых актов. [Administrative Responsibility: Collection of Normative Legal Acts]. Comps. P. V. Anisimov, V. D. Simuzhin. Volgograd: VIUI MVD Rossii, 1999. 188 p. 300 ptd. ISBN 5-7899-0054-2.

Административное право: Для вузов. [Administrative Law: For Institutes of Higher Education]. Eds. Iu. M. Kozlov, L. L. Popov. M.: Iurist', 1999. 726 p. 10000 ptd. ISBN 5-7975-0138-4.

Административно-территориальное устройство Республики Башкортостан на 1 января 1999 года. [Administrative-Territorial Structure of the Republic of Bashkortostan for 1 January 1999]. Ufa: Bashkortostan, 1999. 411 p. 15000 ptd. ISBN 5-85051-142-3.

Agapov, A. B. *Учебник административного права.* [Textbook of Administrative Law]. M.: Gorodets, 1999. 558 p. 6000 ptd. ISBN 5-89391-040-0.

Аграрное законодательство Российской Федерации: Сборник нормативных правовых актов и документов. [Agrarian Legislation of the Russian Federation: Collection of Normative Legal Acts and Documents]. Comp. M. S. Pashova. M.: Iurist', 1999. 701 p. 5000 ptd. ISBN 5-7975-0175-9.

Akbarov, N. G. *Состояние и тенденции преступности*

несовершеннолетних. [Conditions and Tendencies to Criminality by Minors]. Kazan; Izd-vo Kazan. un-ta, 1999. 165 p. 1000 ptd. ISBN 5-7464-0433-0.

Актуальные проблемы гражданского права. [Urgent Problems of Civil Law]. Ed. M. I. Braginskii. M.: Statut, 1999. 464 p. 5000 ptd. ISBN 5-89398-017-4.

Актуальные проблемы миграции. Международные механизмы защиты прав беженцев. [Urgent Problems of Migration. International Mechanisms for the Defence of the Rights of Refugees]. Comps. S. A. Gannushkina, I. A. Zolotarevskaia. M.: Zvenia, 1999. 207 p. 2300 ptd. ISBN 5-7870-0029-3.

Alekhin, A. P., Karmolitskii, A. A., Kozlov, Iu. M. *Административное право Российской Федерации: Для вузов.* [Administrative Law of the Russian Federation: For Institutes of Higher Education]. 2d. rev. ed. M.: Zertsalo, 1999. 672 p. 8000 ptd. ISBN 5-8078-0043-5.

Aleksandrov, A., Kovtun, N. *Апелляция в русском уголовном судопроизводстве.* [Appeal in Russian Criminal Court Proceeding]. N. Novgorod: Izd-vo Volgo-Viat. akad. gos. sluzhby, 1999. 108 p. 250 ptd. ISBN 5-85152-177-5.

Aleksandrov, Iu. K. *Если вас арестовали ...: Справочник для лиц, содержащихся под стражей в следственных изоляторах.* [If They Have Arrested You ...: Manual for Persons Detained Under Guard in Solitary Confinement]. M.: Prava cheloveka, 1999. 279 p. 2000 ptd. ISBN 5-7712-0107-3.

Aleksandrov, Iu. K. *Тюремный закон.* [Prison Law]. M.: Pravovoe prosveshchenie, 1999. 278 p. 5000 ptd. ISBN 5-89-661-008-4.

Aleksandrov, Iu. K., Vezhnina, N. N., Klimenko, S. K. *Туберкулез в тюрьме: Пособие для заключенных.* [Tuberculosis in Prison: Manual for Prisoners]. M.: Prava cheloveka, 1999. 70 p. 5000 ptd. ISBN 5-7712-0105-7.

Alekseev, N. N. *Основы философии права: Для вузов.* [Fundamental

Principles of the Philosophy of Law: For Institutes of Higher Education]. Spb.: Lan, 1999. 252 p. 5000 ptd. ISBN 5-8114-0070-5.

Alekseev, S. S. *Частное право.* [Private Law]. M.: Statut, 1999. 159 p. 5000 ptd. ISBN 5-8354-0007-1.

Alekseev, S. S. *Философия права.* [Philosophy of Law]. M.: NORMA, 1999. 329 p. 3000 ptd. ISBN 5-89123-149-2.

Alekseev, S. S. *Гражданское право в современную эпоху.* [Civil Law in the Contemporary Epoch]. M.: Iurait, 1999. 40 p. 3000 ptd. ISBN 5-85294-082-8.

Alekseev, S. S. *Право: Азбука - теория - философия.* [Law: The Alphabet - Theory -Philosophy]. M.: Statut, 1999. 712 p. 1000 ptd. ISBN 5-8354-0002-0.

Alekseev, S. S. *Право - надежда наша.* [The Law - Our Hope]. Ekaterinburg: Sred.-Ural. kn. izd-vo, 1999. 319 p. 10000 ptd. ISBN 5-7529-0728-4.

Alenichev, V. V. *Страховое законодательство России: Том 1. Зарождение, становление и развитие страхового дела X-XX вв.* [Russian Insurance Legislation: Vol.1. Birth, Formation and Development of the Insurance Business from the 10th-20th Centuries]. Eds. I. A. Isaev, V. V. Shakhov. M.: IUKIS, 1999. 623 p. 300 ptd. ISBN 5-86030-018-2.

Alikperov, Kh. D. *Освобождение от уголовной ответственности: Уголовно-правовые аспекты.* [Release from Criminal Responsibility: Criminal Legal Aspects]. M.: IPK RK Gen. prokuratury RF, 1999. 127 p. 200 ptd.

Aminov, D. I. *Полный курс уголовного права России в таблицах и схемах: Учебное пособие.* [Complete Course on the Criminal Law of Russia in Tables and Diagrams]. Ed. V. P. Revin. M.: Filin', 1999. 427 p. 3000 ptd. ISBN 5-89568-145-X.

Andrianov, V. I., Sokolov, A. V. *Охранные устройства для дома и офиса.* [Protective Equipment for the Home and Office]. Spb.: Lan,

1999. 302 p. 10000 ptd. ISBN 5-8114-0040-X.

Andrichenko, L. V., Belousova, E. V. *В помощь вынужденным переселенцам.* [With Aid for Forced Immigrants]. M.: Zvenia, 1999. 64 p. 15000 ptd. ISBN 5-7870-0024-2.

Anners, E. *История европейского права.* [History of European Law]. Trans. from Swedish. M.: Nauka, 1999. 395 p. 700 ptd. ISBN 5-02-008330-5.

Anokhin, V. S. *Арбитражное процессуальное право России: Учебник.* [Arbitrazh Procedure Law of Russia: Textbook]. M.: VLADOS, 1999. 495 p. 10000 ptd. ISBN 5-691-00352-6.

Anokhin, V. T. *Предпринимательское право.* [Entrepreneurial Law]. M.: VLADOS, 1999. 400 p. 10000 ptd. ISBN 5-691-00354-2.

Antokolskaia, M. V. *Семейное право: Учебник.* [Family Law: Textbook]. 2nd. rev. ed. M.: Iurist', 1999. 336 p. 10000 ptd. ISBN 5-7975-0234-8.

Антология мировой правовой мысли: В 5 томах. [Anthology of World Legal Thought: In 5 Volumes]. Comp. G. Iu. Semigin. M.: Mysl, 1999. 3000 ptd. ISBN 5-244-00935-4.

Vol.1. *Античность. Восточные цивилизации.* [Antiquity. Eastern Civilisations]. Ed. L. R. Siukiianen. 150 p. ISBN 5-244-00936-2.

Vol.2. *Европа: V-XVII вв.* [Europe: 5th-17th Centuries]. 830 p. ISBN 5-244-00937-0.

Vol.3. *Европа. Америка: XVII-XX вв.* [Europe. America: 17th-20th Centuries]. 830 p. ISBN 5-244-00938-9.

Vol.4. *Россия. XI-XIX вв.* [Russia. 11th-19th Centuries]. Ed. E. A. Skrypilev. 813 p. ISBN 5-244-00939-7.

Vol.5. *Россия. Конец XIX-XX в.* [Russia. End 19th-20th Centuries]. Ed. I. A. Isaev. 829 p. ISBN 5-244-00940-0.

Antonian, Iu. M., Tkachenko, A. A., Shostakovich, B. V. *Криминальная сексология.* [Criminal Sexology]. M.: Spark, 1999. 464 p. 4000 ptd. ISBN 5-88914-109-0.

Арбитражная практика за 1998 г. [Arbitrazh Practice for 1998]. Comp. M. G. Rozenberg. M.: Statut, 1999. 269 p. 7000 ptd. ISBN 5-8354-0013-6.

Арбитражный процесс: Практикум. [Arbitrazh Procedure: Practical Work]. Ed. V. V. Iarkov. M.: Iurist', 1999. 186 p. 10000 ptd. ISBN 5-5-7975-0222-4.

Арбитражный процессуальный кодекс Российской Федерации. Федеральный конституционный закон «Об арбитражных судах в Российской Федерации»: Официальные тексты по состоянию на 15 января 1999г. [Code of Arbitrazh Procedure of the Russian Federation. Federal Constitutional Law "On Arbitrazh Courts in the Russian Federation": Official Texts as of 15 January 1999]. M.: EKMOS, 1999. 96 p. 3000 ptd. ISBN 5-88124-036-7.

Арбитражный процессуальный кодекс Российской Федерации. Федеральный конституционный закон «Об арбитражных судах в Российской Федерации»: Официальные тексты по состоянию на 1 февраля 1999 г. [Code of Arbitrazh Procedure of the Russian Federation. Federal Constitutional Law "On Arbitrazh Courts in the Russian Federation": Official Texts from 1 February 1999]. M.: NORMA-INFRA-M, 1999. 156 p. 4000 ptd. ISBN 5-89123-318-5, ISBN 5-86225-972-4.

Арбитражный процессуальный кодекс Российской Федерации: С изменениями и дополнениями на 1 февраля 1999 г. [Code of Arbitrazh Procedure of the Russian Federation: With Changes and Additions for 1 February 1999]. M.: Prospekt, 1999. 96 p. 5000 ptd. ISBN 5-7896-0072-7.

Арбитражный процессуальный кодекс Российской Федерации: С изменениями и дополнениями на 5 апреля 1999 г. [Code of Arbitrazh Procedure of the Russian Federation: With Changes and Additions for 5 April 1999]. M.: Prospekt, 1999. 96 p. 5000 ptd. ISBN 5-8369-0008-6.

Арбитражный процессуальный кодекс Российской Федерации: С изменениями и дополнениями на 1 сентября 1999 г. [Code of Arbitrazh Procedure of the Russian Federation: With Changes and

Additions for 1 September 1999]. M.: Prospekt, 1999. 96 p. 5000 ptd. ISBN 5-8369-0043-4.

Арбитражный процессуальный кодекс Российской Федерации: с изменениями и дополнениями на 15 октября 1999 г. [Code of Arbitrazh Procedure of the Russian Federation: With Changes and Additions for 15 October 1999]. M.: Prospekt, Kodeks, 1999. 96 p. 10000 ptd. ISBN 5-8369-0043-4.

Arkhipov, I. V. *Коммерческое судоустройство и судопроизводство России в XIX веке: Проблемы модернизации.* [Commercial Court Organisation and Court Organisation in Russia in the 19th Century: Problems of Modernisation]. Saratov: Izd-vo SGU, 1999. 214 p. 500 ptd. ISBN 5-292-02341-8.

Astafichev, P. A. *Избирательное право России: современное состояние и перспективы развития.* [Electoral Law of Russia: Contemporary Condition and Development Prospects]. Orel: ORAGS, 1999. 201 p. 500 ptd. ISBN 5-93179-016-0.

Avakian, T. A. *Выборы-99 депутатов Государственной Думы: правила и процедуры.* [Elections-99 of Deputies of the State Duma: Rules and Procedures]. M.: Mezhdunar. obshchesv. fond "Interligal", 1999. 112 p.

Azarkin, N. M. *История юридической мысли России: Курс лекций.* [History of the Legal Thought of Russia: Course of Lectures]. M.: Iurid. lit., 1999. 527 p. 3000 ptd. ISBN 5-7260-0931-2.

Azarova, E. G., Kondratieva, Z. A. *Комментарий к Закону Российской Федерации «О государственных пенсиях в Российской Федерации» (постатейный): Текст Закона по состоянию на 1 декабря 1998 г.* [Commentary to the Russian Federation Law "On State Pensions in the Russian Federation" (Article by Article): Text of Law as of 1 December 1998]. M.: NORMA-INFRA-M, 1999. 215 p. 3000 ptd. ISBN 5-89123-322-3, ISBN 5-86225-979-1.

Bagaets, A. M. *Война не окончена: Книга об истории и людях транспортной милиции Кузбасса.* [The War is Not Over: A Book on the History and People of the Kuzbas Transport Police]. Novosibirsk:

Kn. izd-vo, 1999. 272 p. 1000 ptd. ISBN 5-7620-0834-7.

Baglai, M. V. *Конституционное право Российской Федерации: Учебник.* [Constitutional Law of the Russian Federation: Textbook]. 2nd. rev. ed. M.: NORMA-INFRA-M, 1999. 776 p. 60000 ptd. ISBN 5-89123-329-0, ISBN 5-86225-989-9.

Baimukhametov, S. *Сны золотые: Исповеди наркоманов.* [Golden Dreams: Confessions of Drug Addicts]. M.: PanBinter, 1999. 191 p. ISBN 5-89884-006-0.

Bakhrakh, D. N. *Административная ответственность: Пособие.* [Administrative Responsibility: Manual]. M.: Iurisprudentsiia, 1999. 111 p. 7000 ptd. ISBN 5-86532-049-1.

Barak, A. *Судейское усмотрение.* [Judicial Discretion]. Trans. from English. M.: NORMA, 1999. 364 p. 3000 ptd. ISBN 5-89123-370-3.

Baranov, V. M., Polenina, S. V. *Система права, система законодательства и правовая система: Лекция.* [System of Law, System of Legislation and Legal System: Lecture]. N. Novgorod: Nizhegorod. iurid. in-t MVDRF, 1999. 46 p. 250 ptd.

Barashkov, Iu. *Депутат СССР.* [A Deputy of the USSR]. 2d. rev. ed. Arkhangelsk: Pravda Severa, 1999. 287 p. 300 ptd. ISBN 5-85879-110-8.

Barshchevskii, M. *Адвокатская этика.* [Advocate Ethics]. Samara: Fedorov, 1999. 288 p. 1000 ptd. ISBN 5-8407-0003-7.

Baryshev, V. V. *Правозаступники: Твер. прокуроры. 1764-1917 гг.* [State Advocates: Procurators of Tver. 1764-1917]. Tver, 1999. 80 p. 1000 ptd. ISBN 5-87049-139-8.

Bashkinskas, V. Iu., Dedov, D. I., Karelina, S. A. *Правовое регулирование деятельности акционерных обществ: Учебное пособие.* [Legal Regulation of the Activity of Joint-Stock Societies: Instructional Manual]. Ed. E. P. Gubin. M.: Zertsalo, 1999. 241 p. 5000 ptd. ISBN 5-8078-0029-X.

Baskov, V. I. *Курс прокурорского надзора: Учебник для вузов.* [Procuracy Supervision Course: Textbook for Institutes of Higher Education]. M.: Zertsalo, 1999. 468 p. 8000 ptd. ISBN 5-8078-0004-4.

Beliaev, I. D. *История русского законодательства: Для вузов.* [History of Russian Legislation: For Institutes of Higher Education]. Spb.: Lan, 1999. 640 ptd. ISBN 5-8114-0141-8.

Belkin, A. R. *Теория доказывания: Научно-методическое пособие.* [Theory of Proof: Instructional Methods Manual]. M.: NORMA, 1999. 429 p. 3000 ptd. ISBN 5-89123-323-1.

Belkin, R. S. *История отечественной криминалистики.* [History of National Criminalistics]. M.: NORMA, 1999. 486 p. 3000 ptd. ISBN 5-89123-350-9.

Belkin, R. T. *Криминалистика.* [Criminalistics]. M.: Iurist', 1999. 266 p. 5000 ptd. ISBN 5-7975-0230-5.

Beloglazov, A. V., Mingaleev, I. I., Krylova, G. G. *Страницы истории: Казан. милиция.* [Pages of History: Police of Kazan]. Kazan: Liana, 1999. 159 p. 1000 ptd. ISBN 5-7497-0004-6.

Belov, V. A. *Вексельное законодательство России: Научно-практический комментарий.* [Bill of Exchange Legislation of Russia: Scientific Practical Commentary]. 2d. rev. ed. M.: IurInfoR, 1999. 549 p. 10000 ptd. ISBN 5-89158-026-8.

Belova, S. I. *Административно-правовое регулирование архивного дела в Российской Федерации: Учебное пособие.* [Administrative Legal Regulation of Archive Matters in the Russian Federation: Instructional Manual]. Saratov: Sarat. iurid. in-t, 1999. 68 p. 200 ptd. ISBN 5-7485-0023-X.

Berlin, N. *Записки прокурора.* [A Procurator's Notes]. Perm: Pushka, 1999. 156 p. 3000 ptd.

Безопасность России: Правовые, социально-экономические и научно-технические аспекты. [Russia's Security: Legal, Socio-Economic and Scientific-Technical Aspects]. M.: MGF "Znanie", 1999.

667 p. 1000 ptd. ISBN 5-87633-044-2.

Безопасность России: Правовые, социально-экономические и научно-технические аспекты. Словарь терминов и определений. [Russia's Security: Legal, Socio-Economic and Scientific-Technical Aspects. Dictionary of Terms and Definitions]. 2d. rev. ed. M.: MGF "Znanie", 1999. 368 p. 1000 ptd. ISBN 5-87633-039-6.

Biriukov, P. N. *Международное право: Учебное пособие.* [International Law: Instructional Manual]. 2d. rev. ed. M.: Iurist', 1999. 415 p. 10000 ptd. ISBN 5-7975-0191-0.

Бюджетный кодекс Российской Федерации: От 31 июля 1998 г. Официальный текст. [Budget Code of the Russian Federation: From 31 July 1998. Official Text]. M.: NORMA-INFRA-M, 1999. 144 p. 3000 ptd. ISBN 5-89123-295-2, ISBN 5-86225-937-6.

Бюджетный кодекс Российской Федерации: С изменениями и дополнениями на 15 сентября 1999 г. [Budget Code of the Russian Federation: With Changes and Additions for 15 September 1999]. M.: Prospekt, 1999. 157 p. 5000 ptd. ISBN 5-8369-0009-4.

Бюджетный кодекс Российской Федерации: С изменениями и дополнениями на 15 ноября 1999 г. [Budget Code of the Russian Federation: With Changes and Additions for 15 November 1999]. M.: Prospekt, 1999. 160 p. 5000 ptd. ISBN 5-8369-0009-4.

Blek, B., Krekman, P., Tarasova, A. *Комментарий Федерального закона «Об акционерных обществах».* [Commentary to the Federal Law "On Joint-Stock Societies"]. M.: Labirint, 1999. 720 p. 3000 ptd. ISBN 5-87604-098-3.

Blishchenko, I. P., Doria, Zh. *Прецеденты в международном публичном и частном праве.* [Precedents in International Public and Private Law]. 2d. rev. ed. M.: Izd-vo MNIMP, 1999. 472 p. 1000 ptd. ISBN 5-88720-020-0.

Боевой пост - на магистралях: 80 лет транспортной милиции. [Battle Post - On the Highways: 80 Years of the Transport Police]. Ed. & Comp. S. V. Katkov. Saratov: Letopis, 1999. 159 p.

2500 ptd.

Bogoliubov, S. A. *Экологическое право: Учебник для вузов.* [Ecological Law: Textbook for Institutes of Higher Education]. M.: NORMA-INFRA-M, 1999. 433 p. 50000 ptd. ISBN 5-89123-259-6, ISBN 5-86225-839-6.

Boguslavskii, M. M. *Международное частное право: Практикум.* [International Private Law: Practical Work]. M.: Iurist', 1999. 300 p. 10000 ptd. ISBN 5-7975-0240-2.

Borisov, K. G. *Международный туризм и право: Для вузов.* [International Tourism and Law: For Institutes of Higher Education]. M.: NIMP, 1999. 352 p. 3000 ptd. ISBN 5-88720-024-3.

Borodin, S. V. *Преступления против жизни.* [Crimes Against Life]. M.: Iurist', 1999. 356 p. 5000 ptd. ISBN 5-7975-0221-6.

Braginskii, M. I. *Договор хранения.* [Storage Contract]. M.: Statut, 1999. 157 p. 5000 ptd. ISBN 5-8354-0020-9.

Braginskii, M. I. *Договор подряда и подобные ему договоры.* [Independent-Work Contract and Similar Contracts]. M.: Statut, 1999. 254 p. 10000 ptd. ISBN 5-8354-0003-9.

Braginskii, M. I., Vitrianskii, V. V. *Договорное право: Книга 1.* [Contractual Law: Book 1]. 2nd. rev. ed. M.: Statut, 1999. 841 p. 5000 ptd. ISBN 5-8354-0016-0.

Briachikhin, A. M. *Автобиография префекта.* [Autobiography of a Prefect]. M.: Kontakt RL, 1999. 200 p. 10000 ptd. ISBN 5-86502-035-8.

Brinchuk, M. M. *Экологическое право: Учебник.* [Ecological Law: Textbook]. M.: Iurist', 1999. 351 p. 10000 ptd. ISBN 5-7975-0237-2.

Brusnitsyn, L. V. *Правовое обеспечение безопасности лиц, содействующих уголовному правосудию.* [Legal Ensuring of the Safety of Persons Assisting Criminal Justice]. M.: Spark, 1999. 108 p. 2000 ptd. ISBN 5-88914-110-4.

Cherdantsev, A. F. *Теория государства и права: Учебник для вузов.* [Theory of State and Law: Textbook for Institutes of Higher Education]. M.: Iurait, 1999. 429 p. 10000 ptd. ISBN 5-85294-078-X.

Chernenko, A. G. *Общероссийская национальная идеология и развитие федерализма в России.* [All-Russian National Ideology and the Development of Federalism in Russia]. Spb.: Aleteia, 1999. 274 p. 5500 ptd.ISBN 5-89329-155-7.

Chernichenko, S. V. *Теория международного права: В 2 томах.* [Theory of International Law: In 2 Volumes]. M.: NIMP, 1999. 3000 ptd.

Vol.1. *Современные теоретические проблемы.* [Contemporary Theoretical Problems]. 335 p. ISBN 5-88720-021-9.

Vol.2. *Старые и новые теоретические проблемы.* [Old and New Theoretical Problems]. 526 p. ISBN 5-88720-022-7.

Чернобыль 13: Права и льготы: Сборник нормативных документов о социальной защите граждан, подвергшихся воздействию радиации вследствие катастрофы на Чернобыл. АЕС, ядерных испытаний на Семипалатин. полигоне, аварии в 1957 году на ПО «Маяк» и сбросов радиоактив. отходов в реку Теча. [Chernobyl 13: Rights and Privileges: Collection of Normative Documents on the Social Defence of Citizens Subjected to the Effect of Radiation as a Consequence of the Disaster at the Chernobyl Nuclear Plant, the Nuclear Tests at the Semipalatinsk Site, the Accident in 1957 at the Industrial Combine "Maiak" and the Disposal of Radioactive Waste in the River Techa]. Comps. V. N. Kurashov, N. G. Kurashova. Posad: Melekess, 1999. 242 p. 1000 ptd.

Chernoiarov, A. D. *Защита прав на жилую недвижимость.* [Defence of Rights to a Dwelling Immovable]. Novosibirsk: RIF-servis, 1999. 214 p. 10000 ptd. ISBN 5-85298-032-3.

Chirkin, V. E. *Государствоведение: Учебник.* [Constitutional Law: Textbook]. M.: Iurist', 1999. 398 p. 5000 ptd. ISBN 5-7975-0164-3.

Chirkin, V. E. *Конституционное право зарубежных стран: Практикум.* [Constitutional Law of Foreign Countries: Practical Work]. M.: Iurist', 1999. 429 p. 5000 ptd. ISBN 5-7975-0151-1.

Chirkin, V. E. *Конституционное право зарубежных стран: Учебник.* [Constitutional Law of Foreign Countries: Textbook]. 2nd. rev. ed. M.: Iurist', 1999. 599 p. 10000 ptd. ISBN 5-7975-0267-4.

Chislov, A. I. *Профессионализм и деятельность сотрудников милиции.* [Professionalism and the Activity of Police Personnel]. Ed. V. P. Salnikov. Spb.: Sankt-Peterburg. un-t MVD Rossii, Akad. prava, ekonomiki i bezopasnosti zhiznedetelnosti, 1999. 174 p. 3000 ptd. ISBN 5-93598-002-9.

Chubukov, G. V. *Земельное право России: Курс лекций.* [Land Law of Russia: Course of Lectures]. M.: MAEP, 1999. 128 p. 1000 ptd. ISBN 5-93417-001-5.

Chukovenkov, A. Iu., Iankovaia, V. F. *Оформление документов: Комментарий к ГОСТ, 730-97 «Унифицированные системы документации. Унифицированная система организационно-распорядительной документации. Требования к оформлению документов».* [Formalisation of Documents: Commentary to the All-Union State Standard, 730-97 "Unified Systems of Documentation. Unified System of Organisational-Administrative Documentation"]. M.: Delo, 1999. 232 p. 10000 ptd. ISBN 5-7749-0149-1.

Chukovskaia, E. A. *Аудиовизуальный бизнес: Договорное регулирование. Учебное пособие для вузов.* [Audio-Visual Business: Contractual Regulation. Instructional Manual for Institutes of Higher Education]. M.: Ros-Konsult, 1999. 331 p. 4000 ptd. ISBN 5-89805-005-1.

Chuvilev, A. A. *Оперативно-розыскное право.* [Operational Search Law]. M.: NORMA-INFRA-M, 1999. 75 p. 40000 ptd. ISBN 5-89123-369-X, ISBN 5-86225-603-2.

Chuvilev, A. A. *Прокурорский надзор за исполнением законов при задержании подозреваемых: Учебное пособие.* [Procuracy Supervision over the Execution of Laws During the Detention of Suspects: Instructional Manual]. Eds. R. Z. Livshitz, Iu. P. Orlovskii. M.: NORMA-INFRA-M, 1999. 473 p. 60000 ptd. ISBN 5-89123-175-1, ISBN 5-86225-672-5.

Chuvilev, A. A., Chuvilev, An. A. *Прокурорский надзор: Вопросы и ответы.* [Procuracy Supervision: Questions and Answers]. M.: Novy Iurist, 1999. 136 p. 7000 ptd. ISBN 5-7969-0064-1.

Danilov, E. P. *Наследование: Консультации. Образцы документов. Судебные споры.* [Inheritance: Consultations. Models of Documents. Judicial Disputes]. M.: Novy Iurist', 1999. 239 p. 8000 ptd. ISBN 5-7969-0059-5.

Danilov, E. P. *Справочник адвоката: Консультации, защита в суде, образцы документов.* [An Advocate's Manual: Consultations, Defence in Court, Models of Documents]. 2d. rev. ed. M.: Novy Iurist', 1999. 528 p. 1000 ptd. ISBN 5-7969-0072-2.

Danilov, E. P. *Жилищные споры.* [Housing Disputes]. M.: Pravo i zakon, 1999. 349 p. 5000 ptd. ISBN 5-7858-0031-4.

Danilov, S. Iu. *Правовые демократические государства: очерки истории: Выпуск 1.* [Rule-of-Law Democratic States: History Essays: Issue 1]. M., 1999. 291 p. 3000 ptd. ISBN 5-7856-0117-6.

Dashevskaia, L. M. *Правовые основы хозяйственной деятельности предприятий.* [Legal Fundamental Principles of the Economic Activity of Enterprises]. M.: Kolos, 1999. 224 p. 2000 ptd. ISBN 5-10-003493-9.

David, R., Joffre-Spinozi, K. *Основные правовые системы современности.* [Fundamental Contemporary Legal Systems]. Trans. from French. M.: Mezhdunar. otnosheniia, 1999. 399 p. 2000 ptd. ISBN 5-7133-0997-5.

Действующее международное право: В 3 томах. Учебное пособие для вузов. [Prevailing International Law: In 3 Volumes. Instructional Manual for Institutes of Higher Education]. Comps. Iu. M. Kolosov, E. S. Krivchikova. M.: Izd-vo Mosk. nezavisimogo in-ta mezhdunar. prava, 1999. 3000 ptd.

Vol.1. 864 p. ISBN 5-88720-008-1.
Vol.2. 832 p. ISBN 5-88720-009-X.
Vol.3. 825 p. ISBN 5-88720-012-X.

Деловая переписка: правила написания немецких деловых писем: типовые фразы: образцы писем и документов. [Business Correspondence: Rules for Writing German Business Correspondence: Typical Phrases: Samples of Letters and Documents]. 2d. rev. ed. M.: ETS, 1999. 237 p. 1000 ptd. ISBN 5-86455-045-0.

Demianenko, V. N., Demianenko, V. V. *Сельскохозяйственно-кооперативное право: Курс лекций.* [Agricultural-Cooperative Law: Course of Lectures]. Saratov: Sarat. gos. akad. prava, 1999. 259 p. 500 ptd. ISBN 5-7924-0068-7.

Detkov, M. G. *Тюрьмы, лагеря и колонии России.* [Russian Prisons, Camps and Colonies]. M.: Verdykt-1M, 1999. 447 p. 1000 ptd. ISBN 5-87143-013-9.

Diakov, S. V. *Государственные преступления (против основ конституционного строя и безопасности государства) и государственная преступность.* [State Crimes (Against Fundamental Principles of Constitutional Structure and State Security) and State Criminality]. M.: NORMA, 1999. 307 p. 3000 ptd. ISBN 5-89123-332-0.

Dmitrienko, T. M., Chaadaev, S. G. *Судебная (правовая) бухгалтерия: Учебник.* [Forensic (Legal) Accountancy: Textbook]. M.: Prospekt, 1999. 335 p. 5000 ptd. ISBN 5-7896-0049-2.

Dmitrieva, G. K., Filimonova, M. V. *Международное частное право: Действующие нормативные акты: Учебное пособие.* [International Private Law: Prevailing Normative Acts: Instructional Manual]. M.: In-t mezhdunar. prava i ekonomiki im. A. S. Griboekova, 1999. 624 p. 5000 ptd. ISBN 5-86344-100-3.

Договорные споры: Сборник документов. [Contractual Disputes: Collection of Documents]. Ed. M. Iu. Tikhomirov. M.: Izd. g-na Tikhomirova M. Iu., 1999. 208 p. 3000 ptd. ISBN 5-89194-032-9.

Договоры: Образцы документов, комментарий, практика разрешения споров. [Contracts: Models of Documents, Commentary, Practice of Settling Disputes]. Ed. M. Iu. Tikhomirov. M.: Izd. g-na Tikhomirova M. Iu., 1999. 376 p. 30000 ptd. ISBN 5-89194-030-2.

Документы в земельных правоотношениях. [Documents in Land Relations]. Ed. M. Iu. Tikhomirov. M.: Iurinformtsentr, 1999. 55 p. 3000 ptd. ISBN 5-89194-039-6.

Dolgova, A. I. *Криминология: Учебник для вузов.* [Criminology: Textbook for Institutes of Higher Education]. M.: NORMA-INFRA-M, 1999. 272 p. 40000 ptd. ISBN 5-89123-375-4, ISBN 5-86225-847-7.

Домашняя юридическая энциклопедия: Женщинам. Ответы на все вопросы. [Domestic Legal Dictionary: For Women. Answers to All Questions]. M.: AST, Olimp, 1999. 576 p. 4000 ptd. ISBN 5-7390-0363-X, ISBN 5-7390-0485-3, ISBN 5-237-03950-2.

Dozhdev, D. V. *Римское частное право: Учебник.* [Roman Private Law: Textbook]. Ed. V. S. Nersesiants. 2nd. rev. ed. M.: NORMA-INFRA-M, 1999. 784 p. 40000 ptd. ISBN 5-89123-382-7, ISBN 5-16-000083-6.

Дознание и предварительное следствие в органах Федеральной службы налоговой полиции России: Сборник нормативных актов. [Inquiry and Preliminary Investigation in the Agencies of the Federal Service of the Tax Police of Russia: Collection of Normative Acts]. Ed. V. E. Manuylov. Comps. V. N. Galuzo, M. P. Smirnov. M.: Iurait, 1999. 493 p. 5000 ptd. ISBN 5-85294-075-5.

Drobyshevskii, S. A. *Классические теоретические представления о государстве, праве и политике: Учебное пособие для вузов.* [Classic Theoretical Representations on State, Law and Politics: Instructional Manual for Institutes of Higher Education]. Krasnoiarsk: Krasnoiar. gos. un-t, 1999. 376 p. ISBN 5-7638-0135-0.

Dubovoi, N. *Жилищно-коммунальный комплекс района в условиях экономической реформы: Кн.2. Правовые основы экономических реформ в жилищно-коммунальном хозяйстве.* [Municipal Housing Complex of the District under the Terms of Economic Reform: Book 2. Legal Fundamental Principles of Economic Reforms in the Municipal Housing Economy]. M.: Triada, Ltd, 1998-1999. 1500 ptd.

Part 1. 448 p. ISBN 5-86344-084-8.

Part 2. 572 p. ISBN 5-86344-085-6.
Part 3. 638 p. ISBN 5-86344-086-4.
Part 4. 607 p. ISBN 5-86344-086-4.

Dugin, A. N. *Неизвестный ГУЛАГ: Документы и факты.* [The Unknown GULAG: Documents and Facts]. M.: Nauka, 1999. 103 p. 1000 ptd. ISBN 5-02-008352-6.

240 страниц о недвижимости. [240 Pages on Immovable Property]. M.: Dom. Advokat, 1999. 240 p. (Dom. advokat. Zhilishchnaia entsyklopedia. Issue 4). 100000 ptd. ISBN 5-89156-008-9.

Dyshev, S. *Россия бандитская.* [Gangster Russia]. M.: EKSMO-Press, 1999. 432 p. 10000 ptd. ISBN 5-04-001619-0.

Dziliev, M. I. *Рынок и насилие: Пособие для руководителей силовых и охранных структур, служб безопасности и предпринимателей.* [The Market and Force: Manual for Directors of Power and Protection Structures, the Security Forces and Entrepreneurs]. M.: Izd. dom "Mir bezopastnosti", 1999. 319 p. 3000 ptd. ISBN 5-89258-021-0.

Efremov, A. F. *Принципы и гарантии законности.* [Principles and Guarantees of Legality]. Samara, 1999. 147 p. 600 ptd. ISBN 5-89716-010-4.

Egiazarov, V. A. *Транспортное право: Учебное пособие.* [Transport Law: Instructional Manual]. M.: Iurid. lit., 1999. 272 p. 3000 ptd. ISBN 5-7260-0930-4.

Egorov, Iu. P. *Сделки в гражданском праве: Для вузов.* [Transactions in Civil Law: For Institutes of Higher Education]. Novosibirsk: Nauka, Sib. izd. firma RAN, 1999. 160 p. 500 ptd. ISBN 5-02-032271-7.

Экологическое право России: Сборник материалов научно-практических конференций 1995-1998 гг. [Ecological Law of Russia: Collection of Materials from Scientific-Practical Conferences from 1995-1998]. Comps. I. A. Ignatieva, A. K. Golichenkov. M.: Zertsalo, 1999. 394 p. 2000 ptd. ISBN 5-8078-0044-3.

Elchev, V. A. *Аппарат Государственной Думы и законотворческий процесс.* [Apparatus of the State Duma and the Law Creation Process]. M.: Pamiatniki ist. mysli, 1999. 256 p. 1000 ptd. ISBN 5-88451-073-X.

Электронные документы в корпоративных сетях: второе пришествие Гутенберга. [Electronic Documents in Corporate Networks: The Second Coming of Gutenburg]. S. V. Klimenko et al. M.: Ankei, Eko-Trendz, 1999. 271 p. ISBN 5-88405-014-3.

Emelin, A. S. *История государства и права России: Окт. 1917 - дек. 1991 гг.* [History of State and Law of Russia: October 1917 - December 1991]. M.: Shchyt-M, 1999. 229 p. 1000 ptd. ISBN 5-93004-030-3.

Eminov, V. E., Matskevich, I. M. *Преступность военнослужащих: Исторический, криминологический, социально-правовой анализ.* [Criminality of Military Servicemen: Historical, Criminological, Socio-Legal Analysis]. M.: Penates-Penaty, 1999. 261 p. 2000 ptd.

Engibarian, R. V., Kozlov, Iu. K. *Теория государства и права: Учебное пособие.* [Theory of State and Law: Instructional Manual]. M.: Iurist', 1999. 271 p. 5000 ptd. ISBN 5-7975-0184-8.

Энциклопедия судебной экспертизы. [Encyclopedia of Forensic Expert Examination]. Eds. T. V. Averianovaia, E. R. Rossinskaia. M.: Iurist', 1999. 551 p. 5000 ptd. ISBN 5-7975-0262-3.

Энциклопедический юридический словарь. [Encyclopedic Legal Dictionary]. V. N. Dodonov et al. Ed. V. E. Krutskikh. 2nd. ed. M.: INFRA-M, 1999. 368 p. 5000 ptd. ISBN 5-86225-708-X.

Erdelevskii, A. M. *Финансовые услуги, вексель, недвижимость: анализ и комментарий законодательства и судебной практики.* [Financial Services, Bill of Exchange, Immovable Property: Analysis and Commentary to the Legislation and Judicial Practice]. M.: BEK, 1999. 299 p. 2000 ptd. ISBN 5-85639-255-8.

Erdelevskii, A. M. *Комментарий к Федеральному закону «О*

государственной регистрации прав на недвижимое имущество и сделок с ним». [Commentary to the Federal Law "On State Registration of Rights to Immovable Property and on Transactions with It"]. M.: BEK, 1999. 211 p. 2000 ptd. ISBN 5-89639-260-4.

Erdelevskii, A. M. *Обращение в Европейский Суд.* [Appeal to the European Court]. M.: Iurist', 1999. 156 p. 5000 ptd. ISBN 5-7975-0171-6.

Eremin, S. G., Rezvan, A. P. *Раскрытие и расследование хищений на предприятиях рыбного хозяйства: Учебное пособие.* [Uncovering and Investigation of Stealing at Fish Farming Enterprises: Instructional Manual]. Volgograd: VIUI MVD Rossii, 1999. 104 p. 300 ptd. ISBN 5-7899-0053-4.

Ermakov, V. G. *Федерация как форма государственного устройства России.* [The Federation as a Form of State Structure of Russia]. M.: Bylina, 1999. 192 p. 550 ptd. ISBN 5-88528-238-2.

Ermolaev, V. G., Sivakov, O. V. *Международное частное право: Курс лекций.* [International Private Law: Course of Lectures]. M.: Bylina, 1999. 176 p. 5000 ptd. ISBN 5-88528-238-2.

Erofeev, B. V. *Экологическое право: Учебник для вузов.* [Ecological Law: Textbook for Institutes of Higher Education]. M.: Iurisprudentsiia, 1999. 445 p. 8000 ptd. ISBN 5-86532-044-0.

Erofeev, B. V. *Земельное право.* [Land Law]. 3rd rev. ed. M.: MTSUPL, 1999. 559 p. 5000 ptd. ISBN 5-86095-206-6.

Ershov, V. V., Ershova, E. A. *Трудовой договор: Учебное пособие.* [Labour Contract: Instructional Manual]. M.: Delo, 1999. 351 p. 5000 ptd. ISBN 5-7749-0128-9.

Ershova, I. V. *Имущество и финансы предприятия. Правовое регулирование: Практическое пособие.* [Property and Finances of an Enterprise. Legal Regulation: Practical Manual]. M.: Iurist', 1999. 397 p. 5000 ptd. ISBN 5-7975-0176-7.

Ershova, I. V., Ivanova, T. M. *Предпринимательское право: Учебное пособие.* [Entrepreneurial Law: Instructional Manual]. M.: Iurisprudentsiia, 1999. 336 p. 10000 ptd. ISBN 5-8401-0006-4.

Если вас остановил инспектор: Ваши права. [If an Inspector Stops You: Your Rights]. M.: Avers, 1999. 81 p. 100000 ptd. ISBN 5-7198-0041-7.

Evstigneev, E. N. *Основы налогообложения и налогового права: Учебное пособие.* [Fundamental Principles of Taxation and Tax Law: Instructional Manual]. M.: INFRA-M, 1999. 119 p. 6000 ptd. ISBN 5-86225-992-9.

Ежегодник 98: Государственная служба России. [Annual 98: State Service of Russia]. Ed. F. D. Demidov. M.: Izd-vo, RAGS, 1999. 318 p. 500 ptd. ISBN 5-7729-0041-2.

Fagradiants, I. V. *Переписка с официальными лицами и учреждениями: Образцы писем.* [Correspondence with Officials and Institutions: Models of Letters]. Trans. from German. In German & Russian. M.: ETS, 1999. 207 p. 1000 ptd. ISBN 5-76455-028-0.

Федеральный конституционный закон «О правительстве Российской Федерации»: Комментарий. [Federal Constitutional Law "On the Government of the Russian Federation": Commentary]. Ed. L. A. Okunkov. M.: Iurid. lit., 1999. 480 p. 3000 ptd. ISBN 5-7260-0929-0.

Федеральный закон «О государственной регистрации прав на недвижимое имущество и сделок с ним»: Комментарий в схемах и таблицах. [Federal Law "On the State Registration of Rights to Immovable Property and Transactions with It": Commentary in Diagrams and Tables]. Tiumen: Izd-vo TiumGU, 1999. 140 p. 500 ptd. ISBN 5-88081-154-9.

Федеральный Закон «О несостоятельности (банкротстве): Постатейный комментарий. [Federal Law "On Insolvency (Bankruptcy)": Article by Article Commentary]. Ed. V. V. Vitrianskii. M.: Statut, 1999. 417 p. 15000 ptd. ISBN 5-89398-018-2.

Федеральный закон «О садоводческих, огороднических и дачных некоммерческих объединениях граждан». [Federal Law "On Horticultural, Market Gardening and Suburban Non-Commercial Citizens' Associations"]. M.: Druzhba narodov, 1999. 96 p. 5000 ptd. ISBN 5-285-00339-3.

Федеральный закон «О выборах депутатов Государственной Думы Федерального Собрания Российской Федерации». [Federal Law "On Elections of Deputies of the State Duma of the Federal Assembly of the Russian Federation"]. M.: Tsentr. izbirat. komissiia Ros. Federatsii, 1999. 256 p. 200000 ptd.

Also published:

M.: Tsentr. izbirat. komissii Ros. Federatsii, 1999. 256 p. 1000 ptd.

Федеральный закон «Об основных гарантиях избирательных прав и права на участие в референдуме граждан Российской Федерации»: С изменениями и дополнениями внесенными Федеральным законом от 30 марта 1999 г. No.55-ФЗ «О внесении изменений и доп. в Федеральный закон «Об основных гарантиях избирательных прав и права на участие в референдуме граждан Российской Федерации». [Federal Law "On the Basic Guarantees of Electoral Rights and Rights of Citizens to Participate in the Referendum of the Russian Federation": With Changes and Additions Introduced by the Federal Law of 30 March 1999 No.55-F3 "On the Introduction of Changes and Additions to the Federal Law "On the Basic Guarantees of Electoral Rights and Rights of Citizens to Participate in the Referendum of the Russian Federation"]. M.: Tsentr. izbirat. komis. Ros. Federatsii, 1999. 160 p. 1000 ptd.

Федеральный закон Российской Федерации «О несостоятельности (банкротстве)»: Официальный текст. [Federal Law of the Russian Federation "On Insolvency (Bankruptcy)": Official Text]. 3rd. ed. M.: Filin', 1999. 128 p. 5000 ptd. ISBN 5-89568-087-9.

Fedoseeva, G. Iu. *Международное частное право.* [International Private Law]. M.: Ostozhie, 1999. 295 p. 3000 ptd. ISBN 5-86-095-195-7.

Финансовое право: Учебник. [Financial Law: Textbook]. Ed. N. I. Khimichev. 2nd rev. ed. M.: Iurist', 1999. 20000 ptd. ISBN 7975-0256-9.

Fogelson, Iu. *Введение в страховое право: Учебно-практическое пособие.* [Introduction to Insurance Law: Instructional Practical Manual]. M.: BEK, 1999. 255 p. 3000 ptd. ISBN 5-85639-256-6.

Fogelson, Iu. B. *Комментарий к страховому законодательству.* [Commentary to Insurance Legislation]. M.: Iurist', 1999. 284 p. 5000 ptd.

Fokin, V. M. *Правоохранительные органы Российской Федерации: Учебник для вузов.* [Law Enforcement Agencies of the Russian Federation: Textbook for Institutes of Higher Education]. Ed. M. I. Lepikhov. M.: Bylina, 1999. 219 p. 3000 ptd. ISBN 5-88528-236-6.

Фонды по защите прав вкладчиков и акционеров. [Funds for the Defence of the Rights of Depositors and Stockholders]. Eds. V. F. Ukolov, A. M. Omarov. M.: Luch. Mol. gvardiia, 1999. 108 p. 500 ptd. ISBN 6-235-02360-9.

Frenkel, Z. G. *Волостное самоуправление: Его значение, задачи и взаимоотношения с кооперацией.* [Volost Self-Government: Its Significance, Tasks and Mutual Relationships with Cooperation]. Intro. & Commentary: T. M. Govorenkovaia. Pereizd. M.: Munitsipal. vlast, 1999. 302 p. 3000 ptd. ISBN 5-938158-002-6.

Fursov, D. A. *Предмет, система и основные принципы арбитражного процессуального права: Проблемы теории и практики.* [Subject, System and Fundamental Principles of Arbitrazh Procedure Law: Problems of Theory and Practice]. M.: INFRA-M, 1999. 452 p. 3000 ptd. ISBN 5-86225-970-8.

Gagut, L. *Государственная Дума.* [State Duma]. M.: Rus, 1999. 96 p. 1000 ptd. ISBN 5-89655-014-6.

Galiakbarov, R. R. *Уголовное право Российской Федерации: Общая часть. Конспекты и иные материалы.* [Criminal law of the Russian Federation: General Part Notes and Other Materials]. Krasnodar: Kuban. gos. agrarny un-t, 1999. 280 p. 3000 ptd.

Gelmanov, A. G., Gontar, S. A. *Как установить участие лица в правонарушении.* [How to Establish the Participation of a Person in the Violation of Law]. M.: Mozhaisk. poligraf. komb., 1999. 160 p. 5000 ptd. ISBN 5-8493-0063-5.

Gerosa, L. *Каноническое право в католической церкви.* [Canon Law in the Catholic Church]. Trans. from Italian. M.: Khristian. Rossiia, 1999. 379 p. 2000 ptd. ISBN 5-87468-043-8.

Getsevich, I. *Наедине со всеми: Геннадий Райков. Без ретуши. Выступления, интервью, размышления.* [In Private with Everyone: Genadii Raikov. Without Retouching. Speeches, Interviews, Reflections]. Ekaterinburg: Ural. rabochii, 1999. 151 p. 25000 ptd. ISBN 5-85383-147-X.

Girev, V. N., Zemlin, A. I. *Финансовое право: Практикум.* [Financial Law: Practical Work]. M.: Iurisprudentsiia, 1999. 143 p. 8000 ptd. ISBN 5-8401-0013-7.

Glotov, S. A. *Конституционно-правовые проблемы сотрудничества России и Совета Европы.* [Constitutional and Legal Problems of the Cooperation of Russia and the Council of Europe]. Saratov: Izd-vo Sarat. Gos. Akad. Prava, 1999. 544 p. 2500 ptd. ISBN 5-7924-0062-X.

Glotov, S. A. *Совет Европы как политико-правовой институт.* [The Council of Europe as a Political-Legal Institute]. Krasnodar: Sov. Kuban, 1999. 192 p. 2000 ptd. ISBN 5-7221-0240-7.

Glushchenko, P. P., Chaban, Iu. M. *Сам себе адвокат: Практическое пособие.* [Be Your Own Advocate: Practical Manual]. 2nd. rev. ed. Spb.: Politekhnika, 1999. 246 p. 5000 ptd. ISBN 5-7325-0497-4.

Glushchenko, P. P., Sedov, A. M. *Основы нотариальной деятельности: Учебное пособие.* [Fundamental Principles of

Notarial Activity: Instructional Manual]. Spb.: Izd-vo Mikhailova V. A., 1999. 367 p. 5000 ptd. ISBN 5-8016-0036-1.

Golenko, E. N., Kovalev, V. I. *Право социального обеспечения: Схемы и комментарии.* [Law of Social Security: Diagrams and Commentaries]. M.: Iurisprudentsiia, 1999. 182 p. 8000 ptd. ISBN 5-8401-0002-1.

Golenko, E. N., Kovalev, V. I. *Трудовое право: Схемы и комментарий.* [Labour Law: Diagrams and Commentary]. M.: Iurisprudentsiia, 1999. 176 p. 7000 ptd. ISBN 5-86532-050-5.

Gongalo, B. M. *Обеспечение исполнения обязательств.* [Securing the Performance of Obligations]. M.: Spark, 1999. 152 p. 2000 ptd. ISBN 5-88914-110-4.

Good, R. *Руководство к Унифицированным правилам для гарантий по требованию.* [Guide to Unified Rules for Guarantees on Demand]. Trans. from English. M.: Konsaltbankir, 1999. 166 p. 1100 ptd. ISBN 5-85187-055-9, ISBN 5-85187-085-0.

Goremykin, V. A., Bugulov, E. R. *Недвижимость: регистрация прав и сделок, ипотечное кредитование в схемах.* [Immovable Property: Registration of Rights and Transactions, Mortgage Credit in Diagrams]. 2d. ed. M.: Filin', 1999. 144 p. 5000 ptd. ISBN 5-89568-113-1.

Goshuliak, V. V. *Конституционное и уставное законодательство субъектов Российской Федерации.* [Constitutional and Charter Legislation of Subjects of the Russian Federation]. M.: NORMA, 1999. 439 p. 500 ptd.

Государственная Дума: Стенограмма заседаний. [State Duma: Record of Sessions]. M.: Izvestiia, 1999. 500 ptd.

Vol.7 (30). 1996. Spring Session. 21 June - 17 July. 704 p.
Vol.9 (32). 1996. Autumn Session. 2-16 October. 751 p.
Vol.10 (33). 1996. Autumn Session. 18 October - 11 November. 687 p.
Vol.11 (34). 1996. Autumn Session. 13-29 November. 640 p.
Vol.12 (35). 1996. Autumn Session. 4-15 December. 736 p.

Vol.13 (36). 1996. Autumn Session. 18-28 December. 671 p.
Vol.14 (37). 1997. Spring Session. 15 January-5 February. 816 p.
Vol.15 (38). 1997. Spring Session. 7-20 February. 704 p.
Vol.17 (40). 1997. Spring Session. 19 March - 4 April. 671 p.
Vol.18 (41). 1997. Spring Session. 9-24 April. 831 p.
Vol.49 (72). 1999. Spring Session. 13-15 May. 528 p.

Государственная и муниципальная кадровая политика Республики Адыгея в современных условиях. [State and Municipal Personnel Policy of the Republic of Adigeia under Contemporary Conditions]. A. A. Dzharimov et al. Maikop; Rostov n/D.: Sev.-Kavkaz. akad. gos. sluzhby, 1999. 214 p. ISBN 5-89546-035-6.

Государственная регистрация прав на недвижимое имущество и сделок с ним: правовая форма: В 3 ч. [State Registration of Rights to Immovable Property and Transactions with It: Legal Form: In 3 Parts]. Tiumen: Izd-vo TiumGU, 1999. 500 ptd. ISBN 5-88081-154-9.
Part 1. 171 p.
Part 2. 162 p.
Part 3. 233 p.

Государственная служба: Для вузов. [State Service: For Institutes of Higher Education]. Ed. A. V. Obolonskii. M.: Delo, 1999. 440 p. 5000 ptd. ISBN 5-7749-0153-X.

Государственная служба: Сборник нормативных документов. [State Service: Collection of Normative Documents]. M.: Delo, 1999. 430 p. 3000 ptd. ISBN 5-7749-0157-2.

Государственное социальное страхование. [State Social Security]. Comp. A. V. Verkhovtsev. M.: INFRA-M, 1999. 144 p. 3000 ptd. ISBN 5-16-000091-7.

Государственный служащий: культура поведения и деловой этикет. [State Employee: Behavioural Culture and Professional Etiquette]. 2d. ed. Ed. E. V. Okhotskii. M.: Izd-vo RAGS, 1999. 335 p. 1000 ptd. ISBN 5-7729-0037-4.

Государственные символы и награды Российской Федерации.

[State Symbols and Awards of the Russian Federation]. Comp. Iu. L. Kusher. M.: Knizh. palata, 1999. 171 p. 3000 ptd. ISBN 5-7000-0476-3.

Gracheva, E. Iu. *Финансовое право: Схемы и комментарий.* [Financial Law: Diagrams and Commentary]. M.: Iurisprudentsiia, 1999. 96 p. 7000 ptd. ISBN 5-86532-050-3.

Gracheva, E. Iu. *Финансовое право: Учебное пособие.* [Financial Law: Instructional Manual]. 3rd. rev. ed. M.: Iurisprudentsiia, 1999. 98 p. 8000 ptd. ISBN 5-8401-0020-X.

Gracheva, E. Iu., Sokolova, E. D. *Финансовое право: Вопросы и ответы.* [Financial Law: Questions and Answers]. M.: Iurisprudentsiia, 1999. 189 p. 8000 ptd. ISBN 5-8401-0005-6.

Градостроительный кодекс Российской Федерации: Официальный текст. Введен в действие с 11 мая 1998 г. [Urban Construction Code of the Russian Federation: Official Text. Entered into Operation from 11 May 1998]. M.: NORMA-INFRA-M, 1999. 90 p. 2000 ptd. ISBN 5-89123-366-5, ISBN 5-86225-859-0.

Grankin, I. V. *Парламент России.* [Russia's Parliament]. M.: Konsaltbankir, 1999. 304 p. 1000 ptd. ISBN 5-85187-089-3.

Гражданский кодекс Квебека. [Civil Code of Quebec]. Trans. Eds. O. M. Kozyr, A. A. Makovskaia. M.: Statut, 1999. 471 p. 1000 ptd. ISBN 5-8354-0009-8.

Гражданский кодекс Российской Федерации. [Civil Code of the Russian Federation]. Comp. D. V. Murzin. M.: NORMA-INFRA-M, 1999. 1024 p. 60000 ptd. ISBN 5-89123-353-3, ISBN 5-16-000024-0.

Гражданский кодекс Российской Федерации: Ч. 1, 2. [Civil Code of the Russian Federation: Parts 1 & 2]. M.: OLMA-Press; Novosibirsk: IUKEA, 1999. 559 p. 11000 ptd. ISBN 5-86750-096-9.

Гражданский кодекс Российской Федерации: Части первая и вторая. [Civil Code of the Russian Federation: Parts One and Two]. Intro. Iu. Kh. Kalmykov. 15th ed. M.: NORMA-INFRA-M, 1999. 555 p. 8000 ptd. ISBN 5-89123-387-8, ISBN 5-816-000107-7.

Гражданский кодекс Российской Федерации: Чч.1, 2. С постатейными материалами из практики Высшего Арбитражного Суда Российской Федерации. [Civil Code of the Russian Federation: Parts 1 & 2. With Article by Article Materials from the Practice of the Highest Arbitrazh Court of the Russian Federation]. Comp. D. V. Murzin. M.: NORMA-INFRA-M, 1999. 832 p. 60000 ptd. ISBN 5-89123-304-5, ISBN 5-86225-951-1.

Гражданский кодекс Российской Федерации: Ч.2. Комментарий. Гл.30. Купля-продажа. Кн.1. [Civil Code of the Russian Federation: Part 2. Commentary. Chapter 30. Contract of Sale. Book 1]. Eds. T. E. Abova, A. Iu. Kabalkin. M.: BEK, 1999. 235 p. 3000 ptd. ISBN 5-85639-242-6.

Гражданский кодекс Российской Федерации: Чч. 1 и 2. Официальный текст по состоянию на 1 декабря 1998 г. [Civil Code of the Russian Federation: Parts 1 and 2. Official Text as of 1 December 1998]. M.: NORMA-INFRA-M, 1999. 555 p. 6000 ptd. ISBN 5-89123-317-7.

Гражданский кодекс Российской Федерации: Чч.1 и 2. Официальный текст по состоянию на 1 марта 1999 г. [Civil Code of the Russian Federation: Parts 1 & 2. Official Text as of 1 March 1999]. M.: NORMA-INFRA-M, 1999. 560 p. 10000 ptd. ISBN 5-89123-338-X, ISBN 5-86225-984-8.

Гражданский кодекс Российской Федерации: Чч. 1 и 2. С постатейными материалами из практики Высшего Арбитражного Суда РФ. [Civil Code of the Russian Federation: Parts 1 and 2. With Article by Article Materials from the Practice of the Supreme Arbitrazh Court of the Russian Federation]. M.: NORMA-INFRA-M, 1999. 819 p. 6000 ptd. ISBN 5-89123-304-5, ISBN 5-86225-951-1.

Гражданский кодекс Российской Федерации в схемах. [Civil Code of the Russian Federation in Diagrams]. Ed. T. M. Medvedeva. M.: Gorodets, Formula prava, 1999. 101 p. 5000 ptd. ISBN 5-89391-019-2.

Гражданский процесс: Учебник. [Civil Procedure: Textbook]. 2d.

rev. ed. Eds. V. A. Musin, N. A. Chechinaia, D. M. Chechota. M.: Prospekt, 1999. 472 p. 10000 ptd. ISBN 5-7896-0069-7.

Also published:
M.: Spark, Gorodets, 1999. 544 p. 8000 ptd. ISBN 5-88914-107-4.
M.: Novy Iurist, 1999. 400 p. 2000 ptd. ISBN 5-7969-0076-5.
M.: BEK, 1999. 593 p. 20000 ptd. ISBN 5-85639-264-7.
M.: Prospekt, 1999. 472 p. 10000 ptd. ISBN 5-8369-0049-3. (2nd. rev. ed).

Гражданский процессуальный кодекс РСФСР. [RSFSR Code of Civil Procedure]. M.: NORMA-INFRA-M, 1999.

Официальный текст по состоянию на 15 декабря 1998 г. [Official Text as of 15 December 1998]. 219 p. 8000 ptd. ISBN 5-89123-325-8.

Официальный текст по состоянию на 15 февраля 1999 г. [Official Text as of 15 February 1999]. 219 p. 10000 ptd. ISBN 5-89123-325-8.

Also published:
M.: Iurist', 1999. 176 p. 10000 ptd. ISBN 5-7975-0188-0.

Гражданский процессуальный кодекс РСФСР: Официальный текст с изменениями и дополнениями по состоянию на 1 сентября 1999 г. [RSFSR Code of Civil Procedure: Official Text with Changes and Additions for 1 September 1999]. M.: TANDEM, EKMOS, 1999. 128 p. 3000 ptd. ISBN 5-88124-050-2.

Гражданский процессуальный кодекс РСФСР: С изменениями и дополнениями на 15 мая 1999 г. [RSFSR Code of Civil Procedure: With Changes and Additions for 15 May 1999]. M.: Prospekt, Kodeks, 1999. 166 p. 10000 ptd. ISBN 5-8369-0010-8.

Гражданский процессуальный кодекс РСФСР: С изменениями и дополнениями на 15 сентября 1999 г. [RSFSR Code of Civil Procedure: With Changes and Additions for 15 September 1999]. M.: Prospekt, 1999. 168 p. 10000 ptd. ISBN 5-8369-0010-8.

Гражданский процессуальный кодекс РСФСР с постатейным

приложением судебных документов и комментариями. [RSFSR Code of Civil Procedure with Article by Article Annex of Judicial Documents and Commentaries]. Comp. N. R. Vilchur et al. M.: Prospekt, Kodeks, 1999. 416 p. 5000 ptd. ISBN 5-8369-0036-1.

Гражданский процессуальный кодекс РСФСР с судебными документами. [RSFSR Code of Civil Procedure with Judicial Documents]. N. R. Vilchur et al. M.: Kodeks, Prospekt, 1999. 416 p. 5000 ptd. ISBN 5-8369-0068-X.

Гражданское процессуальное право России: Учебник для вузов. [Law of Civil Procedure of Russia: Textbook for Institutes of Higher Education]. 2d. rev. ed. Ed. M. S. Shakarian. M.: Bylina, 1999. 500 p. 5000 ptd.

Гражданско-правовые документы для оформления сделок с недвижимостью. [Civil Law Documents for Formalising Transactions with an Immovable]. Ed. M. Iu. Tikhomirov. M.: Izd. g-na Tikhomirova M. Iu., Iurinformtsentr, 1999. 86 p. 3000 ptd. ISBN 5-89194-024-8.

Гражданское и предпринимательское право: Сборник документов. Ч.2. [Civil and Entrepreneurial Law: Collection of Documents. Part 2]. Ed. T. V. Bogachevaia. Comp. M. Iu. Savranskii. M.: TON, Ostozhie, 1999. 896 p. 7000 ptd. ISBN 5-86095-125-6.

Гражданское право: Часть 2: Учебник. [Civil Law: Part 2: Textbook]. Ed. A. G. Kalpin. M.: Iurist', 1999. 542 p. 50000 ptd. ISBN 5-7975-0223-2.

Гражданское право: Часть 3. Учебник. [Civil Law: Part 3. Textbook]. Eds. A. P. Sergeev, Iu. K. Tolstoi. M.: Prospekt, 1999. 591 p. 10000 ptd. ISBN 5-8369-0035-3.

Гражданское право: Учебник. [Civil Law: Textbook]. Eds. A. P. Sergeev, Iu. K. Tolstoi. 3rd. rev. ed. M.: Prospekt, 1999. 20000 ptd.

Part 1. 631 p. ISBN 5-8369-0013-2.
Part 2. 782 p. ISBN 5-8369-0014-0.
Vol.1. 4th rev. ed. 610 p. ISBN 5-8369-0051-5.
Vol.2. 720 p. 20000 ptd. ISBN 5-8369-0052-3.
Vol.3. 2nd. rev. ed. 621 p. ISBN 5-8369-0053-1.

Гражданское право России: Часть 1. [Civil Law of Russia: Part 1]. Eds. Z. I. Tsybulenko, P. V. Ramzaev. 2nd. rev. ed. M.: Iurist', 1999. 163 p. 10000 ptd. ISBN 5-7975-0220-8.

Гражданское законодательство: Сборник нормативных актов. [Civil Legislation: Collection of Normative Acts]. Comp. A. P. Sergeev. M.: Kodeks, Prospekt, 1999. 10000 ptd.

Part 1. 688 p. ISBN 5-8369-0002-7.

Part 2. 720 p. ISBN 5-8369-0003-5.

Гражданское законодательство России: Ч.1: Сборник нормативных правовых актов и документов. [Civil Legislation of Russia: Part 1: Collection of Normative Legal Acts and Documents]. Ed. Z. I. Tsybulenko. M.: Iurist', 1999. 620 p. 10000 ptd. ISBN 5-7975-0196-1.

Grigoriev, V. N. *Задержание подозреваемого.* [Detention of Suspect]. M.: IurInfoR, 1999. 541 p. 5000 ptd. ISBN 5-89158-029-2.

Grishaev, T. P. *Гражданское право. Часть первая в вопросах и ответах: Учебное пособие.* [Civil Law. Part One in Questions and Answers: Instructional Manual]. M.: Iurist', 1999. 141 p. 10000 ptd. ISBN 5-7975-0242-9.

Gromov, N. A. *Вновь открывшиеся обстоятельства в уголовном процессе.* [Newly Discovered Circumstances in Criminal Procedure]. M.: Spark, 1999. 220 p. 1500 ptd.

Губернаторы Урала. [Governors of the Urals]. Comps. A. D. Kirillov, B. A. Kirillov. Ekaterinburg: Ural. rabochii, 1999. 248 p. 1000 ptd. ISBN 5-85383-150-X.

Guev, A. N. *Постатейный комментарий Налогового Кодекса Российской Федерации.* [Article by Article Commentary to the Tax Code of the Russian Federation]. M.: IUKANG, 1999. 957 p. 600 ptd. ISBN 5-900749-08-8.

Gusev, A. N. *Постатейный комментарий к части первой Гражданского кодекса Российской Федерации.* [Article by Article Commentary to the First Part of the Civil Code of the Russian

Federation]. 2d. rev. ed. M.: INFRA-M, 1999. 773 p. ISBN 5-86225-900-7.

Gusev, A. N. *Постатейный комментарий к части второй Гражданского кодекса Российской Федерации.* [Article by Article Commentary to the Second Part of the Civil Code of the Russian Federation]. 3rd. rev. ed. M.: INFRA-M, 1999. 820 p. 30000 ptd. ISBN 5-86225-625-3.

Gushchin, V. V. *Теория госдударства и права: Вопрос - ответ.* [Theory of State and Law: Question - Answer]. M.: Pravo i Zakon, 1999. 123 p. 5000 ptd. ISBN 5-7858-0033-0.

Gutsenko, K. F., Kovalev, M. A. *Правоохранительные органы: Хрестоматия.* [Law Enforcement Agencies: Anthology]. Ed. K. F. Gutsenko. M.: Zertsalo, 1999. 368 p. 5000 ptd. ISBN 5-8078-0051-6.

Gutsenko, K. F., Kovalev, M. A. *Правоохранительные органы: Учебник для вузов.* [Law Enforcement Agencies: Textbook for Institutes of Higher Education]. 4th. rev. ed. M.: Zertsalo, 1999. 416 p. 8000 ptd. ISBN 5-8078-0033-8.

Khabarov, A. *Россия ментовская.* [Cop-Shop Russia]. M.: EKSMO-Press, 1999. 480 p. 10000 ptd. ISBN 5-04-001813-4.

Khafizova, R. I. *Управление в Уфимской губернии во второй половине XIX - начале XX в.: Учебное пособие.* [Administration in the Ufimskii Province in the Second Half of the 19th to the Beginning of the 20th Centuries: Instructional Manual]. Ufa: Vos. un-t, 1999. 117 p. 200 ptd. ISBN 5-87865-178-5.

Khalafin, A. *Как прописаться в Москве: Консультации юриста.* [How to Register in Moscow: A Jurist's Advice]. M.: Poznavat. kn. plius, 1999. 175 p.

Khalipov, V. F., Khalipova, E. V., Shishkin, A. N. *Выборы и власть.* [Elections and Power]. M.: Sovershenstvo, 1999. 378 p. 10000 ptd. ISBN 5-8089-0032-8.

Khokhriakov, G. F. *Криминология: Учебник.* [Criminology:

Textbook]. Ed. V. N. Kudriavtsev. M.: Iurist', 1999. 511 p. 10000 ptd. ISBN 5-7975-0192-9.

Хрестоматия по истории государства и права России: Учебное пособие. [Anthology on the History of State and Law of Russia: Instructional Manual]. Comp. Iu. P. Titov. M.: Prospekt, 1999. 472 p. 10000 ptd. ISBN 5-7896-0036-0.

Хрестоматия по истории государства и права зарубежных стран: Древность и сред. века. [Anthology on the History of State and Law of Foreign Countries: Antiquity and the Middle Ages]. Comp. V. A. Tomsinov. M.: Zertsalo, 1999. 467 p. 8000 ptd. ISBN 5-8078-0041-9.

Хрестоматия по истории государства и права зарубежных стран: Новое и Новейшее время. [Anthology on the History of the State and Law of Foreign Countries]. Comp. N. A. Krasheninnikov. M.: Zertsalo, 1999. 563 p. 8000 ptd. ISBN 5-8078-0042-7.

Хрестоматия по уголовному процессу России. [Anthology on Russian Criminal Procedure]. Comp. E. F. Kutsov. M.: Gorodets, 1999. 269 p. 4000 ptd. ISBN 5-89391-033-8.

Khropaniuk, V. N. *Теория государства и права: Учебное пособие для вузов.* [Theory of State and Law: Instructional Manual for Institutes of Higher Education]. Ed. V. G. Strekozov. M.: Interstil, 1999. 377 p. 5000 ptd. ISBN 5-8438-0020-3.

Iakimov, A. Iu. *Статус субъекта административной юрисдикции и проблемы его реализации: Монограмма.* [Status of a Subject of Administrative Jurisdiction and Problems of Its Realisation: Monogram]. M.: Prospekt, 1999. 199 p. 1000 ptd. ISBN 5-8369-0004-3.

Iakovenko, A. V. *Прогрессивное развитие международного космического права: Актуальные проблемы.* [Progressive Development of International Space Law: Urgent Problems]. M.: Mezhundar. otnosheniia, 1999. 166 p. 1000 ptd. ISBN 5-7133-1022-1.

Iakubovskaia, I. *Генерал Дима: Карьера. Тюрьма. Любовь.* [General

Dima: Career. Prison. Love]. M.: Kollektsiia "Sovershenno sekretno", 1999. 255 p. 20000 ptd. ISBN 5-89048-049-9.

Iakubovskie, D. & I. *Что такое арест и как с ним бороться: Практическое пособие.* [What It Is To Be Arrested and How To Fight Against It: Practical Manual]. M.: Politbiuro, 1999. 575 p. 11000 ptd. ISBN 5-89756-016-1.

Iakupov, R. Kh. *Уголовный процесс: Учебник для вузов.* [Criminal Procedure: Textbook for Institutes of Higher Education]. Ed. V. N. Galuzo. M.: Zertsalo, 1999. 464 p. 8000 ptd. ISBN 5-8078-0037-0.

Ianushkevich, I. P. *Нотариат в России: Учебное пособие.* [The Notariat in Russia: Instructional Manual]. M.: INITS Rospatenta, 1999. 83 p. 150 ptd.

Iarkov, V. V. *Комментарий к Федеральному закону «Об исполнительном производстве» (постатейный) и к Федеральному закону «О судебных приставах».* [Commentary to the Federal Law "On Execution Proceeding" (Article by Article) and to the Federal Law "On Bailiffs"]. M.: Iurist', 1999. 384 p. 10000 ptd. ISBN 5-7975-0206-2.

Iaroshik, O. D., Ruslanova, I. N. *Справочник по проблемам дорожно-транспортного происшествия: Дорожно-транспортное происшествие: Кто виноват? Что делать?* [Manual on the Problems of Road Transport Accidents: The Road Transport Accident: Who is to Blame? What is to be Done?]. M.: Atlasy avtomobilei, 1999. 191 p. 30000 ptd. ISBN 5-8245-0004-5.

Ignatenko, V. V., Ishchenko, E. P. *Юридическая ответственность за нарушения избирательного законодательства.* [Legal Responsibility for the Violation of Electoral Legislation]. M.: RTSOIT, 1999. 96 p. 3000 ptd. ISBN 5-93639-002-0.

Ikonitskaia, I. A. *Земельное право Российской Федерации.* [Land Law of the Russian Federation]. In-t gosudarstva i prava RAN. M., 1999. 127 p. 1600 ptd. ISBN 5-88720-058-8.

Illarionov, V. P., Putova, I. V. *Правовые и организационно-*

методические аспекты международного розыска преступников: Для вузов. [Legal and Organisational-Methods Aspects of the International Search for Criminals: For Institutes of Higher Education]. M.: Knizh. mir, 1999. 94 p. 2000 ptd. ISBN 5-8041-0040-8.

Иностранные юридические лица: Налогообложение, учет, отчетность. [Foreign Juridical Persons: Taxation, Settlement of Accounts, Accountability]. M.: Ucheb.-inform. tsentr pri Gos. nalogovoi inspektsii po g. Moskve, 1999. 352 p. 3000 ptd. ISBN 5-86297-107-6.

Институты административного права. [Institutes of Administrative Law]. Eds. I. L. Bachilo, N. Iu. Khamanev. M.: In-t gosudarstva i prava RAN, 1999. 254 p. 1000 ptd. ISBN 5-8339-0008-5.

Ishchenko, A. E., Ishchenko, E. P. *Выбираю в первый раз: Молодому избирателю об основах российского избирательного права и избирательного процесса.* [I Am Voting for the First Time: For the Young Voter About the Fundamental Principles of Russian Electoral Law and the Electoral Process]. M.: RTSOIT, 1999. 25 p. 5000 ptd. ISBN 5-93639-044-7.

Ishchenko, E. P., Ishchenko, P. P., Zotchev, V. A. *Криминалистическая фотография и видеозапись: Учебно-практическое пособие.* [Criminalistics Photography and Video Recording: Instructional Practical Manual]. Ed. E. P. Ishchenko. M.: Iurist', 1999. 436 p. 5000 ptd. ISBN 5-7975-0202-X.

История государства и права: Учебник. [History of State and Law: Textbook]. Ed. Iu. P. Titov. M.: Prospekt, 1999. 542 p. 10000 ptd. ISBN 5-8369-0063-9.

История государства и права зарубежных стран: Учебник для вузов. [History of State and Law of Foreign Countries: Textbook for Institutes of Higher Education]. Eds. O. A. Zhidkov, N. A. Krasheninnikova. 2nd. ed. M.: NORMA-INFRA-M, 1999.

Part 1. 609 p. 30000 ptd. ISBN 5-89123-341-X, ISBN 5-86225-950-3.

Part 2. 703 p. 30000 ptd. ISBN 5-89123-380-0, ISBN 5-16-000081-X.

История отечественного государства и права: Часть 1: Учебник. [History of National State and Law: Part 1: Textbook]. Ed. O. I. Chistiakov. M.: BEK, 1999. 360 p. 10000 ptd. ISBN 5-85639-173-X.

История политических и правовых учений: Учебник для вузов. [History of Political and Legal Doctrines: Textbook]. 2nd. ed. Ed. V. S. Nersesiants. M.: NORMA, INFRA-M, 1999. 727 p. 60000 ptd. ISBN 5-89123-189-1, ISBN 5-86225-633-4.

Also published:

M.: Zertsalo, 1999. 688 p. 10000 ptd. ISBN 5-8078-0054-0.

Iugov, A. A. *Правовые основы публичной власти в Российской Федерации.* [Legal Fundamental Principles of Public Authority in the Russian Federation]. Ekaterinburg: Izd-vo UrGIUA, 1999. 124 p. 600 ptd. ISBN 5-7845-0094-5.

Iuldashbaeva, L. R. *Правовое регулирование оборота эмиссионных ценных бумаг (акций, облигаций).* [Legal Regulation of the Circulation of Emission Securities (Stocks, Obligations)]. M.: Statut, 1999. 204 p. 5000 ptd. ISBN 5-8354-0018-7.

Iusov, S. V., Tkachev, V. N., Kharkovskii, A. I. *Избирательные споры в ходе федеральных, региональных и местных выборов 1993-1999 годов.* [Electoral Disputes in the Course of Federal, Regional and Local Elections in the Years 1993-1999]. M.: Prospekt, 1999. 80 p. 500 ptd. ISBN 5-8369-0075-2.

Юридические консультации по вопросам применения Закона Российской Федерации «О садоводческих, огороднических и дачных некоммерческих объединениях граждан». [Legal Consultations on Questions of the Application of the Russian Federation Law "On Horticultural, Market Gardening and Suburban Non-Commercial Citizens' Associations"]. M.: Druzhba narodov, 1999. 96 p. 5000 ptd. ISBN 5-285-00341-5.

Ivakina, N. N. *Основы судебного красноречия: Риторика для юристов: Учебное пособие.* [Fundamental Principles of Judicial Eloquence: Rhetoric for Jurists: Instructional Manual]. M.: Iurist', 1999. 383 p. 5000 ptd. ISBN 5-7975-0150-3.

Ivanov, E. A. *Отмывание денег и правовое регулирование борьбы с ним.* [Money Laundering and Legal Regulation of the Struggle Against It]. M.: Ros. Iurid. Izdat. Dom, 1999. 176 p. ISBN 5-88635-030-6.

Ivanova, N. R. *Защита права собственности в арбитражном суде: Комментарий арбитраж. практики.* [Defence of the Rights of Ownership in an Arbitrazh Court: Commentary to Arbitrazh Practice]. M.: Kontrakt, INFRA-M, 1999. 295 p. 3000 ptd. ISBN 5-86225-921-X.

Избирательное право и избирательный процесс в Российской Федерации: Для вузов. [Electoral Law and the Electoral Process in the Russian Federation: For Institutes of Higher Education]. S. A. Avakian et al. M.: NORMA, 1999. 841 p. 30000 ptd. ISBN 5-89123-311-8.

Избирательное право России: В документах. Том 1. Федеральные нормативно-правовые акты. [Russian Electoral Law: In Documents. Vol.1. Federal Normative Legal Acts]. Ed. O. E. Kutafin. M.: Mosk. gos. iurid. akad., 1999. 638 p. 1000 ptd. ISBN 5-86095-191-4.

Избирательное право России (в документах): Т.2. Региональные нормативно-правовые акты. [Electoral Law of Russia (in Documents): Vol.2. Regional Normative-Legal Acts]. Comps. N. A. Mikhaleva, A. A. Iashin. M.: Mosk. gos. iurid. akad., 1999. 868 p. 1000 ptd. ISBN 5-86095-192-2.

Избирательное право России: В документах. Т.3. Нормативно-правовые акты Центральной избирательной комиссии Российской Федерации. [Electoral Law of Russia: In Documents. Vol.3. Normative-Legal Acts of the Central Electoral Commission of the Russian Federation]. Ed. O. E. Kutafin. M.: Mosk. gos. iurid. akad., 1999. 836 p. 1000 ptd. ISBN 5-86095-193-0.

Как получить вид на жительство в Чехии. [How to Obtain a Residence Permit in Czechoslovakia]. Ed. D. B. Tolkachev. M.: Kampana, 1999. 153 p. 5000 ptd. ISBN 5-7941-0038-9.

Kalamkarian, R. A. *Поведение государств в международном суде ООН.* [Conduct of States in the International Court of the United Nations]. M.: Nauka, 1999. 160 p. 420 ptd. ISBN 5-02-008276-7.

Канада: Справочник иммигранта. [Canada: The Immigrant's Manual]. Comp. L. Mikhailova. M.: Linor, 1999. 352 p. 5000 ptd. ISBN 5-900889-67-X.

Kananovich, I. V. *Арбитражный процесс: Вопросы и ответы.* [Arbitrazh Procedure: Questions and Answers]. M.: Iurisprudentsiia, 1999. 141 p. 7000 ptd. ISBN 5-8401-0008-0.

Karaseva, M. V. *Финансовое право: Общая часть. Учебник.* [Financial Law: General Part. Textbook]. M.: Iurist', 1999. 253 p. 10000 ptd. ISBN 5-7975-0204-6.

Kartashkin, V. A. *Как подать жалобу в Европейский Суд по правам человека. Комментарий к правилам обращения в органы Совета Европы по защите прав человека.* [How to Lodge an Appeal with the European Court of Human Rights. Commentary to the Rules for Appeal to the Agencies of the Council of Europe for the Defence of Human Rights]. M.: NORMA-INFRA-M, 1999. 96 p. 50000 ptd. ISBN 5-89123-219-7, ISBN 5-86225-718-7.

Karyshev, V. *Жизнь бандитская: История группировки. Взгляд изнутри.* [A Gangster's Life: History of the Group. An Opinion from Within the Group]. M.: EKSMO-Press, 1999. 480 p. 5000 ptd. ISBN 5-04-002559-9.

Kashanina, T. V. *Корпоративное право: Учебник для вузов.* [Corporate Law: Textbook for Institutes of Higher Education]. M.: NORMA-INFRA-M, 1999. 802 p. 30000 ptd. ISBN 5-89123-174-3.

Kashanina, T. V. *Происхождение государства и права: Современные трактовки и новые подходы: Учебное пособие.* [Origin of State and Law: Contemporary Interpretations and New Approaches: Instructional Manual]. M.: Iurist', 1999. 335 p. 5000 ptd. ISBN 5-7975-0184-8.

Kasso, L. A. *Понятие о залоге в современном праве.* [Concept of

Pledge in Contemporary Law]. M.: Statut, 1999. 284 p. 7000 ptd. ISBN 5-89398-025-5.

Katkov, D. B., Korchigo, E. V. *Конституционное право России: Учебное пособие.* [Constitutional Law of Russia: Instructional Manual]. Ed. Iu. A. Vedeneev. M.: Iurisprudentsiia, 1999. 288 p. 8000 ptd. ISBN 5-8401-0007-2.

Kibalnik, A. G. *Иммунитеты в уголовном праве.* [Immunities in Criminal Law]. Stavropol: Stavropolservisshkola, 1999. 173 p. 1000 ptd. ISBN 5-93078-029-3.

Kirsanova, M. V., Aksenov, Iu. M. *Курс делопроизводства: Учебное пособие.* [Clerical Work Course: Instructional Manual]. 2d. ed. M.: INFRA-M; Novosibirsk: NGAEiU, 1999. 271 p. 50000 ptd. ISBN 5-86225-521-4, ISBN 5-7014-0007-7.

Kiselev, I. Ia. *Сравнительное и международное трудовое право: Учебник.* [Comparative and International Labour Law: Textbook]. M.: Delo, 1999. 728 p. 5000 ptd. ISBN 5-7749-0158-0.

Kleandrov, M. I. *Нефтегазовое законодательство в системе российского права.* [Oil and Gas Legislation in the System of Russian Law]. Eds. V. V. Laptev, V. F. Iakovlev. Novosibirsk: Nauka, Sib. izd. firma RAN, 1999. 144 p. 500 ptd. ISBN 5-02-031550-8.

Kleandrov, M. I. *Судья - центральное звено судебной системы: Учебное пособие.* [The Judge - The Central Link of the Judicial System: Instructional Manual]. Tiumen: Izd-vo TiumGU, 1999. 232 p. 500 ptd. ISBN 5-5-88081-168-9.

Klimenko, S. V., Chicherin, A. L. *Основы государства и права: Пособие для поступающих в юридические вузы.* [Fundamental Principles of State and Law: Manual for Those Entering Juridical Institutes]. M.: Zertsalo, 1999. 353 p. 8000 ptd. ISBN 5-8078-0003-6.

Кодекс об административных правонарушениях: С изменениями и дополнениями на 15 сентября 1999 г. [Code on Administrative Violations of Law: With Changes and Additions for 15 September 1999]. M.: Kodeks, Prospekt, 1999. 198 p. 10000 ptd.

ISBN 5-8369-0011-6.

Кодекс РСФСР об административных правонарушениях. [RSFSR Code on Administrative Violations of Law]. 12th ed. M.: NORMA-INFRA-M, 1999. 256 p. 6000 ptd. ISBN 5-89123-291-X, ISBN 5-86225-933-3.

Кодекс РСФСР об административных правонарушениях: Официальный текст. По состоянию на 1 февраля 1999 г. [RSFSR Code on Administrative Violations of Law: Official Text as of 1 February 1999]. M.: NORMA-INFRA-M, 1999. 284 p. 6000 ptd. ISBN 5-89123-291-X.

Кодекс РСФСР об административных правонарушениях: Официальный текст. По состоянию на 22 марта 1999 г. [RSFSR Code on Administrative Violations of Law: Official Text. As of 22 March 1999]. M.: Filin', 1999. 279 p. 5000 ptd. ISBN 5-89568-140-9.

Кодекс РСФСР об административных правонарушениях: Официальный текст по состоянию на 15 мая 1999 г. [RSFSR Code on Administrative Violations of Law: Official Text from 15 May 1999]. M.: TANDEM, EKMOS, 1999. 160 p. 3000 ptd. ISBN 5-88124-051-2.

Also published:
M.: Prospekt, Kodeks, 1999. 198 p. 10000 ptd. ISBN 5-8369-0011-6.

Кодекс РСФСР об административных правонарушениях: По состоянию на 15 февраля 1999 г. [RSFSR Code on Administrative Violations of Law: As of 15 February 1999]. M.: OLMA-Press, Novosibirsk: IUKEA, 1999. 288 p. 11000 ptd. ISBN 5-86750-081-0.

Кодекс торгового мореплавания Российской Федерации. [Merchant Shipping Code of the Russian Federation]. M.: B-chka "Ros. gazety", 1999. 191 p. 10000 ptd.

Also published:
M.: Kontrakt RL, Red. gazety "Morskie vesti Rossii", 1999. 239 p. 5000 ptd. ISBN 5-86502-036-6.

Кодекс торгового мореплавания Российской Федерации:

Принят Государственной Думой 31 марта 1999 г. [Merchant Shipping Code of the Russian Federation: Adopted by the State Duma on 31 March 1999]. Spb.: ZAO "TSNIIMF", 1999. 335 p. 1500 ptd. ISBN 5-8072-0022-5.

Кодекс законов о труде Российской Федерации. [Code of Laws on Labour of the Russian Federation]. M.: NORMA-INFRA-M, 1999. 134 p. 6000 ptd. ISBN 5-86225-998-8.
 Also published:
 M.: Novaia Volna, 1999. 126 p. 5000 ptd. ISBN 5-7864-0032-8.

Кодекс законов о труде Российской Федерации: Официальный текст по состоянию на 15 мая 1999 г. [Code of Laws on Labour of the Russian Federation: Official Text as of 15 May 1999]. M.: Tandem, EKMOS, 1999. 79 p. 3000 ptd. ISBN 5-88124-050-2.

Кодекс законов о труде Российской Федерации: Официальный текст по состоянию на 15 ноября 1999 г. [Code of Laws on Labour of the Russian Federation: Official Text for 15 November 1999]. M.: TANDEM, EKMOS, 1999. 80 p. 5000 ptd. ISBN 5-88124-050-2.

Кодекс законов о труде Российской Федерации: По состоянию на 15 февраля 1999 г. [Code of Laws on Labour of the Russian Federation: As of 15 February 1999]. M.: OLMA-Press, Novosibirsk: IUKEA, 1999. 160 p. 11000 ptd. ISBN 5-224-00281-8, ISBN 5-86750-123-X.

Кодекс Законов о труде Российской Федерации: По состоянию на 1 июля 1999 г. [Code of Laws on Labour of the Russian Federation: For 1 July 1999]. M.: Iurist', 1999. 100 p. 10000 ptd. ISBN 5-7975-0232-1.
 Also published:
 M.: Prospekt, 1999. 95 p. 15000 ptd. ISBN 5-8369-0005-1. (With Changes and Additions for 15 September 1999].

Кодекс законов о труде Российской Федерации: С изменениями и дополнениями на 1 февраля 1999 г. [Code of Laws on Labour of the Russian Federation: With Changes and Additions for 1 February 1999]. M.: Prospekt, 1999. 93 p. 10000 ptd. ISBN 5-7896-0044-1.

Кодекс законов о труде Российской Федерации: С изменениями и дополнениями на 1 апреля 1999 г. [Code of Laws on Labour of the Russian Federation: With Changes and Additions for 1 April 1999]. M.: Prospekt, 1999. 95 p. 1000 ptd. ISBN 5-8369-0005-1.

Кодекс законов о труде Российской Федерации: С изменениями и дополнениями на 15 августа 1999 г. [Code of Laws on Labour of the Russian Federation: With Changes and Additions for 15 August 1999]. M.: Prospekt, 1999. 95 p. 10000 ptd. ISBN 5-8369-0005-1.

Kolganova, M. V. *Введение в юридическую специальность: Краткий курс лекций.* [Introduction to the Legal Profession: A Short Course of Lectures]. M.: Finstatinform, 1999. 85 p. 1000 ptd. ISBN 5-7866-0100-5.

Koliushin, E. I. *Конституционное (государственное) право России: Курс лекций.* [Constitutional (State) Law of Russia: Course of Lectures]. M.: Izd-vo Mosk. un-ta, 1999. 381 p. 3000 ptd. ISBN 5-211-04088-0.

Коллективный договор. [Collective Contract]. Comp. A. V. Verkhovtsev. M.: INFRA-M, 1999. 64 p. 3000 ptd. ISBN 5-16-000017-8.

Komarov, S. A., Malko, A. V. *Теория государства и права: Учебно-методическое пособие.* [Theory of State and Law: Instructional Methods Manual]. M.: NORMA-INFRA-M, 1999. 440 p. 40000 ptd. ISBN 5-89123-313-4.

Комментарий арбитражно-судебной практики по делам, связанным с малым предпринимательством и законодательством о применении контрольно-кассовых машин. [Commentary of Arbitrazh and Judicial Practice on Matters Connected with Small Entrepreneurship and Legislation on the Application of Cash Checking Machines]. Mytishchi: IITS "Alfa-Kompozit", 1999. 48 p. 1000 ptd.

Комментарий Федерального закона «О статусе военнослужащих». [Commentary to the Federal Law "On the Status of Military Servicemen"]. Ed. V. G. Strekozov. M.: Spark, 1999. 576 p. 10000 ptd. ISBN 5-88914-098-1.

Комментарий изменений к Налоговому кодексу Российской Федерации, части первой (постатейный). [Commentary to the Changes to the First Part (Article by Article) of the Tax Code of the Russian Federation]. Ed. A. V. Bryzgalin. M.: Nalogi i fin. pravo, Analitika-Press, 1999. 229 p. 50000 ptd. ISBN 5-7916-0069-0.

Комментарий к Арбитражному процессуальному кодексу Российской Федерации. [Commentary to the Code of Arbitrazh Procedure of the Russian Federation]. Intro. V. F. Iakovlev. 2nd. rev. ed. M.: Kontrakt, INFRA-M, 1999. 516 p. 40000 ptd. ISBN 5-90785-013-2, ISBN 5-86225-676-8.

Комментарий к Бюджетному кодексу Российской Федерации (вводный). [Commentary to the Budget Code of the Russian Federation (Introductory)]. Eds. M. V. Romanovskii, O. V. Vrublevskaia. M.: Iurait, 1999. 221 p. 5000 ptd. ISBN 5-85294-069-0.

Комментарий к Федеральному закону о гарантиях прав коренных малочисленных народов Российской Федерации. [Commentary to the Federal Law on the Guarantees of Rights of Indigenous Small Nations of the Russian Federation]. Ed. B. S. Krylov. M.: Izd. g-na Tikhomirova M. Iu., Iurinformtsentr, 1999. 152 p. 5000 ptd. ISBN 5-89194-040-X.

Комментарий к Федеральному закону «О государственной регистрации прав на недвижимое имущество и сделок с ним». [Commentary to the Federal Law "On the State Registration of Rights to Immovable Property and Transactions with It"]. M.: NORMA-INFRA-M, 1999. 523 p. 50000 ptd. ISBN 5-89123-240-5.

Комментарий к Федеральному закону «О содержании под стражей подозреваемых и обвиняемых в совершении преступлений». [Commentary to the Federal Law "On the Keeping Under Guard of Suspects and Those Accused of the Commission of a Crime"]. Eds. A. S. Mikhlin, V. I. Seliverstov. M.: Spark, 1999. 191 p. 8000 ptd. ISBN 5-88914-125-2.

Комментарий к Федеральному закону «Об акционерных обществах». [Commentary to the Federal law "On Joint-Stock Societies"]. 2d. rev. ed. Ed. M. Iu. Tikhomirov. M.: Izd. g-na

Tikhomirova M. Iu., 1999. 392 p. 20000 ptd. ISBN 5-89194-016-7.

Комментарий к Федеральному закону «Об экологической экспертизе». [Commentary to the Federal Law "On Ecological Expertise"]. Ed. M. M. Brinchuk. M.: BEK, 1999. 203 p. 5000 ptd. ISBN 5-85639-262-0.

Комментарий к Федеральному закону «Об ипотеке (залоге недвижимости)». [Commentary to the Federal Law "On Mortgage (Pledge of an Immovable)"]. Ed. I. D. Grachev. M.: NORMA-INFRA-M, 1999. 325 p. 30000 ptd. ISBN 5-89123-349-5, ISBN 5-16-000021-6.

Комментарий к Федеральному закону «Об обществах с ограниченной ответственностью». [Commentary to the Federal Law "On Limited Responsibility Societies"]. Eds. A. A. Ignatenko, S. N. Movchana. M.: Filin', 1999. 384 p. 5000 ptd. ISBN 5-89568-142-5.

Комментарий к Федеральному закону «Об оперативно-розыскной деятельности». [Commentary to the Federal Law "On Operational Search Activity"]. M.: Izdatel Shumilova I. I., 1999. 263 p. 3000 ptd. ISBN 5-89784-016-4.

Комментарий к Федеральному закону «Об оружии» (с постатейными материалами и образцами документов). [Commentary to the Federal Law "On Weapons" (with Article by Article Materials and Models of Documents)]. Ed. S. A. Karapetian. M.: Gorodets, 1999. 511 p. 5000 ptd. ISBN 5-89391-040-0.

Комментарий к Федеральному закону «Об основах государственной службы Российской Федерации» и законодательству о государственной службе зарубежных государств. [Commentary to the Federal Law "On the Fundamental Principles of State Service of the Russian Federation" and to the Legislation on the State Service of Foreign States]. Ed. L. A. Okunkov. M.: Kontrakt, INFRA-M, 1999. 368 p. 20000 ptd. ISBN 5-900785-23-8, ISBN 5-86225-737-3.

Комментарий к Федеральному закону «Об основных гарантиях избирательных прав и права на участие в референдуме граждан Российской Федерации»: С изменениями и дополнениями внесенными Федерал. законом от 30 марта 1999 г. No.55-ФЗ. [Commentary to the Federal Law "On the Basic Guarantees of Electoral Rights and Rights of Citizens of the Russian Federation to Participate in the Referendum": With Changes and Additions Introduced by the Federal Law of 30 March 1999. No.55-F3]. Eds. V. I. Vasiliev, A. A. Veshniakov, V. I. Lysenko. M.: NORMA, 1999. 760 p. 5000 ptd. ISBN 5-89123-394-0.

Комментарий к Гражданскому кодексу Российской Федерации, части первой (постатейный). [Commentary to the Civil Code of the Russian Federation, Part 1 (Article by Article)]. Ed. O. N. Sadikov. M.: KONTRAKT, INFRA-M, 1999. XXII, 777 p. 60000 ptd. ISBN 5-90785-017-2, ISBN 5-86225-669-5.

Комментарий к Гражданскому кодексу Российской Федерации, части второй (постатейный). [Commentary to the Civil Code of the Russian Federation, Part Two (Article by Article)]. 3rd. rev. ed. Ed. O. R. Sadikov. M.: Kontrakt, INFRA-M, 1999. 781 p. 48000 ptd. ISBN 5-900785-26-2.

Комментарий к Гражданскому процессуальному кодексу РСФСР. [Commentary to the RSFSR Code of Civil Procedure]. 2d. rev. ed. Ed. M. K. Treushnikov. M.: Spark, Gorodets, 1999. 588 p. 10000 ptd. ISBN 5-88914-080-9, ISBN 5-89391-021-4.

Комментарий к Гражданскому законодательству Российской Федерации о хозяйственных обществах. [Commentary to the Civil Legislation of the Russian Federation on Economic Societies]. M.: Izd. g-na Tikhomirova, 1999. 462 p. 20000 ptd. ISBN 5-89194-019-1.

Комментарий к Кодексу РСФСР об административных правонарушениях. [Commentary to the RSFSR Code on Administrative Violations of Law]. Eds. I. I. Veremeenko, N. G. Salishchevaia, M. S. Studenkinaia. 3rd. rev. ed. M.: Prospekt, 1999. 907 p. 20000 ptd. ISBN 5-7986-0022-X.

Комментарий к Кодексу Законов о Труде Российской Федерации. [Commentary to the Code of Laws on Labour of the Russian Federation]. Ed. K. N. Gusov. 3rd. rev. ed. M.: Prospekt, 1999.

605 p. 20000 ptd. ISBN 5-7986-0020-3.
Also published:
M.: Prospekt, 1999. 621 p. 15000 ptd. ISBN 5-8369-0024-8. (4th ed.)

Комментарий к Кодексу законов о труде Российской Федерации (постатейный). [Commentary to the Code of Laws on Labour of the Russian Federation (Article by Article)]. Comp. A. B. Borisov. M.: Knizh. mir, 1999. 824 p. ISBN 5-8041-0045-9.

Комментарий к Кодексу законов о труде Российской Федерации: С изменениями и дополнениями на 5 мая 1999 г. [Commentary to the Code of Laws on Labour of the Russian Federation: With Changes and Additions for 5 May 1999]. Iu. N. Korshunov et al. M.: Spark, 1999. 576 p. 12000 ptd. ISBN 5-88914-121-X.

Комментарий к Кодексу законов о труде Российской Федерации: Текст Кодекса законов о труде РФ приводится по состоянию на 30 сентября 1998 г. [Commentary to the Code of Laws on Labour of the Russian Federation: Text of the RF Code of Laws on Labour from 30 September 1998]. 2d. rev. ed. M.: INFRA-M, 1999. XVI, 784 p. 60000 ptd. ISBN 5-86225-942-2.

Комментарий к постановлениям Пленума Верховного Суда Российской Федерации по гражданским делам. [Commentary to the Decrees of the Plenum of the Supreme Court of the Russian Federation on Civil Cases]. Comps. E. A. Borisova, V. M. Zhuykov. Ed. V. M. Zhuykov. M.: Iurist', 1999. 582 p. 50000 ptd. ISBN 5-7975-0260-7.

Комментарий к постановлениям Пленума Верховного Суда Российской Федерации по уголовным делам. [Commentary to the Decrees of the Plenum of the Supreme Soviet of the Russian Federation on Criminal Matters]. Eds. V. M. Lebedev, B. N. Topornin. M.: Iurist', 1999. 412 p. 40000 ptd. ISBN 5-7975-0194-5.

Комментарий к Налоговому кодексу Российской Федерации, части первой (постатейный). [Commentary to the Tax Code of the Russian Federation, Part One, Article by Article]. Ed. A. V. Bryzgalin. M.: Nalogi i finansovoe pravo, Analitika-Press, 1999. 397

p. 30000 ptd. ISBN 5-7916-0051-8.

Also published:

M.: Knizh. mir, 1999. 184 p. 10000 ptd. ISBN 5-8041-0041-6.

M.: NORMA-INFRA-M, 1999. 425 p. 60000 ptd. ISBN 5-89123-373-8, ISBN 5-86225-928-7.

M.: Knizh. mir, 1999. 327 p. 5000 ptd. ISBN 5-8041-0054-8.

Комментарий к Таможенному кодексу Российской Федерации. [Commentary to the Customs Code of the Russian Federation]. Eds. V. A. Maksimtsev, B. N. Gabrichidze. M.: NORMA, INFRA-M, 1999. 495 p. ISBN 5-89123-100-X, ISBN 5-86225-457-9.

Комментарий к Уголовному кодексу Российской Федерации. [Commentary to the Criminal Code of the Russian Federation]. Ed. A. V. Naumov. 2nd. rev. ed. M.: Iurist', 1999. 864 p. 50000 ptd. ISBN 5-7975-0190-2.

Also published:

M.: NORMA-INFRA-M, 1999. 815 p. 90000 ptd. ISBN 5-89123-193-X.

Комментарий к Уголовно-исполнительному кодексу Российской Федерации. [Commentary to the Criminal Executory Code of the Russian Federation]. Ed. S. V. Stepashin. 2nd. rev. ed. M.: Iurist', 1999. 622 p. 10000 ptd. ISBN 5-7975-0227-5.

Комментарий к Уголовно-процессуальному кодексу РСФСР. [Commentary to the RSFSR Code of Criminal Procedure]. Ed. V. M. Savitskii et al. M.: Prospekt, 1999. 576 p. 15000 ptd. ISBN 5-8369-0048-5.

Also published:

M.: Iurait, 1999. 742 p. 10000 ptd. ISBN 5-85294-087-9.

M.: Iurait, 1999. 729 p. 10000 ptd. ISBN 5-85294-058-5. (2d. rev. ed.)

Комментарий к Закону РФ «О защите прав потребителей». Разъяснения «О некоторых вопросах, связанных с применением закона РФ «О защите прав потребителей»: Официальный текст. [Commentary to the Russian Federation Law "On the Defence of Consumers' Rights". Explanations "On Certain Questions, Connected with the Adoption of the Russian Federation Law "On the Defence of

Consumers' Rights": Official Text]. M.: IVTS "Marketing", 1999. 32 p. 5000 ptd. ISBN 5-7856-0097-8.

Комментарий к Закону Российской Федерации «Об охране окружающей природной среды». [Commentary to the Russian Federation Law "On the Protection of the Environment"]. Ed. S. A. Bogoliubov. M.: NORMA-INFRA-M, 1999. 368 p. 20000 ptd. ISBN 5-89123-067-4.

Комментарий судебно-арбитражной практики: Выпуск 6. [Commentary to Judicial Arbitrazh Practice: Issue 6]. Ed. V. F. Iakovlev. M.: Iurid. lit., 1999. 295 p. 5000 ptd. ISBN 5-7260-0935-5.

Комментарий судебной практики: Выпуск 5. [Commentary to Judicial Practice: Issue 5]. Ed. K. B. Iaroshenko. M.: Iurid. lit., 1999. 256 p. 5000 ptd. ISBN 5-7260-0934-7.

Комментарии и разъяснения к Федеральному закону «О прокуратуре Российской Федерации». [Commentaries and Explanations to the Federal Law "On the Procuracy of the Russian Federation"]. N. P. Kirillova et al. Spb.: Izd-vo Mikhailova V. A., 1999. 175 p. 2000 ptd. ISBN 5-8016-0155-4.

Коммерческое право России: Учебно-методическое пособие. [Commercial Law of Russia: Instructional Methods Manual]. Ed. B. I. Putinskii. M.: Gorodets, 1999. 144 p. 5000 ptd. ISBN 5-89391-051-6.

Компетенция органов местного самоуправления: Сборник извлечений из законов Российской Федерации. По состоянию на 1 ноября 1998 г. [Competence of Agencies of Local Self-Government: Collection of Excerpts of Laws of the Russian Federation. As of 1 November 1998]. Comp. V. A. Shchepachev. Orenburg: Kn. izd-vo, 1999. 704 p. 2000 ptd. ISBN 5-88788-050-3.

Конкурентное право Российской Федерации: Учебное пособие для вузов. [Competition Law of the Russian Federation: Instructional Manual for Institutes of Higher Education]. N. V. Vasileva et al. Eds. N. I. Klein, N. E. Fonarevaia. M.: Logos, 1999. 431 p. 10000 ptd. ISBN 5-88439-128-5.

Konstantinov, A. *Бандитский Петербург-98.* [Gangster St Petersburg-98]. 2d. rev. ed. M.: OLMA-Press, 1999. 559 p. 15000 ptd. ISBN 5-224-00161-7.

Konstantinov, A. & K. *Коррумпированный Петербург-98.* [Corrupt St Petersburg-98]. M.: OLMA-Press, 1999. 543 p. 15000 ptd. ISBN 5-224-00162-5.

Конституция Российской Федерации. [Constitution of the Russian Federation]. M.: Novy Iurist, 1999. 46 p. 10000 ptd. ISBN 5-7969-0066-8.

Also published:
Spb.: Litera, 1999. 48 p. 15000 ptd. ISBN 5-86617-034-5.
M.: Iurait, 1999. 46 p. 10000 ptd. ISBN 5-85294-008-9.
M.: NORMA-INFRA-M, 1999. 75 p. 24000 ptd. ISBN 5-89123-308-8.
M.: Filin', 1999. 64 p. 5000 ptd. ISBN 5-89568-138-7.
M.: Prospekt, 1999. 48 p. 40000 ptd. ISBN 5-7896-0085-9.
M.: Delo, 1999. 40 p. 5000 ptd. ISBN 5-7749-0151-3.
M.: AST 1999. 63 p. 20000 ptd. ISBN 5-237-02346-0.

Конституция Российской Федерации: Принята 12 декабря 1993 г. [Constitution of the Russian Federation: Adopted 12 December 1993]. Intro. V. B. Isakov. M., 1999. 184 p. 5000 ptd. ISBN 5-7918-0043-6.

Конституция Российской Федерации: Принята всенарод. голосованием 12 декабря 1993 г. Официальный текст по состоянию на 1 февраля 1999 г. [Constitution of the Russian Federation: Adopted by All-People's Voting on 12 December 1993. Official Text for 1 February 1999]. M.: NORMA-INFRA-M, 1999. 75 p. 8000 ptd. ISBN 5-89123-337-1, ISBN 5-86225-983-X.

Also published:
Spb.: Izd. Dom A. Gromova, 1999. 63 p. 10000 ptd. ISBN 5-89138-007-2.

Конституционное (государственное) право зарубежных стран: Часть общая. [Constitutional (State) Law of Foreign Countries: General Part]. 3rd. rev. ed. Ed. B. A. Strashun. M.: BEK, 1999. 784 p. 30000 ptd. ISBN 5-85639-276-0.

Конституционное право: Учебник. [Constitutional Law: Textbook]. Ed. V. V. Lazarev. M.: Iurist', 1999. 592 p. 10000 ptd. ISBN 5-7975-0259-3.

Конституционное право России: Схемы, комментарии. Пособие. [Constitutional Law of Russia: Diagrams, Commentaries. Manual]. M.: Iurisprudentsiia, 1999. 64 p. 7000 ptd. ISBN 5-86532-043-2.

Конституционное право в вопросах в ответах. [Constitutional Law in Questions and Answers]. Ed. A. V. Malko. M.: Iurist', 1999. 228 p. 10000 ptd. ISBN 5-7975-0162-7.

Конституционное право зарубежных стран: Учебник. [Constitutional Law of Foreign Countries: Textbook]. Eds. M. V. Baglai, Iu. I. Leibo, L. M. Entin. M.: NORMA-INFRA-M, 1999. 819 p. 60000 ptd. ISBN 5-89123-342-8, ISBN 5-86225-905-8.

Конституционное законодательство России. [Constitutional Legislation of Russia]. Ed. Iu. A. Tikhomirov. M.: Gorodets - Formula prava, 1999. 382 p. ISBN 5-89391-045-1.

Конституции государств-участников СНГ. [Constitutions of the Member States of the CIS]. Ed. L. A. Okunkov et al. M.: NORMA-INFRA-M, 1999. 736 p. 3000 ptd. ISBN 5-89123-355-X, ISBN 5-16-000046-1.

Конституции стран СНГ и Балтии. [Constitutions of the Countries of the CIS and the Baltics]. Comp. & Intro. G. N. Andreev. M.: Iurist', 1999. 639 p. 5000 ptd. ISBN 5-7975-0157-0.

Конвенция о защите прав человека и основных свобод: С поправками, внесенными Протоколом No.11. Вступил в силу 1 ноября 1996 г. [Convention on the Defence of Human Rights and Basic Freedoms: With Amendments Introduced by Protocol No.11. Entered into Force on 1 November 1996]. Comps. V. B. Isakov et al. M.: Iurait, 1999. 189 p. 3000 ptd. ISBN 5-85294-077-1.

Korenevskii, Iu. V. *Как обжаловать приговор суда.* [How to Appeal Against the Judgement of a Court]. M.: Ucheb.-konsultativ. tsentr

"IurInfoR", 1999. 178 p. 5000 ptd. ISBN 5-89158-017-9.

Korneeva, I. L. *Практикум по гражданскому праву: Ч.2.* [Practical Work on Civil Law: Part 2]. M.: Iurist', 1999. 196 p. 5000 ptd. ISBN 5-7975-0125-2.

Kornienko, V., Vagin, O. *Технологии выборных кампаний.* [Technologies of Electoral Campaigns]. Ed. V. Zhirinovskii. 2d. rev. ed. M.: Izd. LDPR, 1999. 72 p. 3000 ptd.

Korolev, Iu. A. *Семейное право России: Учебное пособие.* [Family Law of Russia: Instructional Manual]. M.: Iurid. lit., 1999. 335 p. 5000 ptd. ISBN 5-7260-0937-1.

Korolev, S. V. *Теория муниципального управления.* [Theory of Municipal Administration]. M.: In-t gosudarstva i prava RAN, 1999. 143 p. 900 ptd. ISBN 5-7856-0123-0.

Kovalev, M. I. *Соучастие в преступлении.* [Conspiracy in Crime]. Ekaterinburg: Izd-vo UrGIUA, 1999. 203 p. 500 ptd. ISBN 5-7845-0087-2.

Kovalev, S. *Прагматика политического идеализма.* [Pragmatics of Political Idealism]. M.: In-t prav cheloveka, 1999. 352 p. 1200 ptd. ISBN 5-8013-0067-8.

Koveshnikov, E. M., Marchenko, M. N., Steshenko, L. A. *Конституционное право стран Содружества Независимых Государств: Учебник.* [Constitutional Law of the Countries of the Commonwealth of Independent States: Textbook]. M.: NORMA-INFRA-M, 1999. 446 p. 30000 ptd. ISBN 5-89123-367-3.

Kovler, A. I. *Кандидат и его команда: Организационная структура избирательной кампании: Методическое пособие.* [The Candidate and His Team: The Organisational Structure of the Electoral Campaign: Methods Manual]. 2nd. rev. ed. M.: RTSOIT, 1999. 32 p. 3000 ptd. ISBN 5-93639-003-9.

Kovler, A. I., Zotova, Z. M. *Стратегия избирательной кампании и ее планирование.* [The Strategy of the Electoral Campaign and Its

Planning]. M.: RTSOIT, 1999. 73 p. 3000 ptd. ISBN 5-93639-001-2.

Kozlov, Iu. M. *Административное право России: Учебно-методическое пособие.* [Administrative Law of Russia: Instructional Methods Manual]. Ed. B. I. Putinskii. M.: Gorodets, 1999. 144 p. 5000 ptd. ISBN 5-89391-051-6.

Kozlova, E. I., Kutafin, O. E. *Конституционное право.* [Constitutional Law]. M.: Iurist', 1999. 304 p. 10000 ptd. ISBN 5-7975-0201-1.

Krasheninnikov, P. V. *Сделки с жилыми помещениями.* [Transactions with Dwellings]. M.: Statut, 1999. 286 p. 5000 ptd. ISBN 5-8354-0006-3.

Краткий юридический справочник для журналистов. [A Short Legal Manual for Journalists]. Comp. D. Ibodov. M.: Galeriia, 1999. 136 p. 600 ptd. ISBN 5-8137-0024-2.

Краткий словарь терминов по уголовному праву: Учебное пособие. [A Short Dictionary of Terms on Criminal Law: Instructional Manual]. Eds. B. V. Iatselenko, V. B. Borovikov. M.: MIUI MVD Rossii, Izd-vo "Shchyt-M", 1999. 128 p. 1000 ptd. ISBN 5-13004-032-X.

Kravtsova, S. Iu. *Правовой режим уставного капитала банка.* [Legal Regime of the Charter Capital of a Bank]. M.: Delo, 1999. 117 p. 1000 ptd. ISBN 5-7749-0150-5.

Kriazhkov, V. A. *Конституционное правосудие в субъектах Российской Федерации: Правовые основы и практика.* [Constitutional Justice in the Subjects of the Russian Federation: Legal Fundamental Principles and Practice]. M.: Formula prava, 1999. 768 p. 1000 ptd. ISBN 5-8467-0001-2.

Криминалистика: Для вузов. [Criminalistics: For Institutes of Higher Education]. Ed. A. F. Vorlinskii. M.: Zakon i pravo, IUNITI-DANA, 1999. 615 p. 20000 ptd. ISBN 5-238-00083-9.

Also published:

M.: Iurist', 1999. 718 p. 10000 ptd. ISBN 5-7975-0167-8.

Криминалистика: Схемы и комментарий. [Criminalistics: Diagrams and Commentary]. Ed. A. G. Filippov. M.: Iurisprudentsiia, 1999. 240 p. 8000 ptd. ISBN 5-86532-05-6.

Криминалистика: Учебник. [Criminalistic: Textbook]. Ed. V. A. Obraztsov. 2d. rev. ed. M.: Iurist', 1999. 734 p. 10000 ptd. ISBN 5-7975-0187-2.

Криминалистика: Учебник для вузов. [Criminalistics: Textbook for Institutes of Higher Education]. Ed. R. S. Belkin. M.: NORMA-INFRA-M, 1999. 971 p. 60000 ptd. ISBN 5-89123-302-9, ISBN 5-86225-949-X.
Also published:
M.: Spark, 1999. 543 p. 8000 ptd. ISBN 5-88914-084-1.

Криминология: Для вузов. [Criminology: For Institutes of Higher Education]. Eds. V. N. Kudriavtsev, V. E. Eminov. 2nd. rev. ed. M.: Iurist', 1999. 678 p. 10000 ptd. ISBN 5-7975-0193-7.
Also published:
Spb.: Spb. un-t MVD Rossii, Lan, 1999. 608 p. 10000 ptd. ISBN 5-8114-0059-4.

Криминология: Словарь. [Criminology: Dictionary]. Comp. V. N. Burlakov et al. Spb.: Lan, Izd-vo Spb. un-ta MVD Rossii, 1999. 254 p. 5000 ptd. ISBN 5-8114-0164-7.

Kruglova, N. Iu. *Коммерческое право: Учебник.* [Commercial Law: Textbook]. M.: Rus. delovaia lit., 1999. 848 p. ISBN 5-89247-035-0.

Kucherena, A. *Бал беззакония: Диагноз адвоката.* [Lawlessness Ball: An Advocate's Diagnosis]. M.: Politbiuro, 1999. 351 p. 15000 ptd. ISBN 5-89756-017-X.

Kudriavtsev, V. N. *Общая теория квалификации преступлений.* [General Theory of the Qualification of Crimes]. M.: Iurist', 1999. 302 p. 3000 ptd. ISBN 5-7975-0170-8.

Kulesh, V. A. *Налоговая адвокатура, или Как защищаться от финансовых санкций.* [Tax Advocatura, or How to Defend Oneself from Financial Sanctions]. 2d. rev. ed. M.: Biznes-shkola "Intel-Sintez",

1999. 242 p. 2500 ptd. ISBN 5-87057-135-9.

Kunitsyn, A. R. *Образцы судебных документов: С коммент. законодательства и судебной практики. Практическое пособие.* [Models of Judicial Documents: With a Commentary of the Legislation and Judicial Practice. Practical Manual]. 2d. rev. ed. M.: Soleks, 1999. 370 p. 10000 ptd. ISBN 5-900216-08-X.

Kunitsyn, A. R. *Образцы заявлений и жалоб в суд: Практическое пособие.* [Samples of Applications and Appeals to Court: Practical Manual]. M.: Soleks, 1999. 290 p. 5000 ptd. ISBN 5-900216-25-X.

Kuri, Kh. *Развитие преступности на Востоке и Западе.* [Development of Criminality in the East and the West]. M.: Ros. Iurid. izd. Dom, 1999. 80 p. 1000 ptd. ISBN 5-88635-031-4.

Курс уголовного права: Общая часть. Т.1: Учение о преступности. [Criminal Law Course: General Part. Vol.1: Doctrine on Criminality]. Eds. N. F. Kuznetsovaia, I. M. Tiazhkovaia. M.: Zertsalo, 1999. 577 p. 8000 ptd. ISBN 5-8078-0039-7.

Курс уголовного права: Общая часть: Том 2. [Criminal Law Course: General Part: Vol.2]. Eds. N. F. Kuznetsova, I. M. Tiazhkova. M.: Zertsalo, 1999. 400 p. 8000 ptd. ISBN 5-8078-0047-8.

Kuznetsov, I. N. *История государства и права России: Курс лекций.* [History of State and Law of Russia: Course of Lectures]. Minsk: Amalfeia, 1999. 527 p. 5000 ptd. ISBN 985-441-036-6.

Kuznetsov, S. L. *Делопроизводство на компьютере: Компьютерные технологии в делопроизводстве.* [Clerical Work on a Computer: Computer Technologies in Clerical Work]. 2d. rev. ed. M.: Biznes-shkola "Intel-Sintez", 1999. 200 p. 5000 ptd. ISBN 5-87057-160-X.

Kuznetsov, V. F., Kuznetsova, O. V. *Проблемы применения семейного кодекса.* [Problems of the Application of the Family Code]. 2nd. rev. ed. Cheliabinsk: CHGU, 1999. 211 p. 310 ptd. ISBN 5-230-20051-0.

Kuznetsova, I. M. *Семейное право.* [Family Law]. M.: Iurist', 1999. 118 p. 10000 ptd. ISBN 5-7975-0254-2.

Kuznetsova, N. V. *Экологическое право.* [Ecological Law]. 2nd. rev. ed. M.: Iurisprudentsiia, 1999. 156 p. 7000 ptd. ISBN 5-8401-0022-6.

Lapaeva, V. V. *Право и многопартийность в современной России.* [The Law and Multi-Party System in Contemporary Russia]. M.: NORMA, 1999. 296 p. 3000 ptd.

Laptev, V. V. *Акционерное право.* [Joint-Stock Society Law]. M.: Kontrakt, INFRA-M, 1999. 246 p. 6000 ptd. ISBN 5-86225-993-7.

Larin, V. V. *Акционерное право.* [Joint-Stock Law]. Spb.: Izd-vo Ros. nats. b-ki, 1999. 268 p. 3000 ptd. ISBN 5-8192-0042-X.

Larkov, N. S., Chernova, I. V. *Полицмейстеры, комиссары, начальники: Руководители правоохранительных органов Том. обл. в XIX-XX вв.* [Commissioners of Police, Commissars, Commanders: Heads of Law Enforcement Agencies of the Region of Tomsk in the 19th to 20th Centuries]. Tomsk: Izd-vo Tom. un-ta, 1999. 183 p. 1000 ptd. ISBN 5-7511-1085-4.

Lebedev, A. N. *Статус субъекта Российской Федерации: Основы концепции, конституционная модель, практика.* [Status of a Subject of the Russian Federation: Fundamental Principles of Concept, Constitutional Model, Practice]. M.: In-t gosudarstva i prava RAN, 1999. 197 p. ISBN 5-8339-0003-4.

Lebedev, K. K. *Практикум по коммерческому праву: Учебно-методическое и практическое пособие.* [Practical Work on Commercial Law: Instructional Methods and Practical Manual]. Spb.: Izd-vo Spb. un-ta, 1999. 424 p. 5000 ptd. ISBN 5-93333-007-8.

Lesnin, I. V. *Технология политического успеха, или Как победить на местных выборах.* [Technology of Political Success or How to Win in Local Elections]. Volgograd: Peremena, 1999. 79 p. 150 ptd. ISBN 5-88234-346-1.

Liakhov, E. G., Popov, A. V. *Терроризм: национальный:*

региональный и международный контроль. [Terrorism: National, Regional and International Control]. M.: Rostov n/D: RIUI MVD Rossii, 1999. 435 p. 2200 ptd.

Lifanova, M. V. *Выявление и разоблачение ложных показаний на предварительном следствии: Учебное пособие.* [Disclosure and Unmasking of False Testimony During Preliminary Investigation: Instructional Manual]. Ufa: Vost. un-t, 1999. 43 p. 200 ptd.

Litvinov, N. D. *Террористические организации: формирование и деятельность: Политико-правовой анализ.* [Terrorist Organisations: Formation and Activity: Political Legal Analysis]. Ed. S. E. Bitsin. M.: Golos, 1999. 219 p. 5000 ptd. ISBN 5-7117-0381-1.

Liubimov, A. P. *Правовые институты демократии России и стран Европы, выборы, лоббизм и парламентаризм: Сравнительный анализ.* [Legal Institutes of Democracy of Russia and the Countries of Europe, Elections, Lobbying and Parliamentarism: Comparative Analysis]. M.: In-t Evropy RAN, 1999. 57 p. 500 ptd.

Lonchakov, A. P. *Административно-правовая организация механизма управления собственностью в сфере экономики: Учебное пособие.* [Administrative Legal Organisation of the Mechanism for the Management of Ownership in the Sphere of the Economy: Instructional Manual]. Khabarovsk: DVIUI KHGTU, 1999. 249 p. 2000 ptd. ISBN 5-7389-0050-2.

Lukashuk, I. I., Naumov, A. V. *Международное уголовное право: Учебник для вузов.* [International Criminal Law: Textbook for Institutes of Higher Education]. M.: Spark, 1999. 287 p. 5000 ptd. ISBN 5-88914-129-5.

Lukianenko, A. E., Lukianenko, V. I., Novikov, A. V. *Управление персоналом государственных органов: система организации и функционирования.* [Management of the Personnel of State Agencies: System of Organisation and Functioning]. M.: Nauka, 1999. 573 p. ISBN 5-02-008341-0.

Luneev, V. V. *Юридическая статистика: Учебник.* [Legal Statistics: Textbook]. M.: Iurist', 1999. 399 p. 10000 ptd. ISBN 5-

7975-0156-2.

Luneev, V. V. *Преступность XX века: Мировые, регион. и рос. тенденции. Мировой криминологический анализ.* [Criminality in the 20th Century: World, Regional and Russian Trends. World Criminological Analysis]. M.: NORMA, 1999. 516 p. 1500 ptd. ISBN 5-89123-393-2.

Lunts, L. A. *Деньги и денежные обязательства в гражданском праве.* [Money and Monetary Obligations in Civil Law]. M.: Statut, 1999. 352 p. 5000 ptd. ISBN 5-8354-0012-8.

Lustov, A. V. *Образцы нотариальных документов.* [Models of Notarial Documents]. 3rd. rev. ed. M.: Iurait, 1999. 336 p. 3000 ptd. ISBN 5-85294-053-4.

Machulskaia, E. E. *Практикум по праву социального обеспечения: Для вузов.* [Practical Work on the Right to Social Security: For Institutes of Higher Education]. M.: NORMA-INFRA-M, 1999. 240 p. 30000 ptd. ISBN 5-89123-275-8.

Machulskaia, E. E. *Право социального обеспечения: Для вузов.* [Right to Social Security: For Institutes of Higher Education]. 2d. rev. ed. M.: Knizh. mir, 1999. 239 p. (Vysh. shkola). 4000 ptd. ISBN 5-8041-0006-8.

Makagonova, N. V. *Авторское право: Учебное пособие.* [Copyright: Instructional Manual]. Ed. E. P. Gavrilov. M.: Iurid. lit., 1999. 287 p. 3000 ptd. ISBN 5-7260-0932-0.

Mak-Mak, V. P. *Служба безопасности предприятия: Правовые аспекты деятельности.* [Security Service of the Enterprise: Legal Aspects of Activity]. M.: Mir bezopasnosti, 1999. 159 p. 2000 ptd. ISBN 5-89258-015-6.

Maksimov, A. *Бандиты в белых воротничках: Как разворовывали Россию.* [Bandits in White Collars: How They Plundered Russia]. M.: EKSMO-Press, 1999. 480 p. 20000 ptd. ISBN 5-04-002634-X.

Malko, A. V. *Теория государства и права в вопросах и ответах.* [Theory of State and Law in Questions and Answers]. 3rd. rev. ed. M.: Iurist', 1999. 269 p. 10000 ptd. ISBN 5-7975-0158-9.

Marshunov, M. N. *Федеральный Закон о судебных приставах в схемах: Постатейный комментарий.* [Federal Law on Bailiffs in Diagrams: Article by Article Commentary]. M.: Spb.: Gerda, 1999. 350 p. 5000 ptd. ISBN 5-7978-0047-0.

Marshunov, M. N. *Комментарии к законам «Об оружии», «О частной детективной и охранной деятельности»: Научно-практические рекомендации.* [Commentaries to the Laws "On Weapons", "On Private Detective and Protection Activity": Scientific-Practical Recommendations]. M., Spb.: Gerda, 1999. 248 p. 5000 ptd. ISBN 5-7978-0016-0.

Marshunov, M. N. *Комментарий к Закону Российской Федерации «О милиции»: Научно-практические рекомендации.* [Commentary to the Russian Federation Law "On the Police": Scientific-Practical Recommendations]. M., Spb.: Gerda, 1999. 248 p. 5000 ptd. ISBN 5-7978-0008-X.

Mattei, U., Sukhanov, E. A. *Основные положения права собственности.* [Basic Provisions of the Right of Ownership]. M.: Iurist', 1999. 383 p. 5000 ptd. ISBN 5-7975-0155-4.

Medvedev, M. Iu. *Уголовный процесс: Консультации. Образцы документов. Судебная практика.* [Criminal Procedure: Consultations. Samples of Documents. Judicial Practice]. M.: Iurisprudentsiia, 1999. 394 p. 10000 ptd. ISBN 5-8401-0009-9.

Melnikov, V. M. *Актуальные вопросы развития законодательства Российской Федерации о товарных знаках.* [Urgent Questions on the Development of the Legislation of the Russian Federation on Trademarks]. M.: INITS, 1999. 24 p. 180 ptd.

Melnikovskii, M. S. *Некоторые вопросы методики и тактики осуществления адвокатом защиты осужденных в порядке надзора: Методическое пособие.* [Certain Questions of the Methodology and Tactics of the Effectuation by the Advocate of the

Defence of Convicted Persons in the Supervision Procedure: Methods Manual]. M.: DE-IURE, 1999. 46 p. 1000 ptd. ISBN 5-8549-048-9.

Meshkov, V. M., Popov, V. L. *Оперативно-розыскная тактика и особенности легализации полученной информации в ходе предварительного следствия: Учебно-практическое пособие.* [Operational Search Tactics and Peculiarities of the Legalisation of Received Information During the Course of Preliminary Investigation: Instructional Methods Manual]. M.: Shchyt-M, 1999. 79 p. 1000 ptd. ISBN 5-93004-028-1.

Местное самоуправление: российский путь. [Local Self-Government: The Russian Way]. Iu. G. Volkov et al.: Ed. G. V. Dylnov. Saratov: Region. Privolzh. izd-vo "Det. kn.", 1999. 312 p. 1000 ptd. ISBN 5-8270-0224-0.

Местное самоуправление в Санкт-Петербурге и Литве. [Local Self-Government in St. Petersburg and Lithuania]. Ed. M. B. Gorny. Spb.: Norma, 1999. 166 p. 500 ptd. ISBN 5-87857-029-7.

Местное самоуправление в современной России: права, обязанности и деятельность представительных органов власти. [Local Self-Government in Contemporary Russia: Rights, Duties and Activity of Representative Agencies of Power]. A. S. Avtonomov et al. M.: Fond razvitiia parlamentarizma v Rossii, Ves' Mir, 1999. 79 p. 10000 ptd. ISBN 5-7777-0076-4.

Meteleva, Iu. A. *Правовое положение акционера в акционерном обществе.* [Legal Status of the Stockholder in the Joint-Stock Society]. M.: Statut, 1999. 191 p. 7000 ptd. ISBN 5-8354-0005-5.

Международное авторское право. [International Copyright Law]. Comp. E. M. Buriak. 2nd. ed. M.: INITS Rospatenta, 1999. 95 p. 150 ptd.

Международное космическое право: Учебник для вузов. [International Space Law: Textbook for Institutes of Higher Education]. Eds. G. P. Zhukov, Iu. M. Kolosov. M.: Mezhdunar. otnosheniia, 1999. 358 p. 5000 ptd. ISBN 5-7133-0994-0.

Международное право: Учебник для вузов. [International Law: Textbook for Institutes of Higher Education]. Eds. Iu. M. Kolosov, V. I. Kuznetsov. M.: Mezhdunar. otnosheniia, 1999. 619 p. ISBN 5-7133-0991-6.

Also published:

M.: NORMA-INFRA-M, 1999. 584 p. 50000 ptd. ISBN 5-89123-271-5, ISBN 5-86225-875-2.

M.: Iurid. lit., 1999. 559 p. 5000 ptd. ISBN 5-7260-0933-9.

Международное право: Учебно-метод. комплекс. [International Law: Instructional Methods System]. Comps. S. A. Grigorian, T. I. Strokova. Rostov na Donu, Izd-vo RGEA, 1999. 300 p. 100 ptd.

Международное публичное право: Учебник. [Public International Law: Textbook]. Ed. K. A. Bekiashev. M.: Prospekt, 1999. 608 p. 10000 ptd. ISBN 5-7896-0055-7.

Международное уголовное право: Для вузов. [International Criminal Law: For Institutes of Higher Education]. Ed. V. N. Kudriavtsev. M.: Nauka, 1999. 264 p. 3000 ptd. ISBN 5-02-008292-9.

Mikhailov, D. *Конституционное право граждан на жилище в Российской Федерации.* [Constitutional Rights of Citizens to Housing in the Russian Federation]. M.: Ves' Mir, 1999. 59 p. 500 ptd. ISBN 5-7777-0078-0.

Mikhailov, V. I., Fedorov, A. V. *Таможенные преступления: Уголовно-правовой анализ.* [Customs Crimes: Criminal Law Analysis]. Spb.: Iurid. tsentr deiatelnosti. Spb.: Iurid. tsentr Press, 1999. 324 p. 2000 ptd. ISBN 5-93292-006-8.

Mikhailova, E. P., Taranina, I. V. *Краткий справочник по нотариату.* [A Short Manual About the Notariat]. Novosibirsk: IUKEA, 1999. 128 p. 3000 ptd. ISBN 5-93376-012-9.

Mikheeva, L. Iu. *Доверительное управление имуществом.* [Trust Management of Property]. M.: Iurist', 1999. 176 p. 3000 ptd. ISBN 5-7975-0264-X.

Mikhlin, A. S., Seliverstov, V. I., Shmarov, I. V. *Уголовно-*

исполнительное право: Вопросы и ответы. [Criminal Executory Law: Questions and Answers]. M.: Iurisprudentsiia, 1999. 160 p. 8000 ptd. ISBN 5-5-8401-0001-31.

Мир права в афоризмах, мудрых мыслях, эпиграммах. [The World of Law in Aphorisms, Wise Thoughts, Epigrams]. Nizhegorod. pravovaia akad. Comps. V. M. Baranov, Z. Sh. Idrisov. N. Novgorod, 1999. 152 p. 5000 ptd.

Mironov, M. A. *Власть и народ: обратная связь: Вопросы теории и практики организации работы с обращениями граждан в современных условиях.* [Power and the Nation: A Retroactive Bond: Questions of the Theory and Practice of the Organisation of Work with Citizens' Appeals under Contemporary Conditions]. M.: Iurd. lit., 1999. 312 p. 1000 ptd. ISBN 5-7260-0928-2.

Mironov, O. O. *Доклад о деятельности Уполномоченного по правам человека в Российской Федерации в 1998 году.* [Report on the Activity of the Plenipotentiary for Human Rights in the Russian Federation in 1998]. M.: Respublika, 1999. 78 p. 5000 ptd. ISBN 5-250-02731-8.

Mironov, O. O. *О соблюдении прав граждан, страдающих психическими расстройствами.* [On the Observance of the Rights of Citizens Suffering from Psychological Disorders]. M.: Respublika, 1999. 63 p. 2000 ptd. ISBN 5-250-02735-0.

Mishin, A. A. *Конституционное право зарубежных стран: Учебник для вузов.* [Constitutional Law of Foreign Countries: Textbook for Institutes of Higher Education]. 6th rev. ed. M.: Belyt alvy, 1999. 447 p. 3000 ptd. ISBN 5-7619-0067-X.

Mitrichev, V. C., Khrustalev, V. N. *Криминалистическое исследование лакокрасочных материалов, покрытий и окрашенных предметов: Учебно-методическое пособие для образоват. учерждений МВД России.* [Criminalistics Research of Lacquer and Paint Materials, Coverings and Painted Objects: Instructional Methods Manual for the Educational Institutions of the Russian Ministry for Internal Affairs]. Saratov: Sarat. iurid. in-t, 1999. 148 p. 250 ptd. ISBN 5-7485-0012-4.

Модельный закон о порядке выборов депутатов Палаты Представителей Парламента Союза Беларуси и России первого созыва: Одобрен на заседании секции Науч.-метод. совета по общ. пробл. развития федерал. и регион. законодательства о выборах и референдумах в Российской Федерации 28 июля 1999 г. [Model Law on the Procedure for Elections of Deputies of the Chamber of Representatives of the Parliament of the Union of Belorussia and Russia of the first Convocation: Approved at the Session of the Section of the Instructional Methods Council for General Problems of the Development of Federal and Regional Legislation on Elections and Referenda in the Russian Federation on 28 July 1999]. M., 1999. 191 p. 500 ptd.

Morozova, L. A. *Основы государства и права: Пособие.* [Fundamental Principles of State and Law: Manual]. M.: Novaia Volna, 1999. 351 p. 5000 ptd. ISBN 5-7864-0087-5.

Московское трехсторонние соглашение на 1999 год между Правительством Москвы, московскими объединениями профсоюзов и московскими объединениями предпринимателей (работодателей). [Moscow Three-Sided Agreement for 1999 Between the Government of Moscow, Moscow Associations of Trade Unions and Moscow Associations of Entrepreneurs (Employers)]. M.: Infomart, 1999. 16 p. 20000 ptd.

Motorny, I. D. *Теоретико-прикладные основы применения средств и методов криминалистической взрывотехники в борьбе с терроризмом.* [Theoretical and Practical Fundamental Principles of the Application of Means and Methods of Criminalistics Explosives Technology in the Struggle Against Terrorism]. M.: Izdatel Shumilova I. I., 1999. 199 p. 1000 ptd. ISBN 5-89784-019-9.

Муниципальное право Российской Федерации: Хрестоматия. [Municipal Law of the Russian Federation: Anthology]. Comp. & Intro. E. V. Belousovaia. M.: Iurist', 1999. 543 p. 5000 ptd. ISBN 5-7975-0261-5.

Muratova, S. A. *Семейное право: Схемы, комментарий.* [Family Law: Diagrams, Commentary]. M.: Iurisprudentsiia, 1999. 153 p. 7000 ptd. ISBN 5-8401-0004-8.

Muratova, S. A., Tarsamaeva, N. Iu. *Семейное право: Учебное пособие.* [Family Law: Instructional Manual]. M.: Novy Iurist, 1999. 272 p. 6000 ptd. ISBN 5-7969-0061-7.

Nadeev, R. K., Korolev, A. N. *Путеводитель по Гражданскому кодексу Российской Федерации, Гражданскому кодексу РСФСР и Основам гражданского законодательства Союза ССР и республик: По состоянию на 1 марта 1999 г.* [Guide to the Civil Code of the Russian Federation, the RSFSR Civil Code and the Fundamental Principles of the Civil Legislation of the USSR and Republics: For 1 March 1999]. M., 1999. 182 p. 5000 ptd. ISBN 5-7018-0044-4.

Надежда в беде: Наркотики и наркоманы. [Hope in Misfortune: Drugs and Drug Addicts]. M.: Samarianin, 1999. 118 p. 2000 ptd.

Nafiev, S. Kh. *Корыстное убийство: понятие, виды, квалификация: Уголовно-правовые и криминологические аспекты.* [Mercenary Homicide: Concepts, Types, Classification: Criminal Legal and Criminological Aspects]. Kazan: Tatar. gazetno-kn. izd-vo, 1999. 117 p. 1000 ptd. ISBN 5-85247-095-3.

Налог с продаж: Закон. Инструкция. Разъяснения. [Tax from Sales: Law. Instruction. Explanations]. M.: INFRA-M, 1999. 32 p. 3000 ptd. ISBN 5-86225-826-4.

Налог с продаж в Москве: Вводится в действие с 1 июля 1999 г.: Закон города Москвы «О налоге с продаж». Ответы на вопросы. [Tax from Sales in Moscow: Enters into Operation from 1 July 1999: Law of the City of Moscow "On Tax from Sales". Answers to Questions]. M.: Sovr. ekonomika i pravo, 1999. 32 p. 3000 ptd. ISBN 5-8411-0006-8.

Налоговый кодекс. Налог с продаж: Официальный текст закона. Комментарий к закону. [Tax Code. Tax from Sales: Official Text of the Law. Commentary to the Law]. M.: In-t nalogovogo prava, 1999. 64 p. 5000 ptd. ISBN 5-93212-004-5.

Налоговый кодекс Российской Федерации. [Tax Code of the Russian Federation]. M.: NIPKTS VOSKHOD, 1999. 101 p. ISBN 5-93055-010-7.

Налоговый кодекс Российской Федерации: Ч.1. [Tax Code of the Russian Federation: Part 1]. M.: Prospekt, 1999. 96 p. 5000 ptd. ISBN 5-7896-0082-4.

Also published:

M.: Delo, 1999. 96 p. 5000 ptd. ISBN 5-7749-0139-4.

M.: NORMA-INFRA-M, 1999. 142 p. 10000 ptd. ISBN 5-89123-321-5, ISBN 5-86225-879-3.

M.: OLMA-Press, Novosibirsk: IUKEA, 1999. 144 p. 11000 ptd. ISBN 5-224-00262-1, ISBN 5-86750-121-3.

M.: Izd. g-na Tikhomirova M. Iu., 1999. 93 p. 3000 ptd. ISBN 5-89194-015-9.

M.: Statut, 1999. 125 p. 10000 ptd. ISBN 5-5-8354-0001-2.

M.: Nalogi i finansovoe pravo, Analitik-Press, 1999. 150 p. 5000 ptd. ISBN 5-7916-0055-0.

M.: Finansy i statistika, 1999. 136 p. 4000 ptd. ISBN 5-279-02076-1.

M.: Spb.: Gerda, 1999. 126 p. 5000 ptd. ISBN 5-7978-0050-0.

M.: Filin', 1999. 144 p. 5000 ptd. ISBN 5-89568-136-0.

M.: Slavian. dom knigi, 1999. 128 p. 8000 ptd. ISBN 5-93220-006-5.

Ulianovsk: Knigochei, 1999. 7000 ptd. ISBN 5-855525-017-2.

Ufa: Bashkortostan, 1999. 93 p. 10000 ptd. ISBN 5-8258-0130-8.

M.: Ucheb.-inform. tsentr pri Gos. nalogovoi inspektsii po g. Moskve, 1999. 112 p. 5000 ptd. ISBN 5-86297-106-8.

Налоговый кодекс Российской Федерации: Ч.1: Федеральный закон «О введении в действие части первой Налогового кодекса РФ». Комментарии. [Tax Code of the Russian Federation: Part 1: Federal Law "On the Introduction into Operation of Part 1 of the Russian Federation Tax Code". Commentaries]. Tiumen: Slovo, 1999. 128 p. 5000 ptd. ISBN 5-93030-015-1.

Налоговый кодекс Российской Федерации: Ч.1. Официальный текст по состоянию на 8 февраля 1999 г. [Tax Code of the Russian Federation: Part 1. Official Text as of 8 February 1999]. M.: Filin', 1999. 139 p. 5000 ptd. ISBN 5-89568-136-0.

Налоговый кодекс Российской Федерации: Часть 1: Официальный текст по сост. на 15 августа 1999 г. [Tax Code of the Russian Federation: Part 1: Official Text for 15 August 1999]. M.: INFRA-M, 1999. 107 p. 12000 ptd. ISBN 5-86225-926-0.

Налоговый кодекс Российской Федерации: Часть 1: По состоянию на 15 сентября 1999 г. [Tax Code of the Russian Federation: Part 1: For 15 September 1999]. M., Spb.: Izd. Torgovy Dom "Gerda", 1999. 158 p. 10000 ptd. ISBN 5-7978-0050-0.

Налоговый кодекс Российской Федерации: Ч.1. Постатейный комментарий. [Tax Code of the Russian Federation: Part 1. Article by Article Commentary]. Ed. V. I. Sloma. M.: Statut, 1999. 396 p. 30000 ptd. ISBN 5-89398-024-7.

Налоговый кодекс Российской Федерации: Часть 1: Принят Государственной Думой 16 июля 1998 г.: Одобрен Советом Федерации 17 июля 1998 г. [Tax Code of the Russian Federation: Part 1: Adopted by the State Duma on 16 July 1998: Approved by the Soviet of the Federation on 17 July 1998]. M.: Politekh-4, 1999. 165 p. 5000 ptd. ISBN 5-86297-120-3.

Налоговый кодекс Российской Федерации: Ч.1. С изменениями и дополнениями. [Tax Code of the Russian Federation: Part 1. With Changes and Additions]. Spb.: Izd. Dom A. Gromova, 1999. 142 p. 7500 ptd. ISBN 5-89138-009-9.

Налоговый кодекс Российской Федерации: Часть 1. С изменениями и дополнениями на 15 июля 1999 г. [Tax Code of the Russian Federation: Part 1. With Changes and Additions for 15 July 1999]. Ed. N. M. Golovanov. Spb.: Iurid. tsentr "Press", 1999. 288 p. 5000 ptd. ISBN 5-93292-003-3.

Налоговый кодекс Российской Федерации: Часть 1. С изменениями и дополнениями на 1 августа 1999 г. [Tax Code of the Russian Federation: Part 1: With Changes and Additions for 1 August 1999]. M.: OLMA-Press: Novosibirsk: IUKEA, 1999. 159 p. 20000 ptd. ISBN 5-224-00601-5, ISBN 5-93316-013-7.

Налоговый кодекс Российской Федерации: Часть 1. С

изменениями и дополнениями на 1 октября 1999 г. [Tax Code of the Russian Federation: Part 1. With Changes and Additions for 1 October 1999]. M.: Prospekt, Kodeks, 1999. 128 p. 10000 ptd. ISBN 5-8369-0055-8.

Налоговый кодекс Российской Федерации: Часть 1. С постатейными комментарии к изменениям и дополнениям. [Tax Code of the Russian Federation: Part 1. With Article by Article Commentaries to Changes and Additions]. Comp. V. R. Zakharin. M.: DiS, 1999. 200 p. 5000 ptd. ISBN 5-8018-0069-7.

Налоговый кодекс в схемах: Официальный текст и комментарий. [Tax Code in Diagrams: Official Text and Commentary]. M.: In-t issled. po nalogovomu pravu, 1999. 240 p. 5000 ptd. ISBN 5-93212-003-7.

Налоговые споры: Сборник документов. [Tax Disputes: Collection of Documents]. Ed. M. Iu. Tikhomirov. M.: Iurinformtsentr, Izd. g-na Tikhomirova M. Iu., 1999. 231 p. 3000 ptd. ISBN 5-89194-031-0.

Наложение ареста на имущество. Оценка и распределение активов. [Imposition of Arrest on Property. Valuation and Distribution of Assets]. Eds. V. F. Ukolov, A. M. Omarov. M.: Luch, Mol. gvardiia, 1999. 111 p. 500 ptd. ISBN 5-235-02362-5.

Наркотики в России: преступления и расследование. [Narcotics in Russia: Crimes and Investigation]. Ed. V. P. Salnikov. Spb.: Fond podderzhki i obrazovaniia v obl. pravookhranit. deiatelnosti "Universitet", 1999. 425 p. 5000 ptd. ISBN 5-93598-004-5.

Насилие в семье: Как бороться с ним государству. [Violence in the Family: How the State Should Fight Against It]. Trans. from English. M.: Glas, 1999. 191 p. ISBN 5-7172-0043-9.

Настольная книга государственного служащего: Комментарий к Федеральному закону «Об основах государственной службы Российской Федерации». [A Civil Servant's Manual: Commentary to the Federal Law "On the Fundamental Principles of the Civil Service of the Russian Federation"]. Ed. V. I. Shkatulla. M.: Ekonomika, 1999. 678 p. 5000 ptd. ISBN 5-282-01935-3.

Научно-практический комментарий к части первой Гражданского кодекса Российской Федерации для предпринимателей. [Scientific-Practical Commentary to Part One of the Civil Code of the Russian Federation for Entrepreneurs]. M. I. Braginskii et al. 2d. rev. ed. M.: Spark, Red. zhurn. "Khoz-vo i pravo", 1999. 736 p. 10000 ptd. ISBN 5-88914-115-5.

Научно-практический комментарий к Федеральному закону «О защите населения и территорий от чрезвычайных ситуаций природного и техногенного характера»: С постатейными материалами. [Scientific-Practical Commentary to the Federal Law "On the Defence of the Population and Territories from Extraordinary Situations of a Natural and Technogenic Character": With Article by Article Materials]. Ed. A. P. Moskalets. M.: MCHS Rossii, 1999. 410 p. 500 ptd.

Научно-практический комментарий к Федеральному закону «Об ипотеке (залоге недвижимости)» (постатейный). [Scientific-Practical Commentary to the Federal Law "On Mortgage (Pledge of Immovable)" (Article by Article)]. Ed. M. G. Masevich. M.: KONTRAKT, INFRA-M, 1999. 292 p. 3000 ptd. ISBN 5-86225-850-7.

Научно-практический комментарий к Федеральному закону (залог недвижимости): Постатейный. [Scientific-Practical Commentary to the Federal Law (Pledge of Immovable): Article by Article]. Ed. M. G. Masevich. M.: Kontrakt, INFRA-M, 1999. 292 p. 3000 ptd. ISBN 5-900785-32-7, ISBN 5-86225-850-7.

Научно-практический комментарий к Гражданскому процессуальному кодексу РСФСР. [Scientific Practical Commentary to the RSFSR Code of Civil Procedure]. Ed. M. K. Treushnikov. M.: Gorodets, 1999. 672 p. 10000 ptd. ISBN 5-89391-051-6.

Nemytina, M. V. *Суд в России: вторая половина XIX - начало XX вв.* [The Court in Russia: Second Half of the 19th to the Beginning of the 20th Centuries]. Saratov: SIUI MVD RF, 1999. 256 p. 1000 ptd. ISBN 5-7485-0021-3.

Nersesiants, V. S. *Философия права: Учебник для вузов.* [Philosophy of Law: Textbook for Institutes of Higher Education]. M.: NORMA-INFRA-M, 1999. 652 p. 30000 ptd. ISBN 5-89123-098-4, ISBN 5-86225-452-8.

Nersesiants, V. S. *Юриспруденция: Введение в курс общей теории права и государства.* [Jurisprudence: Introduction to the Course on the General Theory of Law and State]. M.: NORMA - INFRA-M, 1999. 288 p. 30000 ptd. ISBN 5-89123-227-8, ISBN 5-86225-732-2.

Neshataeva, T. N. *Международные организации и право: Новые тенденции в международно-правовом регулировании.* [International Organisations and Law: New Trends and International Law Regulation]. M.: Delo, 1999. 271 p. 2000 ptd. ISBN 5-7749-0058-4.

Netesov, A. V. *Современный трудовой договор (контракт): Нормативные акты.* [Contemporary Labour Contract: Normative Acts]. M.: Spb.: Gerda, 1999. 286 p. 5000 ptd. ISBN 5-7978-0051-9.

Netrevozhko, T. A. *Квартира: покупка, продажа, обмен ...: Руководство по операциям с недвижимостью: 200 практических советов.* [The Flat: Purchase, Sale, Exchange: Guide to Operations with Immovable Property: 200 Items of Practical Advice]. 2nd rev. ed. M.: Kn. mir, 1999. 319 p. 3000 ptd. ISBN 5-8041-0019-X.

Nikonov, A. A. *Комментарий к изменениям в Налоговый кодекс РФ.* [Commentary to the Changes to the Tax Code of the Russian Federation]. M.: “Glavbukh”, 1999. 147 p. 8000 ptd. ISBN 5-88759-065-3.

Novikova, E. V. *Частное право и экологическое законодательство: влияние и соотношение.* [Private Law and Ecological Legislation: Influence and Correlation]. M.: Iurist’, 1999. 63 p. 1000 ptd. ISBN 5-7975-0286-0.

Novikova, E. V. *Теоретические проблемы развития экологического законодательства в Республике Казахстан.* [Theoretical Problems of the Development of Ecological Legislation in the Republic of Kazakhstan]. M.: Iurist’, 1999. 199 p. 1000 ptd. ISBN 5-7975-0287-9.

Novikova, I. Iu. *Аренда зданий и сооружений: Правовое регулирование. Налогообложение.* [Lease of Buildings and Installations: Legal Regulation. Taxation]. Comps. O. V. Volkova, S. D. Kazancheva. M.: Sovr. ekonomika i pravo, 1999. 106 p. ISBN 5-250-00-826-X.

Novogorodtsev, P. I. *Историческая школа юристов: Для вузов.* [Historical School of Jurists: For Institutes of Higher Education]. Comp. Iu. A. Sandulov. Spb.: Lan, 1999. 189 p. 5000 ptd. ISBN 5-8114-0079-9.

Novoselova, L. A. *Вексель в хозяйственном обороте.* [The Bill of Exchange in Economic Turnover]. 3rd. rev. ed. M.: Statut, 1999. 221 p. 3000 ptd. ISBN 5-8354-0017-9.

Новый юридический словарь-справочник. [New Legal Dictionary/ Manual]. Iu. N. Adonka et al. Ed. E. V. Butenko. Smolensk: Rusich, 1999. 512 p. 11000 ptd. ISBN 5-8138-0042-5.

Новый оперативно-розыскной закон России: Учебно-практическое пособие. [New Operational Search Law of Russia: Instructional Practical Manual]. Comp. A. Iu. Shumilov. 5th rev. ed. M.: Izdatel Shumilova I. I., 1999. 48 p. 3000 ptd. ISBN 5-89784-014-8.

Новые правила документирования результатов оперативно-розыскной деятельности. [New Rules for Documenting the Results of Operational-Search Activity]. Comp. A. Iu. Shumilov. M.: Izdatel Shumilova I. I., 1999. 16 p. 3000 ptd. ISBN 5-89784-015-6.

Nozdrachev, A. F. *Государственная служба: Учебник.* [The State Service: Textbook]. M.: Statut, 1999. 592 p. 10000 ptd. ISBN 5-8354-0015-4.

О бухгалтерском учете: Федеральный закон. [On Accountancy: Federal Law]. M.: INFRA-M, 1999. 14 p. 3000 ptd. ISBN 5-86225-692-X.

О конкуренции и ограничении монополистической деятельности на товарных рынках. [On Competition and the Limitation of Monopolistic Activity on Goods' Markets]. M.: Izd. g-na

Tikhomirova M. Iu., 1999. 40 p. 2000 ptd. ISBN 5-89194-105-9.

О лицензировании отдельных видов деятельности: Федеральный закон. [On Licensing Certain Types of Activity: Federal Law]. M.: INFRA-M, 1999. 21 p. 3000 ptd. ISBN 5-86225-698-9.

О лизинге: Федеральный закон Российской Федерации. Официальный текст. [On Finance Leasing: Federal Law of the Russian Federation. Official Text]. M.: Marketing, 1999. 28 p. 3000 ptd. ISBN 5-7856-0074-9.

О милиции: Сборник нормативных актов. [About the Police: Collection of Normative Acts]. M.: Iurait, 1999. 128 p. 3000 ptd. ISBN 5-85294-015-1.

О милиции: Закон РСФСР. [About the Police: RSFSR Law]. 2d. ed. M.: Novy Iurist', 1999. 32 p. 8000 ptd. ISBN 5-7969-0075-7.

О милиции: Закон РСФСР от 18 апреля 1991 г. No.1026-1. [On the Police: RSFSR Law of 18 April 1991. No.1026-1]. M.: Iurisprudentsiia, 1999. 32 p. 7000 ptd. ISBN 5-8401-0016-1.

О потребительской кооперации (потребительских обществах, их союзах) в Российской Федерации: Закон Российской Федерации: Официальный текст. [On Consumer Cooperation (Consumer Societies, Their Unions) in the Russian Federation: Law of Russian Federation: Official Text]. M.: Marketing, 1999. 40 p. 3000 ptd. ISBN 5-7856-0112-5.

О приватизации жилищного фонда в Российской Федерации. [On the Privatisation of the Housing Fund in the Russian Federation]. M.: Izd. g-na Tikhomirova M.Iu., 1999. 13 p. 3000 ptd. ISBN 5-89194-015-9.

О призыве на военную службу: Сборник нормативных актов. [On the Call-Up for Military Service: Collection of Normative Acts]. 3rd. rev. ed. M.: Iurait, 1999. 294 p. 3000 ptd. ISBN 5-85294-070-4.

О рынке ценных бумаг. [On the Securities' Market]. M.: Izdanie g-na Tikhomirova M. Iu., 1999. 51 p. 3000 ptd. ISBN 5-89194-015-9.

О санитарно-эпидемиологическом благополучии населения: Федеральный закон. [On the Sanitary and Epidemiological Welfare of the Population: Federal Law]. M.: INFRA-M, 1999. 40 p. 3000 ptd. ISBN 5-86225-579-6.

О соблюдении прав человека и гражданина в Российской Федерации в 1998 году. [On the Observance of the Rights of a Person and Citizen in the Russian Federation in 1998]. M.: Iurid. lit., 1999. 45 p. 1045 ptd. ISBN 5-7260-0926-6-2.

О средствах массовой информации. Об информации, информатизации и защите информации. [On the Mass Media. On Information, Informatisation and the Defence of Information]. M.: Izd. g-na Tikhomirova M. Iu., 1999. 47 p. 3000 ptd. ISBN 5-89194-027-2.

О валютном регулировании и валютном контроле. [On Currency Regulation and Currency Control]. M.: Izd. g-na Tikhomirova M. Iu., Iurinformtsentr, 1999. 16 p. 3000 ptd. ISBN 5-89194-025-6.

О ветеранах: Федеральный закон. [On Veterans: Federal Law]. M.: INFRA-M, 1999. 33 p. 3000 ptd. ISBN 5-86225-740-3.

О воинской обязанности и военной службе: Федеральный закон. [On Military Duty and Military Service: Federal Law]. M.: INFRA-M, 1999. 51 p. 3000 ptd. ISBN 5-86225-783-7.

О воинской обязанности и военной службе: Федеральный закон от 28 марта 1998 г. No.53-F3. Вопросы прохождения военной службы: Указ Президента РФ от 4 января 1999 г. No.4. [On Military Duty and Military Service: Federal Law of 28 March 1998. No.53-F3. Questions on the Origin of Military Service: Russian Federation Presidential Edict of 4 January 1999. No.4.]. M.: Iurisprudentsiia, 1999. 55 p. 5000 ptd. ISBN 5-86532-048-3.

Об обязательном социальном страховании от несчастных случаев на производстве и профессиональных заболеваний: Федеральный закон Российской Федерации от 24 июля 1998 г. No.125-ФЗ. [On Obligatory Social Insurance from Production Accidents and Occupational Disease: Federal Law of the Russian

Federation of 24 July 1998. No.125-F3]. M.: Aprokhim, 1999. 31 p. 3000 ptd. ISBN 5-89785-024-0.

Об образовании: Закон Российской Федерации. [On Education: Law of the Russian Federation]. M.: INFRA-M, 1999. 52 p. 3000 ptd. ISBN 5-86225-782-9.

Об обществах с ограниченной ответственностью: Федеральный закон от 8 февраля 1998 г. No.14-ФЗ. [On Limited Responsibility Societies: Federal Law of 8 February 1998. No.14-F3]. M.: Iurisprudentsiia, 1999. 48 p. 5000 ptd. ISBN 5-86532-048-3.
Also published:
M.: Iurait, 1999. 47 p. 5000 ptd. ISBN 5-85294-033-X.

Об обжаловании в суд действий и решений, нарушающих права и свободы граждан. [On the Appeal to Court on Actions and Decisions which Violate the Rights and Freedoms of Citizens]. M.: Izd. g-na Tikhomirova M. Iu., 1999. 50 p. 3000 ptd. ISBN 5-89194-015-9.

Об организации страхового дела в Российской Федерации. [On the Organisation of Insurance Business in the Russian Federation]. M.: Izd. g-na Tikhomirova M. Iu., 1999. 29 p. 2000 ptd. ISBN 5-89194-015-9.

Об оружии: Федеральный закон. [On Weapons: Federal Law]. M.: INFRA-M, 1999. 24 p. 3000 ptd. ISBN 5-86225-616-4.

Об основах охраны труда в Российской Федерации: Федеральный закон. Официальный текст. [On the Fundamental Principles of the Protection of Labour in the Russian Federation: Federal Law. Official Text]. M.: Marketing, 1999. 26 p. 5000 ptd. ISBN 5-7856-0104-4.

Об основах охраны труда в Российской Федерации: Федеральный закон Российской Федерации от 17 июля 1999 г. No.181-ФЗ. [On the Fundamental Principles of the Protection of Labour in the Russian Federation: Federal Law of the Russian Federation of 17 July 1999. No.181-F3]. M.: Aprokhim, 1999. 27 p. 2000 ptd. ISBN 5-89785-027-5.

Об основных гарантиях избирательных прав и права на участие в референдуме граждан Российской Федерации: Федеральный закон от 19 сентября 1997 г. No.124-ФЗ. [On the Basic Guarantees of Electoral Rights and Rights to Participate in the Referendum of Citizens of the Russian Federation: Federal Law of 19 September 1997. No.124-F3]. M.: Iurisprudentsiia, 1999. 120 p. 6000 ptd. ISBN 5-8401-0015-3.

Обеспечение прав человека в Содружестве Независимых Государств: Выпуск 1. Основополагающие документы Содружества, договоры России о дружбе и сотрудничестве с государствами СНГ. [Ensuring Human Rights in the Commonwealth of Independent States: Issue 1. Basic Documents of the Commonwealth, Treaties of Russia on Friendship and Cooperation with CIS States]. Ed. O. O. Mironov. M.: Nalogovy vestnik, 1999. 143 p. 10000 ptd. ISBN 5-93094-010-X.

Образовательное право: Учебно-методическое пособие. [Educational Law: Instructional Methods Manual]. Eds. V. M. Syrykh, V. I. Shkatulla. Ufa: Vost. un-t, 1999. 119 p. 1000 ptd. ISBN 5-87865-190-4.

Образцы нотариальных документов. [Models of Notarial Documents]. Comp. A. P. Ryzhakov. M.: Gorodets, Formula prava, 1999. 381 p. ISBN 5-89391-050-8.

Also published:

M.: Iurait, 1999. 336 p. 5000 ptd. ISBN 5-85294-053-4.

Образцы уголовно-процессуальных документов. [Models of Criminal Procedure Documents]. Eds. E. F. Kutsovaia, Iu. K. Orlov. M.: Iurist', 1999. 426 p. 7500 ptd. ISBN 5-7975-0173-2.

Общая теория права и государства: Для вузов. [General Theory of Law and State: For Institutes of Higher Education]. Ed. V. V. Lazarev. 3rd. rev. ed. M.: Iurist', 1999. 517 p. 10000 ptd. ISBN 5-7357-0123-1.

Общероссийские избирательные объединения накануне выборов депутатов Государственной Думы Федерального Собрания Российской Федерации третьего созыва: Справочник. [All-Russian Electoral Associations on the Eve of Elections of Deputies of the State Duma of the Federal Assembly of the Russian Federation of the Third Convocation: Manual]. Ed. O. K. Zastrozhnaia. M.: Ves' Mir, 1999. 183 p. 6500 ptd. ISBN 5-7777-0053-5.

Очерки истории кубанской прокуратуры: Материалы и документы. [Essays on the History of the Kuban Procuracy: Materials and Documents]. Ed. & Comp. N. N. Grigorieva et al. Krasnodar: Sov. Kuban, 1999. 336 p. 3000 ptd. ISBN 5-7221-0228-8.

Очерки конституционного права иностранных государств: Учебник. [Essays on the Constitutional Law of Foreign States: Textbook]. Ed. D. A. Kovachev. M.: Spark, 1999. 303 p. 2000 ptd. ISBN 5-88914-116-3.

Odintsov, S. *Правовое регулирование деятельности дистрибьютора в сфере многоуровневого (сетевого) маркетинга.* [Legal Regulation of Activity of the Distributor in the Sphere of Multi-Level (Computer Network) Marketing]. M.: BINOM, 1999. 314 p. 4000 ptd. ISBN 5-7989-0148-3.

Okunkov, L. A. Roshchin, V. A. *Вето Президента: Научно-практическое пособие.* [The President's Veto: Scientific-Practical Manual]. M.: Gorodets, Formula prava, 1999. 347 p. 1500 ptd. ISBN 5-89391-043-5.

Организация и производство расследования преступлений. [Organisation and Conducting of Investigation of Crimes]. Eds. I. A. Kopylov, V. F. Shcherbatov. Volgograd: VIUI MVD RF, 1999. 208 p. 400 ptd. ISBN 5-7899-0069-0.

Osmaev, I. B. *Международные и национальные правовые средства борьбы с отмыванием преступных доходов.* [International and National Legal Means for the Struggle Against the Laundering of Criminal Revenues]. M.: Izd-vo RUDN, 1999. 296 p. 1000 ptd. ISBN 5-209-973-4.

Основные институты гражданского права зарубежных стран. [Principal Institutes of Civil Law of Foreign Countries]. Author V. V. Zaleskii. M.: NORMA, 1999. 645 p. 3000 ptd. ISBN 5-89123-245-6.

Основы экологического права: Учебное пособие. [Fundamental Principles of Ecological Law: Instructional Manual]. Ed. I. A. Eremichev. M.: MIUI MVD Rossii, Shchyt-M, 1999. 117 p. 3000 ptd. ISBN 5-93004-049-4.

Основы местного самоуправления и муниципального управления: В 2 ч. Учебное пособие. [Fundamental Principles of Local Self-Government and Municipal Administration: In 2 Parts. Instructional Manual]. M.: Munitsipalnaia vlast, 1999. 1000 ptd. ISBN 5-93158-004-2.

Part 1. *Российское и зарубежное наследие.* [Russian and Foreign Legacy]. 209 p.

Part 2. *Правовые, организационные и финансовые основы самоуправления.* [Legal, Organisational and Financial Fundamental Principles of Local Self-Government]. 158 p.

Основы оперативно-розыскной деятельности: Учебник. [Fundamental Principles of Operational Search Activity: Textbook]. Ed. S. V. Stepashin. Spb.: Lan, 1999. 704 p. 5000 ptd. ISBN 5-8114-0153-1.

Основы права: Учебник. [Fundamental Principles of Law: Textbook]. Ed. A. V. Mitskevich. M.: NORMA-INFRA-M, 1999. 317 p. 50000 ptd. ISBN 5-89123-214-6, ISBN 5-86225-701-2.

Also published:

M.: Vysh. shk., 1999. 319 p. 10000 ptd. ISBN 5-06-003645-6.

Основы права: Учебное пособие для студ. дистанционной формы обучения. [Fundamental Principles of Law: Instructional Manual for Correspondence Courses]. Ed. Z. G. Krylova. M.: RITs MGIU, 1999. 388 p. 350 ptd. ISBN 5-276-00018-2.

Основы управления в органах внутренних дел: Учебник. [Fundamental Principles of Administration in the Internal Affairs Agencies: Textbook]. Ed. A. P. Korenev. 3rd. rev. ed. M.: MIUI MVD Rossii, Shchyt-M, 1999. 354 p. 5000 ptd. ISBN 5-93004-051-6.

Отечественное законодательство XI-XX веков: Ч.1. XI-XIX вв. [National Legislation of the 11th-20th Centuries: Part 1. 11th-19th Centuries]. Ed. O. I. Chistiakov.

Отечественное законодательство XI-XX веков: Ч.11. XX век: Пособие для семинаров. [National Legislation of the 11th-20th Centuries: Part 11. 20th Century: Manual for Seminars]. Ed. O. I. Chistiakov. M.: Iurist', 1999. 352 p. 5000 ptd. ISBN 5-7975-0153-8. M.: Iurist', 1999. 463 p. 5000 ptd. ISBN 5-7975-0146-5.

Ovchinnikov, I. I. *Местное самоуправление в системе народовластия.* [Local Self-Government in the System of Sovereignty]. M.: In-t gosudarstva i prava RAN, 1999. 329 p. 1000 ptd. ISBN 5-8339-0006-9.

Panchenko, A. I. *Учись защищать себя.* [Learn to Defend Yourself]. M.: Mir bezopasnosti, 1999. 80 p. 2000 ptd. ISBN 5-89258-012-1.

Panskov, V. G. *Комментарии к Налоговому кодексу Российской Федерации: Ч.1. Вводится в действие с 1 января 1999 г.* [Commentaries to the Tax Code of the Russian Federation: Part 1. Enters into Operation from 1 January 1999]. M.: Finansy i statistika, 1999. 62 p. 3000 ptd. ISBN 5-279-02074-5.

Also published:

M.: Finansy i statistika, 1999. 78 p. 5000 ptd. ISBN 5-279-02164-4. (2d. rev. ed.)

Парламентское право России. [Russian Parliamentary Law]. Eds. I. M. Stepanov, T. Ia. Khabrievaia. M.: Iurist', 1999. 391 p. 5000 ptd. ISBN 5-7975-0127-9.

Pavlov, V. G. *Субъект преступления в уголовном праве: Ист.-правовое исследование.* [Subject of Crime in Criminal Law: Historical-Legal Investigation]. M.: Spb.: Spb, iurid. akad. Gerda, 1999. 118 p. 4000 ptd. ISBN 5-7978-0049-7.

Pchelintseva, L. M. *Комментарий к Семейному кодексу Российской Федерации.* [Commentary to the Family Code of the Russian Federation]. M.: NORMA-INFRA-M, 1999. 689 p. 6000 ptd. ISBN 5-89123-333-9, ISBN 5-86225-994-5.

Pchelintseva, L. M. *Практикум по семейному праву.* [Practical Work on Family Law]. 2d. rev. ed. M.: NORMA-INFRA-M, 1999. 248 p. 30000 ptd. ISBN 5-89123-314-2.

Pchelintseva, L. M. *Семейное право России: Учебник для вузов.* [Family Law of Russia: Textbook for Institutes of Higher Education]. M.: NORMA-INFRA-M, 1999. 672 p. 60000 ptd. ISBN 5-89123-287-1, ISBN 5-86225-929-5.

Perminov, O. G. *Уголовно-исполнительное право: Для вузов.* [Criminal-Executory Law: For Institutes of Higher Education]. M.: Bylina, 1999. 238 p. 3000 ptd. ISBN 5-88528-238-2.

Petrov, V. *Россия. Кризис федерации: Прошлое, настоящее, будущее.* [Russia. Crisis of the Federation: Past, Present, Future]. M., 1999. 281 p.

Petrova, G. V. *Налоговое право: Учебник для вузов.* [Tax Law: Textbook for Institutes of Higher Education]. M.: NORMA-INFRA-M, 1999. 271 p. 30000 ptd. ISBN 5-89123-181-6, ISBN 5-86225-638-5.

Petrukhin, I. L. *Человек и власть (в сфере борьбы с преступностью).* [Man and Power (in the Sphere of the Struggle Against Criminality]. M.: Iurist', 1999. 391 p. 1500 ptd. ISBN 5-7975-0255-0.

Petukhov, V. N. *Корпорации в российской промышленности: законодательство и практика: Научно-практическое пособие.* [Corporations in Russian Industry: Legislation and Practice]. M.: Gorodets, 1999. 208 p. 2000 ptd. ISBN 5-89391-052-4.

Pisarevskii, E. L. *Туристская деятельность: Проблемы правового регулирования.* [Tourist Activity: Problems of Legal Regulation]. Vladivostok: In-t mezhdunar. turizma, 1999. 283 p. 1000 ptd. ISBN 5-93304-002-9.

Piskarev, I. K. *Образцы судебных документов: Практическое пособие.* [Models of Judicial Documents: Practical Manual]. 2d. rev. ed. M.: Gorodets, 1999. 248 p. 5000 ptd. ISBN 5-89391-015-X.

Pleskachevskii, V. M. *Оружие в криминалистике. Понятие и классификация.* [Weapons in Criminalistics. Concept and Classification]. M.: NIPKTS VOSKHOD, 1999. 383 p. ISBN 5-93055-011-5.

Pliev, E. G. *Правовые проблемы предпринимательства в России.* [Legal Problems of Entrepreneurship in Russia]. M.: Prospekt, 1999. 119 p. 1000 ptd. ISBN 5-8369-0038-8.

Подоходный налог с физических лиц. [Income Tax from Physical Persons]. M.: Marketing, 1999. 268 p. 5000 ptd. ISBN 5-7856-0131-1.

Pokrovskii, I. A. *История римского права.* [History of Roman Law]. Spb.: Letnii sad, Zhurn. "Neva", 1999. 532 p. 2500 ptd. ISBN 5-89740-023-7, ISBN 5-89740-123-X.

Полный сборник кодексов Российской Федерации: С изменениями и дополнениями на 1 марта 1999 г. [Complete Collection of Codes of the Russian Federation: With Changes and Additions for 1 March 1999]. 768 p. 8000 ptd. ISBN 5-93220-002-2.

Полный сборник кодексов Российской Федерации: С изменениями и дополнениями на 1 мая 1999 г. [Complete Collection of Codes of the Russian Federation: With Changes and Additions for 1 May 1999]. M.: AST, 1999. 928 p. 10000 ptd. ISBN 5-237-02360-6.

Полный сборник кодексов Российской Федерации: С изменениями и дополнениями на 1 сентября 1999 г. [Complete Collection of Codes of the Russian Federation: With Changes and Additions for 1 September 1999]. M.: Slavian. dom knigi, 1999. 800 p. 10000 ptd. ISBN 5-93220-002-2.

Положение о составе затрат с постатейными материалами. [Statute on the Elements of Expenditure with Article by Article Materials]. 2d. ed. M.: INFRA-M, 1999. 120 p. 3000 ptd. ISBN 5-16-000009-7.

Положение по ведению бухгалтерского учёта и бухгалтерской отчётности в Российской Федерации: Утверждено Приказом Министерства финансов Российской Федерации (вводится в действие с 1 января 1999 г.). Официальный текст. [Statute on Conducting Bookkeeping Registration and Bookkeeping Accountability in the Russian Federation: Confirmed by Order of the Finance Ministry of the Russian

Federation (Enters into Operation from 1 January 1999). Official Text]. M.: Marketing, 1999. 34 p. 5000 ptd. ISBN 5-7856-0073-0.

Popenko, V. N. *Война без правил.* [War Without Rules]. M.: Boguchar, 1999. 128 p. 6000 ptd. ISBN 5-88276-029-X.

Порядок и условия прохождения муниципальной службы: Учебно-методическое пособие. [Procedure and Conditions of Municipal Service: Instructional-Methods Manual]. Eds. A. F. Murashko, O. L. Savranskaia, V. A. Stoliarovaia. M.: RITS "Munitsipal. vlast", 1999. 149 p. 10000 ptd. ISBN 5-93158-006-9.

Пособие для следователя. [Manual for the Investigator]. Eds. N. A. Selivanov, A. I. Dvorkin. 2nd. rev. ed. M.: Liga Razum, 1999. 505 p. 3000 ptd. ISBN 5-89795-008-3.

Постатейный комментарий к Федеральному закону «О судебных приставах». [Article by Article Commentary to the Federal Law "On Bailiffs"]. Ed. E. N. Sidorenko. M.: Statut, 1999. 127 p. 5000 ptd. ISBN 5-8354-0019-5.

Postovoi, N. V. *Муниципальное право: Вопросы и ответы.* [Municipal Law: Questions and Answers]. M.: Novy Iurist, 1999. 117 p. 5000 ptd. ISBN 5-7969-0058-7.

Практическое пособие по арбитражному управлению предприятием. [Practical Manual on the Arbitration Management of Enterprises]. G. K. Tal et al. M.: Statut, 1999. 379 p. 300 ptd.

Практика проведения демократических выборов в Московской области: Учебное пособие. [Practice of Conducting Democratic Elections in the Moscow Region: Instructional Manual]. Ed. V. I. Smirnovaia. M.: Sovr. tetradi, 1999. 143 p. 2000 ptd. ISBN 5-88289-114-0.

Практикум по гражданскому праву: Ч. 1. [Practical Work on Civil Law: Part 1]. Eds. A. G. Kalpin, A. Iu. Kabalkin, V. V. Dolinskaia. M.: Iurist', 1999. 172 p. 5000 ptd. ISBN 5-7975-0046-9.

Практикум по гражданскому процессуальному праву: Учебное

пособие. [Practical Work on the Law of Civil Procedure: Instructional Manual]. Ed. M. K. Treushnikov. M.: Gorodets, Formula prava, 1999. 288 p. 5000 ptd. ISBN 5-89393-003-6.

Практикум по российскому трудовому праву: Для вузов. [Practical Work on Russian Labour Law: For Institutes of Higher Education]. A. A. Abramova et al. M.: NORMA-INFRA-M, 1999. 688 p. 30000 ptd. ISBN 5-89123-343-6, ISBN 5-86225-906-6.

Практикум по уголовному праву. [Practical Work on Criminal Law]. Ed. I. Ia. Kozachenko. M.: NORMA-INFRA-M, 1999. 539 p. 30000 ptd. ISBN 5-89123-250-2, ISBN 5-86225-822-1.

Права человека: Учебник для вузов. [Human Rights: Textbook for Institutes of Higher Education]. Ed. E. A. Lukasheva. M.: NORMA-INFRA-M, 1999. 573 p. 30000 ptd. ISBN 5-89123-352-5, ISBN 5-16-00023-2.

Права человека в России: проблемы гарантий на современном этапе. [Human Rights in Russia: Problems of Guarantees in the Contemporary Stage]. Ed. P. V. Anisimov. Volgograd: VIUI MVD Rossii, 1999. 130 p. 100 ptd. ISBN 5-7899-0068-2.

Права ребёнка: Сборник международных и российских законодательных актов. [Rights of the Child: Collection of International and Russian Legislative Acts]. M.: Novaia Volna, 1999. 127 p. 5000 ptd. ISBN 5-7864-0099-9.

Правила оформления документов в Государственной Думе Федерального Собрания Российской Федерации. [Rules for the Formulation of Documents in the State Duma of the Federal Assembly of the Russian Federation]. M.: Izd. Gos. Dumy, 1999. 79 p. 1500 ptd.

Право: история, теория, практика: Выпуск 3. [Law: History, Theory, Practice: Issue 3]. Briansk: Izd-vo BGPU, 1999. 214 p. 300 ptd. ISBN 5-88543-099-3.

Право Европейского Союза: правовое регулирование торгового оборота: Учебное пособие. [Law of the European Union: Legal Regulation of Trade Turnover: Instructional Manual]. Eds. V. V.

Bezbakh, A. Ia. Kapustin, V. K. Puchinskii. M.: Zerstalo, 1999. 389 p. 3000 ptd. ISBN 5-8078-0035-8.

Правоохранительные органы и организации России: Учебное пособие. [Law Enforcement Agencies and Organisations of Russia]. Ed. A. P. Guliaev. M.: Sobranie, 1999. 144 p. 1250 ptd. ISBN 5-86605-011-0.

Правоохранительные органы Российской Федерации: Сборник нормативных актов. [Law Enforcement Agencies of the Russian Federation: Collection of Normative Acts]. 2nd. rev. ed. M.: Iurait, 1999. 394 p. 6000 ptd. ISBN 5-85294-089-5.

Правоохранительные органы Российской Федерации: Учебник для вузов. [Law Enforcement Agencies of the Russian Federation: Textbook for Institutes of Higher Education]. 2d. rev. ed. Ed. V. P. Bozhiev. M.: Spark, 1999. 399 p. 8000 ptd. ISBN 5-88914-079-5.
Also published:
M.: Spark, 1999. 414 p. 10000 ptd. ISBN 5-88914-127-9. (3rd. rev. ed.)

Правоохранительные органы Российской Федерации: Учебное пособие. [Law Enforcement Agencies of the Russian Federation: Instructional Manual]. Ed. V. K. Bobrov. M.: Shchyt-M, 1999. 212 p. 2000 ptd. ISBN 5-93004-042-7.

Правоведение: Практикум: Учебное пособие. [Jurisprudence: Practical Work: Instructional Manual]. Ed. V. A. Vasenkov. M.: Iurist', 1999. 126 p. 5000 ptd. ISBN 5-7975-0195-3.

Правоведение: Учебное пособие. [Jurisprudence: Instructional Manual]. Ed. S. A. Bogoliubova. M.: Znanie, 1999. 320 p. 20000 ptd. ISBN 5-07-002848-0.

Правовое государство: реальность, мечты, будущее. [Rule-of-Law State: Reality, Aspirations, the Future]. V. M. Boer et al. Spb.: Aleteia, Izd-vo Spb. un-ta MVD Rossii, 1999. 245 p. 2400 ptd. ISBN 5-89329-143-3.

Правовые основы бухгалтерского учёта и аудиторской

деятельности: Учебник. [Legal Fundamental Principles of Accountancy and Auditor Activity: Textbook]. Ed. S. G. Chaadaev. M.: Iurist', 1999. 415 p. 10000 ptd. ISBN 5-7975-0141-4.

Правовые основы обеспечения прав вкладчиков. [Legal Fundamental Principles of Ensuring the Rights of Depositors]. Eds. V. F. Ukolov, A. M. Omarov. M.: Luch. Mol. gvardiia, 1999. 110 p. 500 ptd. ISBN 5-235-02361-7.

Правовые проблемы организации рынка ипотечного кредитования в России. [Legal Problems of the Organisation of the Mortgage Credits Market in Russia]. Ed. V. S. Em. M.: Statut, 1999. 256 p. 10000 ptd. ISBN 5-8354-0008-X.

Предпринимательское (хозяйственное) право: Учебник. В 2 томах. Том 1. [Entrepreneurial (Economic) Law: Textbook. In 2 Volumes. Vol.1]. Ed. O. M. Oleinik. M.: Iurist', 1999. 727 p. 50000 ptd. ISBN 5-7975-0231-3.

Предпринимательское (хозяйственное) право: Сборник нормативных актов: Учебное пособие для вузов. [Entrepreneurial (Economic) Law: Collection of Normative Acts: Instructional Manual for Institutes of Higher Education]. Comp. & Ed. I. V. Doinikov. 2d. rev. ed. M.: Bylina, 1999. 636 p. 10000 ptd. ISBN 5-88528-2420.

Преступность и культура. [Criminality and Culture]. Ed. A. I. Dolgovaia. M.: Kriminol. Assots., 1999. 159 p. 1000 ptd. ISBN 5-87817-019-1.

Проблема обеспечения прав граждан на доступ к правовой информации: Материалы международного «круглого стола». Москва, Государственная Дума, 25-26 ноября 1997 г. [The Problem of Safeguarding the Rights of Citizens for Access to Legal Information: Materials from the International "Round Table". Moscow, State Duma, 25-26 November 1997]. M.: Izd. Gos. Dumy, 1999. 583 p. 1500 ptd. ISBN 5-89686-008-0.

Проблемы формирования уголовно-розыскного права: Выпуск 2. [Problems of the Formation of Criminal Executory Law: Issue 2].

Ed. A. Iu. Shumilov. M.: Izdatel Shumilova I. I., 1999. 136 p. 500 ptd. ISBN 5-89784-023-7.

Проблемы общей теории права и государства: Учебник. [Problems of the Universal Theory of Law and State: Textbook]. Ed. V. S. Nersesiants. M.: NORMA-INFRA-M, 1999. 813 p. 60000 ptd. ISBN 5-89123-361-4, ISBN 5-86225-910-4.

Проблемы правоприменительной практики в предпринимательской деятельности. [Problems of Law Application Practice in Entrepreneurial Activity]. Eds. A. V. Chernykh, D. V. Goloverov. M.: Kn. mir, 1999. 223 p. ISBN 5-8041-0047-5.

Проблемы правового регулирования государственного протекционизма аграрного сектора экономики в России. [Problems of the Legal Regulation of State Protectionism of the Agrarian Sector of the Economy in Russia]. Ed. G. G. Faizullin. Ufa: Poligrafkomb., 1999. 415 p. 1000 ptd. ISBN 5-85051-144-X.

Проблемы реализации суверенитета Республики Башкортостан (1557-1998 гг.): Документы. Нормативные акты. [Problems of the Realisation of the Sovereignty of the Republic of Bashkortostan (1557-1998): Documents. Normative Acts]. Comp. M. K. Malikov. Sterlitamak: Izd-vo Bashkir. un-ta, 1999. 511 p. 1000 ptd. ISBN 5-7477-0261-0.

Проблемы судебно-правовой реформы в России: история и современность: Выпуск 6. [Problems of Judicial Legal Reform in Russia: History and the Present-Day: Issue 6]. Ed. T. V. Klenova. Samara: Izd-vo Samar. gumanitar. akad., 1999. 246 p. 200 ptd. ISBN 5-86465-020-X.

Проблемы теории государства и права: Учебное пособие. [Problems of the Theory of State and Law: Instructional Manual]. Ed. M. N. Marchenko. M.: Prospekt, 1999. 504 p. 10000 ptd. ISBN 5-8369-0007-8.

Профессиональная этика сотрудников правоохранительных органов: Учебное пособие. [Professional Ethics of Personnel of Law Enforcement Agencies: Instructional Manual]. Eds. G. B. Dubov, A. V.

Opalev. 2d. rev. ed. M.: Shchyt-M, 1999. 227 p. 1000 ptd. ISBN 5-93004-027-3.

Prokhorov, L. A., Prokhorova, M. L. *Уголовное право: Учебник.* [Criminal Law: Textbook]. M.: Iurist', 1999. 479 p. 10000 ptd. ISBN 5-7975-0203-8.

Прокурорский надзор в Российской Федерации: Учебное пособие для вузов. [Procuracy Supervision in the Russian Federation: Instructional Manual for Institutes of Higher Education]. Ed. A. A. Chuvileva. M.: Iurist', 1999. 398 p. 10000 ptd. ISBN 5-7975-0189-9.

Protasov, V. N. *Теория государства и права. Проблемы теории права и государства: Вопросы и ответы.* [Theory of State and Law. Problems of the Theory of Law and State: Questions and Answers]. M.: Novy Iurist, 1999. 238 p. 10000 ptd. ISBN 5-7969-0068-4.

Puchkov, O. A. *Социальная свобода. Теоретико-правовые вопросы сущности.* [Social Freedom. Theoretical-Legal Questions of Essence]. Ekaterinburg: Izd-vo UrGIUA, 1999. 161 p. 400 ptd. ISBN 5-7845-0090-2.

Pukhan, I., Polenak-Akimovskaia, M. *Римское право: Базовый учебник.* [Roman Law: Standard Textbook]. Trans. from Macedonian. M.: Zertsalo, 1999. 411 p. 5000 ptd. ISBN 5-8078-0040-0.

Pustogarov, V. V. *Ф. Ф. Мартенс - юрист, дипломат.* [F. F. Martens - Jurist, Diplomat]. 2d. rev. ed. M.: Mezhdunar. otnosheniia, 1999. 287 p. 2500 ptd. ISBN 5-7133-0975-4.

Pustozerova, V. M. *Комментарий КЗоТ РФ: С изменениями и дополнениями.* [Commentary to the Code of Laws on Labour of the Russian Federation: With Changes and Additions]. M.: PRIOR, 1999. 512 p. 14000 ptd. ISBN 5-7990-0151-6.

Рабочее место: права и право. [Place of Work: Rights and the Law]. A. Gerasimov et al. M.: Dom. advokat, 1999. 208 p. 20000 ptd. ISBN 5-89156-009-7.

Rarog, A. I., Stepalin, V. P. *Уголовное право: Общая часть в вопросах и ответах.* [Criminal Law: General Part in Questions and Answers]. M.: Iurist', 1999. 228 p. 10000 ptd. ISBN 5-7975-0144-9.

Район в городе. [District in the City]. A. V. Petrov et al. M.: Tsentr, 1999. 192 p. 5000 ptd. ISBN 5-88860-058-X.

Расследование контрабанды: Практическое пособие. [Investigation into Smuggling: Practical Manual]. Ed. K. F. Skvortsov. M.: Iurist', 1999. 206 p. 7500 ptd. ISBN 5-7975-0116-3.

Расследование неправомерного доступа к компьютерной информации: Научно-практическое пособие. [Investigation of Unlawful Access to Computer Information: Scientific-Practical Manual]. Ed. N. G. Shurukhnova. M.: Shchyt-M, 1999. 254 p. 1500 ptd. ISBN 5-93004-035-4.

Расследование преступлений, связанных с незаконным оборотом наркотических средств и психотропных веществ: В 2 ч. Учебное пособие. [Investigation of Crimes Connected with the Illegal Turnover of Narcotics and Psychotropic Substances: In 2 Parts. Instructional Manual].

Часть 1. Уголовно-правовая и криминалистическая характеристика преступлений. [Part 1. Criminal-Legal and Criminalistics Characteristics of Crimes]. V. P. Prikazchikov et al. 76 p. ISBN 5-7899-0056-9.

Часть 2. В. П. Приказчиков, А. П. Резван, В. Н. Косарев. Организация расследования и особенности производства отдельных следственных действий. [Part 2. V. P. Prikazchikov, A. P. Rezvan, V. N. Kosarev. Organisation of Investigation and Peculiarities of Conducting Separate Investigative Actions]. 68 p. ISBN 5-7899-0059-3.

Расследование преступлений в сфере экономики: Руководство для следователей. [Investigation of Crimes in the Sphere of the Economy: Guide for the Investigator]. Ed. I. N. Kozhevnikov. M.: Spark, 1999. 415 p. 12000 ptd. ISBN 5-88914-118-X.

Rassolov, M. M. *Информационное право: Учебное пособие.* [Informational Law: Instructional Manual]. M.: Iurist', 1999. 400 p. 5000 ptd. ISBN 5-7975-0179-1.

Регламент Центральной избирательной комиссии Российской Федерации. [Reglament of the Central Electoral Commission of the Russian Federation]. M.: Tsentr. izbirat. komis. Ros. Federatsii, 1999. 55 p. 500 p.

Repetskaia, A. L., Rybalskaia, V. Ia. *Криминология: Общая часть: Учебное пособие.* [Criminology: General Part: Instructional Manual]. Irkutsk: Izd-vo IGEA, 1999. 237 p. 700 ptd. ISBN 5-7253-0303-9.

Repin, V. S. *Комментарий к Основам законодательства Российской Федерации о нотариате.* [Commentary to the Fundamental Principles of Russian Federation Legislation on the Notariat]. M.: NORMA-INFRA-M, 1999. 291 p. 30000 ptd. ISBN 5-89123-207-3, ISBN 5-86225-681-4.

Reshetnikova, I. V., Iarkov, V. V. *Гражданское право и гражданский процесс в современной России.* [Civil Law and Civil Procedure in Contemporary Russia]. Ekaterinburg. M.: NORMA, 1999. 302 p. 15000 ptd. ISBN 5-89123-233-2.

Reshetnikova, I. V. *Доказательственное право Англии и США.* [Law of Evidence of England and the USA]. 2d. rev. ed. M.: Gorodets, 1999. 283 p. 1500 ptd. ISBN 5-89391-039-7.

Riapisov, S. V., Ryzhakov, A. P. *Уголовно-процессуальный кодекс РСФСР с постатейными материалами.* [RSFSR Code of Criminal Procedure with Article by Article Materials]. M.: PRIOR, 1999. 750 p. 5000 ptd. ISBN 5-7990-0366-7.

Римское частное право: Учебник. [Roman Private Law: Textbook]. Eds. I. B. Novitskii, I. S. Pereterskii. M.: Iurisprudentsiia, 1999. 509 p. 6000 ptd. ISBN 5-86532-045-9.

Also published:

M.: Iurist', 1999. 544 p. 10000 ptd. ISBN 5-7975-0154-6.

Rogozhin, M. Iu. *Документы делового общения.* [Business Relations Documents]. M.: Rus. delovaia lit., 1999. 204 p. 3000 ptd. ISBN 5-89247-027-X.

Romanov, S. *Мошенничество в России: Как уберечься от*

аферистов. [Swindling in Russia: How to Protect Oneself from Swindlers]. M.: EKSMO-Press, 1999. 751 p. 5000 ptd. ISBN 5-04-000829-5.

Российская юридическая энциклопедия. [Russian Legal Encyclopedia]. Ed. A. Ia. Sukharev. M.: INFRA-M, 1999. 1110 p. 100000 ptd. ISBN 5-86225-925-2.

Российский конституционализм: проблемы и решения: Материалы международных конфер. [Russian Constitutionalism: Problems and Decisions: Materials from International Conferences]. M.: In-t gosudarstva i prava RAN, 1999. 247 p. 1200 ptd. ISBN 5-8339-0004-2.

Российское административное право: Часть общая. Книга 1. Сборник нормативных актов. [Russian Administrative Law: General Part. Book 1. Collection of Normative Acts]. Comp. N. M. Konin et al. Saratov: SGAP, 1999. 544 p. 1000 ptd. ISBN 5-7924-0056-3.

Российское гражданское право: Учебник. [Russian Civil Law: Textbook]. Eds. Z. G. Krylova, E. P. Gavrilov. M.: IurInfoR, 1999. 416 p. 5000 ptd. ISBN 5-89158-019-5.

Российское полицейское (административное) право: Конец XIX - нач. XX в.: Хрестоматия. [Russian Police (Administrative) Law: From the End of the 19th Century to the Beginning of the 20th Century: An Anthology]. Comp. & Intro. Iu. N. Starilov. Voronezh: Izd-vo VGU, 1999. 624 p. 1500 ptd. ISBN 5-7455-1065-X.

Российское служебное право: Сборник нормативных актов. Учебное пособие. [Russian Employment Law: Collection of Normative Acts. Instructional Manual]. Comp. Iu. N. Starilov. Voronezh: Izd-vo Voronezh. gos. un-ta, 1999. 800 p. 1000 ptd. ISBN 5-7455-1044-7.

Российское таможенное право: Учебник. [Russian Customs Law: Textbook]. Ed. B. N. Gabrichidze. M.: NORMA, INFRA-M, 1999. 511 p. 60000 ptd. ISBN 5-89123-097-6, ISBN 5-86225-451-X.

Российское трудовое право: Учебник. [Russian Labour Law:

Textbook]. Ed. A. D. Zaikin. M.: NORMA-INFRA-M, 1999. 415 p. 50000 ptd. ISBN 5-89123-127-1, ISBN 5-86225-538-9.

Российское уголовное право: Курс лекций: Том 1: Преступление. [Russian Criminal Law: Course of Lectures: Vol.1: Crime]. Ed. A. I. Korobeev. Vladivostok: Izd-vo Dalnevost, un-ta, 1999. 604 p. 5000 ptd. ISBN 5-7444-0874-2.

Российское уголовное право: Общая часть. Учебник. [Russian Criminal Law: General Part. Textbook]. Ed. M. P. Zhuravlev. M.: Shchyt-M, 1999. 280 p. 500 ptd. ISBN 5-93004-040-0.

Rossinskaia, E. R. *Криминалистика: Вопросы и ответы: Учебное пособие для вузов.* [Criminalistics: Questions and Answers: Instructional Manual for Institutes of Higher Education]. M.: IUNITI-DANA, 1999. 351 p. 10000 ptd. ISBN 5-238-00116-9.

Rossinskaia, E. R. *Профессия - эксперт.* [Profession - An Expert]. M.: Iurist', 1999. 192 p. 3000 ptd. ISBN 5-7975-0128-7.

Rovny, V. V. *Проблемы единства российского частного права.* [Problems of the Unity of Russian Private Law]. Irkutsk: Izd-vo Irkut. un-ta, 1999. 310 p. 1000 ptd. ISBN 5-7430-0592-3.

Rozenberg, M. G. *Исковая давность в международном коммерческом обороте: практика применения.* [Limitation of Action in International Commercial Turnover: Practice of Application]. M.: Statut, 1999. 142 p. 5000 ptd. ISBN 5-8354-0022-5.

Ручное огнестрельное оружие и патроны к нему. [Manual Firearms and Their Cartridges]. M.: Mozhaisk-Terra, 1999. 301 p. 1200 ptd. ISBN 5-7542-0050-1.

Rudinskii, F. M. *«Дело КПСС» в Конституционном Суде: Записки участника процесса.* ["Case of the Communist Party of the Soviet Union" in the Constitutional Court": Notes of a Participant of the Trial]. M.: Bylina, 1999. 503 p. 2000 ptd.

Rulan, N. *Юридическая антропология: Учебник для вузов.* [Legal Anthropology: Textbook for Institutes of Higher Education]. Trans.

from French. Eds. V. S. Nersesiants. M.: NORMA, 1999. 301 p. 3000 ptd. ISBN 5-89123-303-7.

Русская Православная Церковь и право: Комментарий. [The Russian Orthodox Church and the Law. Commentary]. Ed. M. V. Ilichev. M.: BEK, 1999. 464 p. 6000 ptd. ISBN 5-85639-271-X.

Русские выборы. [Russian Elections]. M.: RIA "Novosti", 1999. 174 p. 5000 ptd.

Ryzhakov, A. P. *Окончание предварительного расследования: Учебное пособие.* [Completion of Preliminary Investigation: Instructional Manual]. M.: Gorodets, Formula prava, 1999. 255 p. ISBN 5-89391-049-4.

Ryzhakov, A. P. *Органы дознания в уголовном процессе.* [Agencies of Inquiry in the Criminal Procedure]. M.: Gorodets, Formula prava, 1999. 356 p. 2000 ptd. ISBN 5-89391-042-7.

Ryzhakov, A. P. *Уголовный процесс: Учебник для вузов.* [Criminal Procedure: Textbook for Institutes of Higher Education]. M.: PRIOR, 1999. 592 p. 8000 ptd. ISBN 5-7990-0284-9.

Ryzhakov, A. P., Sergeev, D. A. *Постатейный комментарий к Гражданскому процессуальному кодексу РСФСР.* [Article by Article Commentary to the RSFSR Code of Civil Procedure]. M.: Statut, 1999. 718 p. 10000 ptd. ISBN 5-8354-0011-X.

Sakhnova, T. V. *Судебная экспертиза.* [Forensic Expert Examination]. M.: Gorodets, Formula prava, 1999. 367 p. 1500 ptd. ISBN 5-89391-052-4.

Samokhvalova, Iu. N. *Лизинг в России: правовые основы, бухгалтерский учёт, налогообложение.* [Finance Leasing in Russia: Legal Fundamental Principles, Accountancy, Taxation]. Eds. V. F. Ukolov, A. M. Omarov. M.: Luch. Mol. gvardiia, 1999. 110 p. 500 ptd. ISBN 5-235-02361-7.

Sannikova, L. V. *Договор найма труда в России.* [Contract for Hired Labour in Russia]. M.: MT-Press, 1999. 120 p. 3000 ptd. ISBN

5-86567-024-8.

Sapozhnikov, N. V. *Валютные операции коммерческих банков. Правовое регулирование: Практическое пособие.* [Currency Operations of Commercial Banks. Legal Regulation: Practical Manual]. M.: Iurist', 1999. 254 p. 3000 ptd. ISBN 5-7975-0161-9.

Sarbash, S. V. *Договор банковского счета: проблемы доктрины и судебной практики.* [Banking Account Contract: Problems of Doctrine and Judicial Practice]. M.: Statut, 1999. 270 p. 5000 ptd. ISBN 5-8354-0010-1.

Savitskii, V. M., Larin, A. M. *Уголовный процесс: Словарь-справочник.* [Criminal Procedure: Dictionary-Manual]. Ed. V. M. Savitskii. M.: Kontrakt, INFRA-M, 1999. 271 p. 6000 ptd. ISBN 5-900785-31-9, ISBN 5-16-000020-8.

Saviuk, L. K. *Правовая статистика: Для вузов.* [Legal Statistics: For Institutes of Higher Education]. M.: Iurist', 1999. 587 p. 10000 ptd. ISBN 5-7975-0135-X.

Сборник действующих постановлений Пленумов Верховных Судов СССР, РСФСР и Российской Федерации по уголовным делам с комментариями и пояснениями. [Collection of Prevailing Decrees of the Plenums of the Supreme Courts of the USSR, RSFSR and Russian Federation on Criminal Cases with Commentaries and Explanations]. Eds. V. I. Radchenko, A. S. Mikhlin. M.: BEK, 1999. 684 p. 3000 ptd. ISBN 5-85639-266-3.

Сборник договоров: Все виды договоров, предусмотренные новым ГК РФ. [Collection of Contracts: All Types of Contracts Provided for by the New Civil Code of the Russian Federation]. Comp. A. N. Dolzhenko et al. M.: Prospekt, 1999. 560 p. 15000 ptd. ISBN 5-8369-0028-0.

Сборник договоров с дискетой. [Collection of Contracts with Diskette]. Comp. A. N. Dolzhenko. 2d. rev. ed. M.: Prospekt, 1999. 232 p. 10000 ptd. ISBN 5-8369-0034-5.

Сборник документов и материалов Специальной комиссии

Государственной Думы Федерального Собрания Российской Федерации по оценке соблюдения процедурных правил и фактической обоснованности обвинения, выдвинутого против Президента Российской Федерации, и их рассмотрения Государственной Думой 13-15 мая 1999 года. [Collection of Documents and Materials of the Special Commission of the State Duma of the Federal Assembly of the Russian Federation for the Appraisal of Observance of Procedural Rules and the Actual Justification of the Accusation Brought Against the President of the Russian Federation and Their Examination by the State Duma on 13-15 May 1999]. Comps. V. D. Filimonov, T. V. Lazarev, P. P. Lopata. Ed. V. D. Filimonov. M.: Izd. Gos. Dumy, 1999. 999 p. 1000 ptd. ISBN 5-86656-093-3.

Сборник документов органов самоуправления города Чебоксары, устанавливающих порядок управления муниципальной собственностью. [Collection of Documents of Organs of Self-Government of the City of Cheboksary, which Establish the Procedure for the Administration of Municipal Ownership]. Cheboksary: Chuvash. kn. izd-vo, 1999. 781 p. 1000 ptd. ISBN 5-7670-1120-6.

Сборник кодексов Российской Федерации: Кн.3. [Collection of Codes of the Russian Federation: Book 3]. M.: Delo, 1999. 208 p. 2000 ptd. ISBN 5-7749-0061-4.

Сборник кодексов Российской Федерации: На 1 марта 1999 г. [Collection of Codes of the Russian Federation: For 1 March 1999]. 9th ed. M.: Filin', 1999. 778 p. 10000 ptd. ISBN 5-89568-124-7.

Сборник кодексов Российской Федерации: В 2 книгах. [Collection of Codes of the Russian Federation: In 2 Books]. M.: Delo, 1999. 6000 ptd.

Book 1. 718 p. ISBN 5-7749-0073-8.
Book 2. 624 p. ISBN 5-7749-0049-5.

Сборник нормативных актов о труде. [Collection of Normative Acts on Labour]. Comp. N. P. Sharilo. M.: Iurid. lit., 1999. 704 p. 5000 ptd. ISBN 5-7260-0904-5.

Сборник нормативных актов по конституционному праву Российской Федерации: Том 4. [Collection of Normative Acts on the Constitutional Law of the Russian Federation: Vol.4]. Comps. A. P. Vorobiev, P. G. Shchekochikhin. Ed. P. G. Shchekochikhin. Ekaterinburg. FGUIPP "Ural. rabochii", 1999. 1045 p. 2000 ptd. ISBN 5-85383-159-3.

Vol.5. Ekaterinburg: Ural. rabochii, 1999. 956 p. 2000 ptd. ISBN 5-85383-163-1.

Сборник нормативных актов Центральной избирательной комиссии Российской Федерации по вопросам выборов депутатов Государственной Думы Федерального Собрания Российской Федерации: Выпуск 2. [Collection of Normative Acts of the Central Electoral Commission of the Russian Federation on Questions of the Elections of Deputies of the State Duma of the Federal Assembly of the Russian Federation: Issue 2]. M.:Izd. Tsentr. izbirat. komissii RF, 1999. 80 p. 5000 ptd.

Сборник нормативно-правовых документов по охране труда. [Collection of Normative Legal Documents on the Protection of Labour]. Ed. Iu. I. Kadochnikov. Tiumen: Tium. izd. dom, 1999. 472 p. 10000 ptd. ISBN 5-88131-111-6.

Сборник основных приказов и указаний Генерального прокурора Российской Федерации. [Collection of Basic Orders and Instructions of the Procurator General of the Russian Federation]. M.: NORMA, 1999. 632 p. 10000 ptd. ISBN 5-89123-327-4.

Сборник постановлений Пленума Высшего Арбитражного Суда Российской Федерации. 1992-1998. [Collection of Decrees of the Plenum of the Supreme Arbitrazh Court of the Russian Federation. 1992-1998]. Ed. A. K. Bolshovaia. M.: Iurid. Dom "Iustitsinform", 1999. 203 p. 10000 ptd. ISBN 5-7205-0393-5, ISBN 5-89568-134-4.

Сборник постановлений Пленумов Верховного Суда и Высшего Арбитражного Суда Российской Федерации по гражданским делам. [Collection of Decrees of the Plenums of the Supreme Court and the Highest Arbitrazh Court of the Russian Federation on Civil Affairs]. Comp. A. P. Sergeev. M.: Prospekt, 1999. 832 p. 5000 ptd. ISBN 5-8369-0033-7.

Сборник постановлений Пленумов Верховных Судов СССР и РСФСР (Российской Федерации) по гражданским делам. [Collection of Decrees of the Plenums of the USSR and RSFSR (Russian Federation) Supreme Courts on Civil Cases]. Comps. A. Ia. Kachanov, S. N. Zabarin, A. L. Soloviev. M.: Spark, 1999. 399 p. 10000 ptd. ISBN 5-88914-018-3.

Сборник постановлений Пленумов Верховных Судов СССР и РСФСР(Российской Федерации) по уголовным делам. [Collection of Decrees of Plenums of the USSR and RSFSR (Russian Federation) Supreme Courts on Criminal Cases]. M.: Spark, 1999. 560 p. 6000 ptd. ISBN 5-88914-011-6.

Сборник судебных документов с дискетой. [Collection of Judicial Documents with Diskette]. N. R. Vilchur et al. M.: Prospekt, 1999. 376 p. 10000 ptd. ISBN 5-8369-0058-2.

Сборник типовых договоров. [Collection of Standard Contracts]. 3rd. rev. ed. Comp. V. M. Prudnikov. M.: INFRA-M, 1999. 318 p. 100000 ptd. ISBN 5-86225-534-6.

Сборник задач по гражданскому процессуальному праву. [Collection of Tasks on the Law of Civil Procedure]. Ed. M. S. Shakarian. M.: Iurist', 1999. 144 p. 10000 ptd. ISBN 5-7975-0021-3.

Сборник задач по уголовному праву: Общая часть. Учебное пособие. [Collection of Tasks on Criminal Law: General Part. Instructional Manual]. Ed. V. B. Borovikov. M.: Shchyt-M, 1999. 172 p. 1000 ptd. ISBN 5-93004-037-0.

Сборник законодательных актов об охране окружающей среды. [Collection of Legislative Acts on the Protection of the Environment]. Orel: Izdatel Pikalin, 1999. 312 p. 500 ptd.

Сборник законов Иркутской области: В 2 ч. [Collection of Laws from the Irkutsk Region: In 2 Parts]. Comp. E. V. Lopatina. Irkutsk: Vost.-Sib. kn. izd-vo, 1999. 500 ptd.

Ч.1. Законодательство о финансах и кредите и экономическое законодательство: С изменениями и дополнениями на 13.01.99. [Part 1. Legislation on Finances and

Credit and Economic Legislation: With Changes and Additions for 13 January 1999]. 336 p.
Ч.2. Государственное устройство области: С изменениями и дополнениями на 13.01.99. [Part 2. State Structure of a Region: With Changes and Additions for 13 January 1999]. 414 p. ISBN 5-7424-0766-1.

Сборник законов Российской Федерации. [Collection of Laws of the Russian Federation]. M.: Slavian. dom knigi, 1999. 688 p. 9000 ptd. ISBN 5-93220-005-7.

Сборник законов Российской Федерации: С изменениями и дополнениями на 1 августа 1999 г. [Collection of Laws of the Russian Federation: With Changes and Additions for 1 August 1999]. M.: AST, 1999. 1200 p. 10000 ptd. ISBN 5-237-03015-7.

Segela, J. *Национальные особенности охоты за голосами.* [National Peculiarities of the Hunt for Votes]. Trans. from French. M.: VAGRIUS, 1999. 263 p. 5000 ptd. ISBN 5-264-00109-X.

Семейный кодекс Российской Федерации. [Family Code of the Russian Federation]. M., Spb.: Gerda, 1999. 112 p. 5000 ptd. ISBN 5-7978-0032-2.
Also published:
M.: Iurist', 1999. 85 p. 10000 ptd. ISBN 5-7975-0209-7.

Семейный кодекс Российской Федерации: С изменениями и дополнениями на 15 февраля 1999 г. [Family Code of the Russian Federation: With Changes and Additions for 15 February 1999]. M.: Prospekt, 1999. 72 p. 7000 ptd. ISBN 5-7896-0075-1.

Семейный кодекс Российской Федерации: С изменениями и дополнениями на 1 мая 1999 г. [Family Code of the Russian Federation: With Changes and Additions for 1 May 1999]. M.: Prospekt, 1999. 72 p. 5000 ptd. ISBN 5-8369-0023-X.

Семейный кодекс Российской Федерации: С изменениями и дополнениями на 15 августа 1999 г. [Family Code of the Russian Federation: With Changes and Additions for 15 August 1999]. M.:

Prospekt, 1999. 72 p. 5000 ptd. ISBN 5-8369-0040-X.

Семейный кодекс Российской Федерации: С изменениями и дополнениями на 15 сентября 1999 г. [Family Code of the Russian Federation: With Changes and Additions for 15 September 1999]. M.: Prospekt, 1999. 72 p. 10000 ptd. ISBN 5-8369-0040-X.

Семейный кодекс Российской Федерации. Федеральный закон «Об актах гражданского состояния»: Официальные тексты по состоянию на 15 апреля 1999 г. [Family Code of the Russian Federation. Federal Law "On Certificates of Registration": Official Texts as of 15 April 1999]. M.: Tandem, EKMOS, 1999. 96 p. 3000 ptd. ISBN 5-88124-022-7.

Serebriakov, D. *Особенности национального следствия: Лучшие комментарии к Уголовно-процессуальному кодексу Российской Федерации.* [Peculiarities of National Investigation: Best Commentaries to the Code of Criminal Procedure of the Russian Federation]. Spb.: Izd: dom "Neva". M.: OLMA-Press, 1999. 15000 ptd.

Chapter 1. 352 p. ISBN 5-5-7654-0256-9, ISBN 5-224-00204-4.
Chapter 2. 400 p. ISBN 5-7654-0257-7, ISBN 5-5-224-00205-2.

Serebriakov, D. *Особенности национального суда. 1: Лучшие комментарии к Уголовно-процессуальному Кодексу Российской Федерации.* [Peculiarities of the National Court. 1: Best Commentaries to the Code of Criminal Procedure of the Russian Federation]. Spb.: Izd. Dom "Neva", OLMA-Press, 1999. 320 p. 15000 ptd. ISBN 5-7654-0258-5, ISBN 5-224-00206-0.

Seregin, V. P., Khalevinskaia, E. D. *Организация, учёт и налогообложение лизинговых операций.* [The Organisation, Registration and Taxation of Finance Leasing Operations]. M.: Iurist', 1999. 174 p. 1000 ptd. ISBN 5-7975-0168-6.

Sergeev, A. P. *Право интеллектуальной собственности в Российской Федерации: Учебник.* [Law of Intellectual Property in the Russian Federation: Textbook]. 2nd. rev. ed. M.: Prospekt, 1999. 751 p. ISBN 5-8369-0032-9.

Sergevnin, S. *Субъект федерации: статус и законодательная деятельность.* [Subject of the Federation: Status and Legislative Activity]. Spb.: Izd-vo in-ta, 1999. 215 p. 1500 ptd. ISBN 5-86247-025-5.

Shaio, A. *Самоограничение власти: Краткий курс конституционализма.* [Self-Limitation of Power: A Short Course on Constitutionalism]. Trans. from Hungarian. M.: Iurist', 1999. 292 p. 3000 ptd. ISBN 5-7975-0235-6.

Shatalov, S. D. *Комментарий к Налоговому кодексу Российской Федерации части первой (постатейный): Учебное пособие для вузов.* [Commentary to the First Part (Article by Article) of the Tax Code of the Russian Federation: Instructional Manual for Institutes of Higher Education]. M.: MTSFER, 1999. 637 p. ISBN 5-7709-0109-8.

Shkatulla, V. I., Nadvikova, V. V., Sytinskaia, M. V. *Основы правовых знаний: Для вузов.* [Fundamental Principles of Legal Knowledge: For Institutes of Higher Education]. M.: Akademiia, 1999. 336 p. 30000 ptd. ISBN 5-7695-0403-X.

Школа муниципального служащего. 1-13 ноября 1998 г. [School of the Municipal Employee. 1-13 November 1998]. Obninsk: Metod. materialy. Ed. & Comp. A. E. Balobanov. M.: Mosk. obshchestv. nauch. fond, 1999. 253 p. 1000 ptd. ISBN 89554-088-0.

Shatalov, A., Vaksian, A. *Фальсификация, подделка, подлог ...* [Falsification, Simulation, Forgery ...]. M.: Liga Razum, 1999. 160 p. 6000 ptd. ISBN 5-89795-006-7.

Shikin, A. S. *Как уберечь себя от взрыва.* [How to Guard Against an Explosion]. M.: Mir bezopasnosti, 1999. 79 p. 2000 ptd. ISBN 5-89258-013-X.

Shilokhvost, O. Iu., *Отступное в гражданском праве России.* [Release Money in the Civil Law of Russia]. M.: Statut, 1999. 251 p. 5000 ptd. ISBN 5-8354-0025-X.

Shokhin, A. *Шестая Государственная Дума: законотворчество и политика.* [Sixth State Duma: Law Creation and Politics].

M., 1999. 183 p. 3000 ptd.

Shugrina, E. S. *Муниципальное право.* [Municipal Law]. M.: Delo, 1999. 496 p. 5000 ptd. ISBN 5-7749-0144-0.

Shulzhenko, Iu. L. *Конституционный статус прокуратуры Российской Федерации.* [Constitutional Status of the Procuracy of the Russian Federation]. In-t gosudarstva i prava RAN. M., 1999. 42 p. 1600 ptd. ISBN 5-88720-057-X.

Shumilov, A. Iu. *Частное детективное и охранное право.* [Private Detective and Protection Law]. M.: NORMA-INFRA-M, 1999. 43 p. 40000 ptd. ISBN 5-89123-368-1, ISBN 5-86225-552-4.

Shumilov, A. Iu. *Юридические основы оперативно-розыскных мероприятий: Учебное пособие.* [Legal Fundamental Principles of Operational Search Measures: Instructional Manual]. M.: Izdatel Shumilova I. I., 1999. 128 p. 2000 ptd. ISBN 5-89784-018-0.

Shumilov, A. Iu. *Новый оперативно-розыскной закон России: Учебно-практическое пособие.* [New Operational Search Law of Russia: Instructional Practical Manual]. 6th rev. ed. M.: Izd. Shumilova I. I., 1999. 48 p. 3000 ptd. ISBN 5-89784-020-2.

Shumilov, A. Iu. *Новый закон о милиции: Учебно-практическое пособие.* [New Law on the Police: Instructional-Methods Manual]. M.: Izdatel Shumilova I. I., 1999. 56 p. 5000 ptd. ISBN 5-89784-017-2.

Shumilov, A. Iu., Ivasenko, V. B. *Новый закон о наркотиках и терминология противодействия наркобизнесу.* [New Law on Narcotics and the Terminology of Opposition to the Narcotics' Business]. 2nd. rev. ed. M.: Izdatel Shumilova I. I., 1999. 72 p. 2000 ptd. ISBN 5-89784-021-0.

Shumilov, V. M. *Международное экономическое право: Учебно-методическое пособие.* [International Economic Law: Instructional-Methods Manual]. M.: DeKA, 1999. 399 p. 1000 ptd. ISBN 5-89645-011-7.

Shurukhnov, N. G. *Расследование краж: Практическое пособие.*

[Investigation of Thefts: Practical Manual]. M.: Iurist', 1999. 111 p. 5000 ptd. ISBN 5-7975-0114-7.

Shutak, I. D. *Правовые оговорки в доктрине международного права.* [Legal Clauses in the Doctrine of International Law]. Spb.: Aleteia, 1999. 251 p. 2200 ptd. ISBN 5-89329-186-7.

Shutak, I. D. *Теория и практика оговорок в праве: система понятий: Терминологический словарь.* [Theory and Practice of Clauses in Law: Terminological Dictionary]. Spb.: Aleteia, 1999. 203 p. 2200 ptd. ISBN 5-89329-187-5.

Shutak, I. D. *Правовые оговорки: практика применения: Научно-методическое пособие.* [Legal Clauses: Practice of Application: Instructional Methods Manual]. Spb.: Aleteia, 1999. 155 p. 2200 ptd. ISBN 5-89329-187-5.

Sitkovskaia, O. D. *Психологический комментарий к Уголовному кодексу Российской Федерации.* [Psychological Commentary to the Criminal Code of the Russian Federation]. M.: Zertsalo, 1999. 89 p. 3000 ptd. ISBN 5-8078-0048-6.

Sklovskii, K. I. *Собственность в гражданском праве.* [Ownership in Civil Law]. M.: Delo, 1999. 511 p. 3000 ptd. ISBN 5-7749-0141-6.

Skorchenko, P. T. *Криминалистика: Учебное пособие.* [Criminalistics: Instructional Manual]. M.: Bylina, 1999. 270 p. 3000 ptd. ISBN 5-93384-002-5.

Skripilev, E. A. *В. Д. Спасович - король русской адвокатуры.* [V. D. Spasovich -King of the Russian Advokatura]. In-t gosudarstva i prava RAN. Ed. & intro. G. M. Reznik. M., 1999. 101 p. 2500 ptd. ISBN 5-88720-060-X.

Skvortsov, O. Iu. *Приватизационное право: Учебное пособие.* [Privatisation Law: Instructional Manual]. M.: ZAO "Biznes-shkola "Intel-Sintez", 1999. 272 p. 3000 ptd. ISBN 5-87057-173-1.

Следственные действия. [Investigative Actions]. Ed. V. A.

Obraztsov. M.: Iurist', 1999. 499 p. 5000 ptd. ISBN 5-7975-0115-5.

Словарь административного права. [Dictionary of Administrative Law]. I. L. Bachilo et al. M.: Pravovaia kultura, 1999. 328 p. 5000 ptd. ISBN 5-87759-033-2.

Smakhtin, E. V. *Расследование контрабанды стратегически важных сырьевых товаров.* [Investigation of Smuggling of Strategically Important Raw Goods]. Tiumen: Izd-vo Iu. Mandriki, 1999. 255 p. 500 ptd. ISBN 5-93020-031-9.

Smirnov, V. V., Lukina, Z. P. *Комментарий к Федеральному закону об ипотеке (залоге недвижимости).* [Commentary to the Federal Law on Mortgage (Pledge of Immovable)]. M.: Fond "Pravovaia kultura", 1999. 245 p. 5000 ptd. ISBN 5-93094-080-0.

Smirnov, V. N., Usmanov, R. R. *История адвокатуры Среднего Урала.* [History of the Advokatura of the Central Urals]. Ekaterinburg: Gumanitar. un-t, 1999. 360 p. 4000 ptd. ISBN 5-7741-0033-2.

Собрание нормативных правовых актов Орловской области: Выпуск 1-2. Том 1. [Collection of Normative Legal Acts of the Orlov Region: Issue 1-2. Vol.1]. Ed. A. S. Aksiutich et al. Orel: ORAGS, 1999. 765 p. 1000 ptd. ISBN 5-93179-018-7.

Соглашение между Федеративной Республикой Германия и Российской Федерацией об избежании двойного налогообложения в отношении налогов на доходы и имущество. [Agreement Between the Federal Republic of Germany and the Russian Federation on the Avoidance of Dual Taxation in Relation to Taxes on Revenues and Property]. Comment. P. Bazedov. M.: ETS, 1999. 95 p. 1000 ptd. In Russian and German. ISBN 5-86455-002-9.

Soldatenko, B. *Москва криминальная.* [Criminal Moscow]. M.: Tsentrpoligraf, 1999. 409. 15000 ptd. ISBN 5-227-00256-8.

Soloviev, O. M., Iarulin, I. F. *Институты государства и гражданского общества: Учебное пособие.* [Institutes of State and Civil Society: Instructional Manual]. Khabarovsk: Izd-vo KHGTU,

1999. 123 p. 300 ptd. ISBN 5-7389-0232-7.

Sotov, P. V., Kamenetskii, R. A. *Адвокатура и нотариат: Учебно-практическое пособие.* [The Advocatura and Notariat: Instructional Manual]. M.: Prospekt, Kodeks, 1999. 400 p. 10000 ptd. ISBN 5-8369-0001-9.

Sotov, P. V., Tikhomirov, A. N. *Делопроизводство.* [Clerical Work]. M.: Prospekt, 1999. 80 p. 10000 ptd. ISBN 5-7896-0079-4.

Современные проблемы криминалистики. [Contemporary Criminalistics Problems]. Ed. B. P. Smagorinskii. Volgograd: VIUI MVD Rossii, 1999. 224 p. 200 ptd. ISBN 5-7899-0043-7.

Spiridonov. L. I. *Теория государства и права: Учебник.* [Theory of State and Law: Textbook]. M.: Prospekt, 1999. 301 p. 10000 ptd. ISBN 5-7986-0008-4.

Споры о возмещении имущественного ущерба и компенсации морального вреда: Сборник документов. [Disputes on Compensation for Property Damage and Compensation for Moral Harm: Collection of Documents]. Comp. O. M. Ogloblina. Ed. M. Iu. Tikhomirov. M.: Iurinform-tsentr, 1999. 155 p. 3000 ptd. ISBN 5-89194-037-X.

Справочник по административно-территориальному устройству Московской области. [Manual on the Administrative and Territorial Structure of the Moscow Region]. M.: RIO Upr. izdatelstv poligrafii i knizh. torgovli Mosk. obl., 1999. 334 p. 1500 ptd. ISBN 5-89752-019-4.

Справочник по арбитражному процессу. [Manual on Arbitrazh Procedure]. 3rd. rev. ed. Intro. V. F. Iakovlev. Ed. V. V. Antonov. M.: DiS, IUKEA, 1999. 761 p. 7000 ptd. ISBN 5-86750-124-8.

Становление местного самоуправления в Российской Федерации. [Formation of Local Self-Government in the Russian Federation]. Ed. & Comp. O. L. Savranskaia. M.: Mosk. obshestv. nauch. fond, 1999. 377 p. 2000 ptd. ISBN 5-89554-066-X.

Stanovskii, M. N. *Назначение наказания.* [Assignment of Punishment]. Spb.: Iurid. tsentr Press, 1999. 480 p. 2000 ptd. ISBN 5-93292-004-1.

Статус малочисленных народов России: Кн.2. Правовые акты. [The Status of Small (in Numbers) Nations of Russia: Book 2. Legal Acts]. Comp. V. A. Kriazhkov. M.: Izd. g-na Tikhomirova M. Iu., 1999. 396 p. 1500 ptd. ISBN 5-89194-018-3.

Stepanov, V. V. *Несостоятельность (банкротство) в России, Франции, Англии, Германии.* [Insolvency (Bankruptcy) in Russia, France, England, Germany]. M.: Statut, 1999. 204 p. 10000 ptd. ISBN 5-8354-0004-7.

Stetstovskii, Iu. I. *Судебная власть: Учебное пособие.* [Judicial Power: Instructional Manual]. M.: Delo, 1999. 399 p. 3000 ptd. ISBN 5-7749-0121-1.

100-летие инициативы России: от Первой конференции мира 1899 г. к Третьей конференции мира 1999 г.: Сборник материалов. [100th Anniversary of the Initiative of Russia: From the First World Conference of 1899 to the Third World Conference of 1999: Collection of Materials]. Comp. & Ed. V. S. Ivanenko. Spb.: SpbGU, 1999. 167 p. 1000 ptd. ISBN 5-93333-006-X.

Стратегический выбор города: научное обоснование и механизм реализации: На примере г. Тольятти, Самар. обл. [Strategic Choice of a City: Scientific Justification and Mechanism for Realisation: After the Example of the City of Toliatti, Samar. Region]. Eds. V. E. Rokhchin, S. F. Zhilkin. Spb.: ISEP RAN, 1999. 182 p. 1000 ptd. ISBN 5-85991-023-1.

Суд и правоохранительные органы: Хрестоматия. [The Court and Law Enforcement Agencies: Anthology]. Comps. Iu. K. Orlov, G. V. Kruchinina. M.: Iurist', 1999. 476 p. 10000 ptd. ISBN 5-7975-0169-4.

Судебная и административная защита прав интеллектуальной собственности в странах-членах Европейского Сообщества. [Judicial and Administrative Defence of Intellectual

Ownership Rights in the Member Countries of the European Community]. Trans. M.: Ros. agentstvo po patentam i tovarnym znakam, FIPS, 1999. 460 p. 300 ptd.

Судебная практика по гражданским делам. [Judicial Practice in Civil Affairs]. Ed. V. M. Zhuykov. M.: Gorodets - Formula prava, 1999. 445 p. 7000 ptd. ISBN 5-89391-042-7.

Судебная практика по жилищным спорам: Сборник постановлений, решений и определений федеральных судов. [Judicial Practice on Housing Disputes: Collection of Decrees, Decisions and Rulings of Federal Courts]. Comp. P. V. Krasheninnikov et al. M.: NORMA-INFRA-M, 1999. 585 p. 6000 ptd. ISBN 5-89123-143-3.

Судебные документы: Сборник образцов более 450 документов. [Judicial Documents: Collection of Models of Over 450 Documents]. N. R. Vilchur et al. M.: Prospekt, 1999. 569 p. 10000 ptd. ISBN 5-8369-0074-4.

Судебные приставы. Исполнительное производство. [Bailiffs. Execution Proceeding]. 2d. rev. ed. Intro. Iu. N. Vlasov. Comps. Iu. N. Vlasov, A. P. Dolina. M.: Iurait, Propaganda Biznes Media, 1999. 174 p. (Ros. pravovaia biblioteka). 2000 ptd. ISBN 5-85294-055-0.

Судебные приставы и исполнительное производство в законодательстве Российской Федерации: Сборник нормативных актов и документов. Том 1. [Bailiffs and Execution Proceeding in the Legislation of the Russian Federation: Collection of Normative Acts and Documents. Vol.1]. Ed. B. P. Kondrashov. M.: Mir bezopasnosti, 1999. 800 p. 10000 ptd. ISBN 5-89258-018-0.

Судебные приставы и исполнительное производство в законодательстве Российской Федерации: Сборник нормативных актов и документов. Том 2. [Bailiffs and Execution Proceeding in the Legislation of the Russian Federation: Collection of Normative Acts and Documents. Vol.2]. Ed. B. P. Kondrashov. M.: Mir bezopasnosti, 1999. 904 p. 10000 ptd. ISBN 5-89258-019-9.

Suntsov, A. P. *Избирательная система субъекта Российской Федерации.* [Electoral System of the Subject of the Russian

Federation]. Tiumen: Tium. iurid. in-t MVD RF, 1999. 163 p. 150 ptd.

Свод хозяйственных договоров и документооборота предприятий с юридическим комментарием: В 2 томах. [Digest of Economic Contracts and Circulation of Documents of Enterprises with a Legal, Arbitrazh and Tax Commentary: In 2 Volumes]. Ed. A. V. Bryzgalin. 2nd. rev. ed. M.: Tsentr "Nalogi in fin. pravo", Analitika-Press, 1999. 30000 ptd.

Vol.1. 613 p. ISBN 5-7916-0063-1.
Vol.2. 581 p. ISBN 5-7916-0064-X.

Syrykh, V. M. *История государства и права России. Советский и современный периоды: Учебное пособие.* [History of State and Law of Russia. Soviet and Contemporary Periods: Instructional Manual]. M.: Iurist', 1999. 488 p. 10000 ptd. ISBN 5-7975-0101-5.

Таможенное дело в Саратовском крае: К 10-летию либерализации внешнеэкономической деятельности. [Customs Matters on the Territory of Saratov: For the 10th Anniversary of the Liberalisation of Foreign Economic Activity]. G. A. Kartashov et al. Saratov: KADR, 1999. 167 p. 1000 ptd.

Таможенное право: Курс лекций: В 2 томах. [Customs Law: Course of Lectures: In 2 Volumes]. Ed. V. G. Draganov. M.; Ekonomika, 1999. 10000 ptd. ISBN 5-282-01983-3.

Vol.1. General Part. 406 p.
Vol.2. Particular Part. 656 p.

Таможенное право: Нормативные акты по Таможенному законодательству. [Customs Law: Normative Acts on Customs Legislation]. M.: TargO, 1999. 819 p. 500 ptd. ISBN 5-8141-0005-2.

Таможенный энциклопедический справочник: В 2 томах. [Customs Encyclopedic Manual: In 2 Volumes]. Ed. I. Iu. Krasnianskii. M.: Letopisets, 1999. 828 p. 3000 ptd. ISBN 5-93186-002-9.

Таможенный кодекс Российской Федерации: Официальный текст по состоянию на 1 декабря 1998 г. [Customs Code of the

Russian Federation: Official Text as of 1 December 1998]. M.: NORMA-INFRA-M, 1999. 279 p. 3000 ptd. ISBN 5-89123-319-3, ISBN 5-86225-973-2.

Таможенный кодекс Российской Федерации: По состоянию на 15 февраля 1999 г. Федеральный закон «О службе в таможенных органах Российской Федерации». [Customs Code of the Russian Federation: As of 15 February 1999. Federal Law "On Service in the Customs Agencies of the Russian Federation"]. M.: OLMA-Press, Novosibirsk, 1999. 336 p. 11000 ptd. ISBN 5-224-00279-6.

Таможенный кодекс Российской Федерации: С изменениями и дополнениями на 15 февраля 1999 г. [Customs Code of the Russian Federation: With Changes and Additions for 15 February 1999]. M.: Prospekt, 1999. 220 p. 5000 ptd. ISBN 5-7896-0074-3.

Таможенный кодекс Российской Федерации: С изменениями и дополнениями на 15 октября 1999 г. [Customs Code of the Russian Federation: With Changes and Additions for 15 October 1999]. M.: Prospekt, Kodeks, 1999. 220 p. 5000 ptd. ISBN 5-8369-0047-7.

Таможенный тариф Российской Федерации. [Customs Tariff of the Russian Federation]. M.: ZAO "Gruppa TARGO", 1999. 905 p. 500 ptd. ISBN 5-8141-0004-4.

Таможня в системе государственной внешнеэкономической политики России: региональный аспект. [Customs in the System of the Russian State Foreign Economic Policy: Regional Aspect]. Ed. S. G. Gorshenin. Orenburg: Kn. izd-vo, 1999. 299 p. 1000 ptd. ISBN 5-88788-060-0.

Tarabrin, A. *Беспредел.* [Chaos]. Intro. A. Aleksakhin, I. Riasny. M.: Panorama, 1999. 320 p. 7000 ptd. ISBN 5-85220-556-7.

Tarabrin, A. *Детоторговцы.* [Traders in Children]. M.: Panorama, 1999. 333 p. 7000 ptd. ISBN 5-85220-404-8.

Taranina, I. V. *Краткий справочник по гражданскому процессу.* [A Short Manual on Civil Procedure]. Novosibirsk: IUKEA, 1999. 159

p. 3000 ptd. ISBN 5-93376-016-1.

Тарифно-квалификационные характеристики по должностям служащих. [Tariff Qualification Characteristics for Employees' Posts]. M.: INFRA-M, 1999. 108 p. 40000 ptd. ISBN 5-86225-402-1.

Tarusina, N. N. *Очерки теории российского семейного права.* [Essays on the Theory of Russian Family Law]. Iaroslav: IAGU, 1999. 93 p. 200 ptd. ISBN 5-8397-0006-1.

Технологии власти и управления в современном государстве. [Technologies of Power and Management in the Contemporary State]. M.: Universitet. gumanitar. litsei, 1999. 250 p. 200 ptd. ISBN 5-88387-031-7.

Teliukina, M. V. *Гражданское право: Т.1: Схемы.* [Civil Law: Vol.1: Diagrams]. Ed. E. A. Sukhanov. M.: BEK, 1999. 120 p. 3000 ptd. ISBN 5-85639-259-0.

Теоретические и практические аспекты охраны промышленной собственности в Российской Федерации. [Theoretical and Practical Aspects of the Protection of Industrial Ownership in the Russian Federation]. Ed. A. D. Korchagin. M.: INITS Rospatent, 1999. 552 p. 900 ptd.

Теоретические проблемы формирования правовой России. [Theoretical Problems of the Formation of a Legal Russia]. Ed. A. K. Chernenko. Novosibirsk: Nauka, 1999. 208 p. 325 ptd. ISBN 5-02-031092-1.

Теория государства и права: Курс лекций. [Theory of State and Law: Course of Lectures]. 2d. rev. ed. Ed. M. N. Marchenko. M.: Zertsalo, 1999. 475 p. 8000 ptd. ISBN 5-8078-0001-X.

Теория государства и права: Схемы, комментарий. [Theory of State and Law: Diagrams, Commentary]. M.: Iurisprudentsiia, 1999. 77 p. 6000 ptd. ISBN 5-86532-047-5.

Теория государства и права: Учебник. [Theory of State and Law: Textbook]. Ed. V. K. Babaev. M.: Iurist', 1999. 591 p. 10000 ptd.

ISBN 5-7975-0239-9.

Tikhomirov, Iu. A., Kotelevskaia, I.V. *Правовые акты: Учебно-практическое пособие.* [Legal Acts: Instructional-Practical Manual]. M.: Izd. g-na Tikhomirova M. Iu., 1999. 381 p. 20000 ptd. ISBN 5-89194-014-0.

Tikhomirov, M. Iu. *Доверенности.* [Powers of Attorney]. M.: Izd. g-na Tikhomirova M. Iu., Iurinformtsentr, 1999. 29 p. 3000 ptd. ISBN 5-89194-026-4.

Tikhomirov, M. Iu. *Гражданско-правовые договоры.* [Civil Law Contracts]. M.: Izd. g-na Tikhomirova, 1999. 141 p. 3000 ptd. ISBN 5-89194-022-1.

Tikhomirov, M. Iu. *Исковые заявления в суд общей юрисдикции.* [Petition to Sue in the Court of General Jurisdiction]. M.: Izd. g-na Tikhomirova M. Iu., 1999. 89 p. 3000 ptd. ISBN 5-89194-029-9.

Tikhomirov, M. Iu. *Трудовые договоры (контракты): Образцы документов, комментарий, нормативные акты.* [Labour Contracts: Models of Documents, Commentary, Normative Acts]. M.: Izdanie g-na Tikhomirova M. Iu., 1999. 324 p. 20000 ptd. ISBN 5-89194-009-4.

Tikhomirov, M. Iu. *Трудовые контракты.* [Labour Contracts]. M.: Izd. g-na Tikhomirova M. Iu., 1999. 54 p. 3000 ptd. ISBN 5-89194-023-X.

Titov, A. A. *Комментарий к Закону РФ «Об основах федеральной жилищной политики» (постатейный).* [Commentary to the RF Law "On the Fundamental Principles of the Federal Housing Policy" (Article by Article)]. Ed. V. B. Isakov. M.: Iurait, 1999. 301 p. 10000 ptd. ISBN 5-85294-067-4.

Titov, A. A. *Комментарий к Жилищному кодексу РСФСР: Постатейный.* [Commentary to the RSFSR Housing Code: Article by Article Commentary]. Ed. V. B. Isakov. M.: Iurait, 1999. 310 p. 10000 ptd. ISBN 5-85294-065-8.

Titov, A. A. *Комментарий к жилищному законодательству Российской Федерации: Постатейный комментарий к основным законам: Закону РФ «Об основах федеральной жилищной политики». Жилищному кодексу РСФСР. Закону РФ «О приватизации жилищного фонда в Российской Федерации».* [Commentary to the Housing Legislation of the Russian Federation: Article by Article Commentary to the Fundamental Laws: Law of the Russian Federation "On the Fundamental Principles of Federal Housing Policy". RSFSR Housing Code. Law of the Russian Federation "On the Privatisation of the Housing Fund in the Russian Federation"]. Ed. V. B. Isakov. M.: Iurait, 1999. 603 p. 10000 ptd. ISBN 5-85294-066-6.

Tiunov, O. I. *Международное гуманитарное право: Учебник для вузов.* [International Humanitarian Law: Textbook for Institutes of Higher Education]. M.: NORMA-INFRA-M, 1999. 315 p. 30000 ptd. ISBN 5-89123-270-7, ISBN 5-86225-873-6.

Tkachuk, I. B. *Коммерческая тайна: Организация защиты, расследование посягательств.* [Commercial Secret: Organisation of Defence, Investigation of Infringements]. M.: Shchyt-M, 1999. 165 p. 1000 ptd. ISBN 5-93004-044-3.

Tolkachenko, A. A. *Судебная бухгалтерия: Учебно-практическое пособие.* [Forensic Bookkeeping: Instructional Practical Manual]. M.: Pravovoe prosveshchenie, 1999. 122 p. 5000 ptd. ISBN 5-89-661-009-2.

Tolstoi, Iu. K. *Наследственное право: Учебное пособие.* [Inheritance Law: Instructional Manual]. M.: Prospekt, 1999. 222 p. 5000 ptd. ISBN 5-8369-0042-6.

Topilskaia, E. V. *Организованная преступность.* [Organised Criminality]. Spb.: Iurid. tsentr Press, 1999. 233 p. 5000 ptd. ISBN 5-93292-005-X.

Topilskaia, E. V. *Записки сумасшедшего следователя.* [Notes of a Mad Investigator]. Spb.: Izd-vo Spb. un-ta, 1999. 151 p. 1000 ptd. ISBN 5-288-02253-4.

Toporkov, A. A. *Словесный портрет: Практическое пособие.* [Description: Practical Manual]. M.: Iurist', 1999. 111 p. 5000 ptd. ISBN 5-7975-0149-X.

Tosunian, G. A., Vikulin, A. Iu. *Постатейный комментарий к Федералному закону «О несостоятельности (банкротстве) кредитных организаций».* [Article by Article Commentary to the Federal Law "On the Insolvency (Bankruptcy) of Credit Organisations"]. M.: BEK, 1999. 332 p. 3000 ptd. ISBN 5-85639-273-6.

Treushnikov, M. K. *Судебные доказательства.* [Judicial Evidence]. 2nd. rev. ed. M.: Gorodets, 1999. 288 p. ISBN 5-89391-014-1.

Trubnikova, T. V., Iakimovich, Iu. K. *Организация и деятельность мировых судей в России.* [Organisation and Activity of Justices of the Peace in Russia]. Tomsk: Izd-vo Tom. un-ta, 1999. 82 p. 500 ptd. ISBN 5-7511-1111-7.

Труд молодежи: Комментарий к КЗоТ. [The Labour of Youth: Commentary to the Code of Laws on Labour]. M.: INFRA-M, 1999. 107 p. 3000 ptd. ISBN 5-16-000041-0.

Труд женщин. [Women's Labour]. M.: INFRA-M, 1999. 64 p. 3000 ptd. ISBN 5-16-000040-2.

Трудовое и социальное право России: Для вузов. [Labour and Social Law of Russia: For Institutes of Higher Education]. Ed. L. N. Anisimov. M.: VLADOS, Mosk. gos. sotsialny un-t, 1999. 431 p. 10000 ptd. ISBN 5-691-00347-X.

Трудовое право: Учебник. [Labour Law: Textbook]. Ed. O. V. Smirnov. 3rd. rev. ed. M.: Prospekt, 1999. 512 p. 10000 ptd. ISBN 5-8369-0031-0.

Трудовое право России: Учебник для вузов. [Labour Law of Russia: Textbook for Institutes of Higher Education]. Eds. R. Z. Livshitz, Iu. P. Orlovskii. M.: NORMA-INFRA-M, 1999. 473 p. 60000 ptd. ISBN 5-89123-175-1, ISBN 5-86225-672-5.

Трудовое законодательство: Сборник нормативных актов по состоянию на 15 августа 1999 г. [Labour Legislation: Collection of Normative Acts for 15 August 1999]. Comp. K. N. Gusov. 4th rev. ed. M.: Prospekt, 1999. 406 p. 5000 ptd. ISBN 5-8369-0039-6.

Трудовой кодекс Российской Федерации: Проект федерального закона. [Labour Code of the Russian Federation: Draft of the Federal Law]. M.: Marketing, 1999. 171 p. 5000 ptd. ISBN 5-7856-0105-2.

Трудовые споры: Сборник документов. [Labour Disputes: Collection of Documents]. Ed. M. Iu. Tikhomirov. Comp. O. M. Ogliblin. M.: Izd. g-na Tikhomirova M. Iu.. Iurinformtsentr, 1999. 200 p. 3000 ptd. ISBN 5-89194-035-3.

Труды Московской государственной юридической академии: No.4. [Scholarly Work of the Moscow State Juridical Academy: No.4]. Ed. O. E. Kutafin. M.: Iurist', 1999. 326 p. 300 ptd. ISBN 5-7975-0174-0.

Turusov, A. A. *Осторожно: КоАП - защищайтесь!: Административные правонарушения.* [Be Careful: The Code on Administrative Violations of Law - Defend Yourselves!: Administrative Violations of Law]. M.: AST: Rostov n/D: Feniks, 1999. 319 p. 10000 ptd. ISBN 5-222-00801-0.

Turusov, A. A. *Осторожно: ГПК - защищайтесь! Защита прав граждан в процессе применения Гражданского процессуального кодекса.* [Be Careful: The Code of Civil Procedure - Defend Yourselves! Defence of the Rights of Citizens During the Process of the Application of the Code of Civil Procedure]. Rostov n/D: Feniks, 1999. 318 p. 10000 ptd. ISBN 5-222-00766-9.

Учебные программы дисциплин и курсов по специальности «Юриспруденция»: Для вузов. [Educational Programmes of Disciplines and Courses Specialising in "Jurisprudence": For Institutes of Higher Education]. Ed. S. A. Komarov et al. M.: Zertsalo, 1999. 608 p. 3000 ptd. ISBN 5-8078-0045-1.

Учиться государственной службе. [To Study the Civil Service]. Ed. V. V. Bakushev. M.: Svarog i Ko., 1999. 1050 p. ISBN 5-93070-

012-5.

Учредительные и внутренние документы общества с ограниченной ответственностью. [Constitutive and Internal Documents of a Limited Responsibility Society]. M.: M. Iu. Tikhomirov, 1999. 76 p. 3000 ptd. ISBN 5-89194-020-5.

Уголовная ответственность несовершеннолетних: Научно-практическое пособие. [Criminal Responsibility of Minors: Scientific-Practical Manual]. Ed. V. P. Kashepov. M.: Iurid, lit., 1999. 159 p. 3000 ptd. ISBN 5-7260-0924-X.

Уголовное право: Часть Общая. Часть Особенная. Учебник. [Criminal Law: General Part. Particular Part. Textbook]. Eds. L. D. Gaukhman, L. M. Kolodkin, S. V. Maksimov. M.: Iurisprudentsiia, 1999. 784 p. 15000 ptd. ISBN 5-8401-0003-X.

Уголовное право. Особенная часть: Учебник. [Criminal Law. Particular Part: Textbook]. Ed. V. N. Petrashev. M.: Prior, 1999. 607 p. 4000 ptd. ISBN 5-7990-03-71-3.

Уголовное право: Учебник. [Criminal Law: Textbook]. Ed. V. N. Petrasheva. M.: Prior, 1999. 544 p. 8000 ptd. ISBN 5-7990-0228-8.
Also published:
M.: NORMA-INFRA-M, 1999. 405 p. 40000 ptd. ISBN 5-89123-376-2, ISBN 5-86225-849-3.

Уголовное право России: Часть Общая: Учебник для вузов. [Criminal Law of Russia: General Part. Textbook for Institutes of Higher Education]. Ed. L. L. Kruglikov. M.: BEK, 1999. 558 p. 3000 ptd. ISBN 5-85639-247-7.

Уголовное право России: Часть Особенная: Учебник для вузов. [Criminal Law of Russia: Special Part: Textbook for Institutes of Higher Education]. Ed. L. L. Kruglikov. M.: BEK, 1999. 832 p. 6000 ptd. ISBN 5-85639-249-3.

Уголовное право России и Особенная часть: Для вузов. [Criminal Law of Russia and Particular Part: For Institutes of Higher Education]. Eds. V. N. Kudriavtsev, A. V. Naumov. 2nd. rev. ed. M.:Iurist', 1999.

492 p. 10000 ptd. ISBN 5-7975-0186-4.

Уголовное право Российской Федерации. [Criminal Law of the Russian Federation]. M.: Iurist', 1999. 10000 ptd.
General Part. Ed. L. D. Ermakovaia. 267 p. ISBN 5-7975-0177-5.
Particular Part. Ed. A. V. Gladkov. 251 p. ISBN 5-7975-0178-3.

Уголовное право Российской Федерации: Для вузов. [Criminal Law of the Russian Federation: For Institutes of Higher Education]. 2d. rev. ed. Ed. B. V. Zdravomyslov. M.: Iurist', 1999. 5000 ptd. General Part. 480 p. ISBN 5-7975-0136-8. Special Part. 550 ptd. ISBN 5-7975-0137-6.

Уголовное право Российской Федерации: Учебно-методическое пособие. [Criminal Law of the Russian Federation: Instructional Methods Manual]. Spb.: Lenizdat, 1999. 170 p. 5000 ptd. ISBN 5-289-01862-X.

Уголовное законодательство зарубежных стран: Англии, США, Франции, Германии, Японии: Сборник законодательных материалов. [Criminal Legislation of Foreign Countries: England, USA, France, Germany, Japan: Collection of Legislative Materials]. Ed. I. D. Kozochkin. M.: Zertsalo, 1999. 346 p. 3000 ptd. ISBN 5-8078-0031-1.

Уголовно-исполнительное право России: Учебник для вузов. [Criminal Executory Law of Russia: Textbook]. M. G. Detkov et al. M.: NORMA-INFRA-M, 1999. 599 p. 6000 ptd. ISBN 5-89123-135-2, ISBN 5-86225-548-6.

Уголовно-исполнительный кодекс Российской Федерации: Официальный текст по состоянию на 1 февраля 1999 г. [Criminal Executory Code of the Russian Federation: Official Text for 1 February 1999]. M.: NORMA-INFRA-M, 1999. 144 p. 3000 ptd. ISBN 5-89123-295-2, ISBN 5-86225-937-6.

Уголовно-исполнительный кодекс Российской Федерации: Официальный текст по состоянию на 15 марта 1999 г. [Criminal Executory Code of the Russian Federation: Official Text for 15 March 1999]. M.: NORMA, INFRA-M, 1999. 139 p. 3000 ptd.

ISBN 5-89123-295-2, ISBN 5-86225-937-6.

Уголовно-исполнительный кодекс Российской Федерации: С изменениями и дополнениями на 15 августа 1999 г. [Criminal Executory Code of the Russian Federation: With Changes and Additions for 15 August 1999]. M.: Prospekt, 1999. 108 p. 5000 ptd. ISBN 5-8369-0030-2.

Уголовно-исполнительный кодекс Российской Федерации: С изменениями и дополнениями на 15 октября 1999 г. [Criminal Executory Code of the Russian Federation: With Changes and Additions for 15 October 1999]. M.: Kodeks, Prospekt, 1999. 108 p. 7000 ptd. ISBN 5-8369-0030-2.

Уголовно-процессуальный кодекс: По состоянию на 15 февраля 1999 г. [Code of Criminal Procedure: As of 15 February 1999]. M.: Biznes-Inform, 1999. 177 p. 4000 ptd. ISBN 5-89563-005-4.

Уголовно-процессуальный кодекс РСФСР. [RSFSR Code of Criminal Procedure]. M.: Iurist', 1999. 229 p. 10000 ptd. ISBN 5-7975-0207-0.

Уголовно-процессуальный кодекс РСФСР: Официальный текст с изменениями и дополнениями по состоянию на 1 марта 1999 г. [RSFSR Code of Criminal Procedure: Official Text with Changes and Additions as of 1 March 1999]. M.: Tandem, EKSMOS, 1999. 176 p. 3000 ptd. ISBN 5-88124-049-9.

Уголовно-процессуальный кодекс РСФСР: С изменениями и дополнениями на 15 февраля 1999 г. [RSFSR Code of Criminal Procedure: With Changes and Additions for 15 February 1999]. M.: Prospekt, 1999. 208 p. 10000 ptd. ISBN 5-7896-0077-8.

Уголовно-процессуальный кодекс РСФСР: С изменениями и дополнениями на 15 августа 1999 г. [RSFSR Code of Criminal Procedure: With Changes and Additions for 15 August 1999]. M.: Prospekt, 1999. 208 p. 10000 ptd. ISBN 5-8369-0029-9.

Уголовно-процессуальный кодекс РСФСР: С изменениями и дополнениями на 1 октября 1999 г. [RSFSR Code of Criminal Procedure: With Changes and Additions for 1 October 1999]. M.:

Prospekt, 1999. 208 p. 10000 ptd. ISBN 5-8369-0029-9.

Уголовный кодекс Российской Федерации. [Criminal Code of the Russian Federation]. Ulianovsk: Knigochei, 1999. 191 p. 5000 ptd. ISBN 5-85525-018-0.

Also published:
M.: Novaia Volna, 1999. 192 p. 5000 ptd. ISBN 5-7864-0040-9.
M.: NIPKTS VOSKHOD, 1999. 147 p. ISBN 5-93055-002-6.
M.: Iurist', 1999. 191 p. 10000 ptd. ISBN 5-7975-02-08-9.
Spb.: Izd. dom "Litera", 1999. 208 p. 10000 ptd. ISBN 5-86617-035-3.
With Changes and additions for 1 April 1999. M.: Prospekt, 1999. 158 p. 7000 ptd. ISBN 5-8369-0006-X.
Official Text for 15 March 1999. M.: NORMA, INFRA-M, 1999. 205 p. 10000 ptd. ISBN 5- 89123-335-5, ISBN 5-86225-981-3.

Уголовный кодекс Российской Федерации: Научно-практический комментарий. [Criminal Code of the Russian Federation: Scientific-Practical Commentary]. M.: NORMA-INFRA-M, 1999. 205 p. 10000 ptd. ISBN 5-89123-335-5; ISBN 5-86225-981-3.

Also published:
M.: Novaia Volna, 1999. 191 p. 5000 ptd. ISBN 5-7864-0040-9.

Уголовный кодекс Российской Федерации: По состоянию на 15 февраля 1999 г. [Criminal Code of the Russian Federation: As of 15 February 1999]. M.: OLMA-Press, Novosibirsk: IUKEA, 1999. 288 p. 11000 ptd. ISBN 5-224-00278-8.

Уголовный кодекс Российской Федерации: С изменениями и дополнениями на 1 февраля 1999 г. [Criminal Code of the Russian Federation: With Changes and Additions for 1 February 1999]. M.: Prospekt, 1999. 158 p. 7000 ptd. ISBN 5-7896-0081-6.

Уголовный кодекс Российской Федерации: С изменениями и дополнениями на 15 августа 1999. [Criminal Code of the Russian Federation: With Changes and Additions for 15 August 1999]. M.: Prospekt, 1999. 160 p. 7000 ptd. ISBN 5-8369-0006-X.

Уголовный кодекс Российской Федерации: С изменениями и

дополнениями на 15 сентября 1999 г. [Criminal Code of the Russian Federation: With Changes and Additions for 15 September 1999]. M.: Prospekt, Kodeks, 1999. 158 p. 10000 ptd. ISBN 5-8369-0006-X.

Уголовный процесс: Сборник задач. [Criminal Procedure: Collection of Tasks]. Ed. V. S. Shadrin. Volgograd: VIUI MVD Rossii, 1999. 156 p. 500 ptd. ISBN 5-7899-0070-4.

Уголовный процесс: Учебник для вузов. [Criminal Procedure: Textbook for Institutes of Higher Education]. Ed. K. F. Gutsenko. 3rd. rev. ed. M.: Zertsalo, 1999. 608 p. 8000 ptd. ISBN 5-8078-0030-3.
Also published:
M.: NORMA-INFRA-M, 1999. 384 p. 60000 ptd. ISBN 5-89123-344-4, ISBN 5-86225-951-1.

Уголовные установления Тан с разьяснениями («Тан люй шу и»). [Criminal Enactments of Tan with Explanations ("Tan Liu shu i"). Trans. from Chinese, intro. & commentary: V. M. Rybakov. Spb.: Peterburg. Vostokovedenie, 1999. 376 p. 1000 ptd. ISBN 5-85803-113-7.

Uporov, I. V. *Профессия - юрист.* [Profession - A Jurist]. M.: AST; Rostov n/D.: Feniks, 1999. 416 p. 10000 ptd. ISBN 5-222-00789-8.

Управление и корпоративный конторль в акционерном обществе: Практическое пособие. [Management and Corporative Control in a Joint-Stock Society: Practical Manual]. Ed. E. P. Gubin. M.: Iurist', 1999. 247 p. 5000 ptd. ISBN 5-7975-0147-3.

Usmanov, U. A. *Комментарий к Уголовному кодексу Российской Федерации.* [Commentary to the Criminal Code of the Russian Federation]. M.: PRIOR, 1999. 496 p. 5000 ptd. ISBN 5-7990-0263-0.

Устав и внутренние документы садоводческого (огороднического, дачного) некоммерческого партнерства. [Charter and Internal Documents of a Horticultural (Market Garden, Country) Non-Commercial Partnership]. M.: M. Iu. Tikhomirov, 1999. 52 p. 3000 ptd. ISBN 5-89194-021-3.

Utiashev, M. M. *Курс лекций по истории политических и правовых учений.* [Course of Lectures on the History of Political and Legal Doctrines]. Ufa: Poligrafkomb., 1999. 320 p. 1000 ptd. ISBN 5-85051-141-5.

В помощь вынужденным переселенцам. [To the Aid of Forced Immigrants]. L. V. Andrichenko, E. V. Belousova. Ed. M. E. Petrosian. M.: Zvenia, 1999. 63 p. 15000 ptd. ISBN 5-7870-0024-2.

Vandyshev, V. V., Dernova, D. V. *Арбитражный процесс: Сборник схем с комментарий: Учебное пособие.* [Arbitrazh Procedure: Collection of Models with Commentary: Instructional Manual]. Spb.: Paritet, 1999. 223 p. 5000 ptd. ISBN 5-89715-005-2.

Varydvin, V. A. *Учебно-методический комплекс. Основы права: Альбом схем, таблиц и определений.* [Instructional Methods System. Fundamental Principles of Law: Album of Diagrams, Tables and Definitions]. 2d. rev. ed. M.: Noosfera, 1999. 164 p. 5000 ptd. ISBN 5-93134-030-0.

Vasetskii, N. A., Krasnov, Iu. K. *Парламентаризм в действии: Государственная Дума Федерального Собрания РФ в 1994-1998 гг.* [Parliamentarism in Action: State Duma of the Federal Assembly of the Russian Federation in 1994-1998]. M.: Izd. Gos. Dumy, 1999. 55 p. 1000 ptd.

Vasiliev, V. I. *Местное самоуправление: Учебное и научно-практическое пособие.* [Local Self-Government: Instructional and Scientific-Practical Manual]. M.:Izd. g-na Tikhomirova M. Iu., 1999. 453 p. 5000 ptd. ISBN 5-89194-017-5.

Vedenin, N. N. *Экологическое право: Вопросы и ответы.* [Ecological Law: Questions and Answers]. M.: Iurisprudentsiia, 1999. 126 p. 7000 ptd. ISBN 5-8401-0014-5.

Vedenin, N. N. *Земельное право: Вопросы и ответы.* [Land Law: Questions and Answers]. M.: Novy Iurist, 1999. 104 p. 5000 ptd. ISBN 5-7969-0063-3.

Also published:

M.: Iurisprudentsiia, 1999. 112 p. 6000 ptd. ISBN 5-8401-

0017-X. (2nd. rev. ed.)

Velichko, A. M. *Государственные идеалы России и Запада. Параллели правовых культур.* [State Ideals of Russia and the West. Parallels of Legal Cultures]. Spb.: Izd-vo iurid. in-ta, 1999. 235 p. 1500 ptd. ISBN 5-86247-024-7.

Vengerov, A. B. *Теория государства и права: Учебник.* [Theory of State and Law: Textbook]. 3rd. ed. M.: Iurisprudentsiia, 1999. 522 p. 12000 ptd. ISBN 5-8401-0023-4.

Verin, V. P. *Преступления в сфере экономики: Учебное пособие.* [Crimes in the Sphere of the Economy: Instructional Manual]. M.: Delo, 1999. 199 p. 5000 ptd. ISBN 5-7749-0127-0.

Vernadskii, G. V. *История права: Для вузов.* [History of Law: For Institutes of Higher Education]. Spb.: Spb. un-t MVD Rossii, Lan, 1999. 176 p. 3000 ptd. ISBN 5-0114-0172-8.

Vetrov, N. I. *Уголовное право: Общая часть: Учебник.* [Criminal Law: General Part: Textbook]. M.: IUNITI, 1999. 415 p. 20000 ptd. ISBN 5-238-00121-5.

Vetrov, N. I. *Уголовное право: Общая и Особенная части. Для вузов.* [Criminal Law: General and Particular Parts. For Institutes of Higher Education]. M.: Knizh. mir, 1999. 221 p. 5000 ptd. ISBN 5-8041-0036-X.

Vikut, M. A., Zaitsev, I. M. *Гражданский процесс России: Учебник для вузов.* [The Civil Procedure of Russia: Textbook for Institutes of Higher Education]. M.: Iurist', 1999. 383 p. 10000 ptd. ISBN 5-7975-0238-0.

Visson, L. *Чужие и близкие в русско-американских браках.* [Disparities and Similarities in Russian-American Marriages]. Trans. from English by S. N. Anisimova. M.: Valent, 1999. 206 p. 3000 ptd. ISBN 5-85677-147-8.

Vitrianskii, V. V. *Договор аренды и его виды: прокат, фрахтование на время, аренда зданий, сооружений и предприятий, лизинг.* [Contract of Lease and Its Types: Hire, Chartering for Time, Lease of Buildings, Installations and Enterprises, Leasing]. M.: Statut, 1999. 299 p. 5000 ptd. ISBN 5-8354-0021-7.

Vlasov, Iu. N., Kalinin, V. V. *Наследование по закону и по завещанию.* [Inheritance According to the Law and According to Testaments]. M.: Iurait, 1999. 247 p. 5000 ptd. ISBN 5-85294-072-0.

Vlasov, V. I., Krapivin, O. M. *Комментарий к законодательству о занятости и трудоустройстве населения.* [Commentary to the Legislation on the Employment and Arrangement of Labour of the Population]. M.: NORMA-INFRA-M, 1999. 357 p. 30000 ptd. ISBN 5-89123-362-2, ISBN 5-86225-916-3.

Власть и пресса: К истории правового регулирования отношений. 1700-1917. Хрестоматия. [Power and the Media: Towards a History of the Legal Regulation of Relations. 1700-1917. Anthology]. Comp. T. S. Ularionov et al. M.: Izd-vo RAGS, 1999. 237 p. 1000 ptd. ISBN 5-7729-0042-0.

Водный кодекс Российской Федерации: Официальный текст по состоянию на 15 февраля 1999 г. [Water Code of the Russian Federation: Official Text for 15 February 1999]. M.: NORMA-INFRA-M, 1999. 87 p. 2000 ptd. ISBN 5-89123-298-7, ISBN 5-86225-943-0.

Водный кодекс Российской Федерации: С изменениями и дополнениями по состоянию на 1 октября 1999 г. [Water Code of the Russian Federation: With Changes and Additions for 1 October 1999]. 4th ed. M.: NORMA-INFRA-M, 1999. 78 p. 2000 ptd. ISBN 5-89123-298-7, ISBN 5-86225-943-0.

Volgin, V. V. *Дорожно-транспортные происшествия. От причины до расплаты: Практическое пособие.* [Road Transport Accidents. From Cause to Payment: Practical Manual]. M.: Livr, 1999. 112 p. 10000 ptd. ISBN 5-89104-057-3.

Volzhenkin, B. V. *Экономические преступления.* [Economic Crimes]. Spb.: Iurid. tsentr Press, 1999. 299 p. 10000 ptd. ISBN 5-93292-001-7.

Вопросы государственной регистрации прав на недвижимое имущество и сделок с ним: Сборник. Выпуск 5. [Questions of the State Registration of Rights to Immovable Property and Transactions with It: Collection. Issue 5]. Comp. E. A. Kindeeva et al. Ed. V. V. Ogorodnikov. M.: Violanta, 1999. 399 p. 6000 ptd. ISBN 5-88803-011-2.

Вопросы квалификации и расследования преступлений в сфере экономики. [Questions of Classification and Investigation of Crimes in the Sphere of the Economy]. Eds. N. A. Lopashenko, V. M. Iurin, A. B. Nekhoroshev. Saratov: SIUI MVD Rossii, 1999. 240 p. 1500 ptd. ISBN 5-7485-0033-7.

Воздушный кодекс Российской Федерации: Официальный текст по состоянию на 1 ноября 1998 г. [Air Code of the Russian Federation: Official Text as of 1 November 1998]. M.: NORMA-INFRA-M, 1999. 75 p. 2000 ptd. ISBN 5-89123-299-5, ISBN 5-86225-944-9.

Воздушынй кодекс Российской Федерации: Официальный текст по состоянию на 1 января 1999 г. [Air Code of the Russian Federation: Official Text as of 1 January 1999]. M.: NORMA-INFRA-M, 1999. 75 p. 3000 ptd. ISBN 5-89123-330-4, ISBN 5-86225-990-2.

Воздушный кодекс Российской Федерации: С изменениями и дополнениями по состоянию на 1 октября 1999 г. [Air Code of the Russian Federation: With Changes and Additions for 1 October 1999]. 4th ed. M.: NORMA-INFRA-M, 1999. 75 p. 3000 ptd. ISBN 5-89123-330-4, ISBN 5-86225-990-2.

Всеобщая история государства и права: Учебник для вузов. [Universal History of State and Law: Textbook for Institutes of Higher Education]. Ed. K. I. Batyr. M.: Bylina, 1999. 495 p. 10000 ptd. ISBN 5-93384-004-1.

Вторая международная конференция по федерализму: Москва, 16-17 декабря 1997 г. [Second International Conference on Federalism: Moscow, 16-17 December 1997]. Trans. from English. Eds. S. S. Artobolevskii, V. V. Klimanov. M.: Editorial URSS, 1999. 316 p. 1500 ptd. ISBN 5-8360-0019-0.

Введение в юриспруденцию: Учебное пособие. [Introduction to Jurisprudence: Instructional Manual]. Eds. V. N. Kartashov, L. L. Kruglikov, N. N. Tarusinaia. 2nd. rev. ed. Iaroslav: Iarosl. gos. un-t, 1999. 284 p. 1500 ptd. ISBN 5-230-20486-9.

Vydrin, I. V., Kokotov, A. N. *Муниципальное право России: Учебник для вузов.* [Municipal Law of Russia: Textbook for Institutes of Higher Education]. M.: NORMA-INFRA-M, 1999. 359 p. 50000 ptd. ISBN 5-86225-520-6.

Забайкальская транспортная ...: Штрихи к истории Забайкал. трансп. милиции. [Beyond the Baikal Transport ...: Features of the History of Beyond the Baikal Transport]. Ed. V. G. Prudnikov. Comp. E. O. Khavkin. Chita, Poisk, 1999. 304 p. 3000 ptd. ISBN 5-93119-026-0.

Zakharova, N. N. *Комментарий к Федеральному закону «Об ипотеке (залоге недвижимости)»: Постатейный.* [Commentary to the Federal Law "On Mortgage (Pledge of an Immovable)": Article by Article]. M.: Iurait, 1999. 192 p. 6000 ptd. ISBN 5-85294-076-3.

Zaikin, A. D., Remizov, K. S. *Экономико-правовое регулирование труда и заработной платы: Учебник для вузов.* [Economical-Legal Regulation of Labour and Wages: Textbook for Institutes of Higher Education]. M.: NORMA-INFRA-M, 1999. 315 p. 30000 ptd. ISBN 5-89123-345-2, ISBN 5-16-000010-0.

Закон города Москвы о социальном партнерстве. [Law of the City of Moscow on Social Partnership]. M.: Informart, 1999. 16 p. 5000 ptd.

Закон о защите детства: Законодательство Российской Федерации о защите прав ребенка. [Law on the Defence of Childhood: Legislation of the Russian Federation on Defence of the Rights of the Child]. Comps. E. M. Rybinskii, N. A. Ivanova. M.: NII detstva Ros. det. fonda, 1999. 352 p. 4000 ptd. ISBN 5-85201-347-1.

Закон Российской Федерации о милиции. [Law of Russian Federation on the Police]. M.: Prospekt, Kodeks, 1999. 40 p. 10000 ptd. ISBN 5-8369-0025-6.

Закон Российской Федерации «О статусе судей в Российской Федерации». Федеральный конституционный закон «О судебной системе Российской Федерации». Федеральный закон «Об исполнительном производстве». [Law of Russian Federation "On the Status of Judges in the Russian Federation". Federal Constitutional Law "On the Judicial System of the Russian Federation". Federal Law "On Execution Proceeding"]. M.: Iurlit, 1999. 96 p. 3500 ptd. ISBN 5-93342-001-8.

Законодательство Норвегии по нефти и газу. [Legislation of Norway on Oil and Gas]. Unofficial trans. M.: EPItsentr, 1999. 379 p. 1000 ptd. ISBN 5-89069-016-7.

Законодательство России об оружии. Частная охранная и детективная деятельность: Сборник нормативных актов. [Legislation of Russia on Weapons. Private Protection and Detective Activity. Collection of Normative Acts]. Ed. V. L. Mironov. M.: Mir bezopasnosti, 1999. 607 p. 10000 ptd. ISBN 5-89258-020-2.

Законодательство Калининградской области. [Legislation of the Region of Kaliningrad]. Kaliningrad: Iantar. skaz, 1999. 360 p. 1500 ptd.

Законодательство о государственной регистрации прав на недвижимое имущество и сделок с ним. [Legislation on the State Registration of Rights on Immovable Property and Transactions With It]. Comp. P. V. Krasheninnikov. 2d. rev. ed. M.: Spark, 1999. 143 p. 8000 ptd. ISBN 5-88914-123-6.

Законодательство о труде: надзор и контроль. [Legislation on Labour: Supervision and Control]. Comp. A. V. Verkhovtsev. M.: INFRA-M, 1999. 72 p. 3000 ptd. ISBN 5-16-000093-3.

Законы города Москвы. Постановления Московской городской Думы. 1998. [Laws of the City of Moscow. Decrees of the Moscow Municipal Duma. 1998]. Ed. A. V. Petrov. M.: In-t zakonodatelstva i sravnit. pravovedeniia pri Pravitelstve RF, 1999. 519 p. 3000 ptd. ISBN 5-85299-006-X.

Законы Тюменской области. 1994-1998: В 2 томах. [Laws of

the Tiumen Region. 1994-1998: In 2 Volumes]. Comps. B. U. Agishev et al. 2nd. rev. ed. Tiumen: Izd. Tiumen. obl. Dumy, 1999. 2000 ptd.
Vol.1. 632 p. ISBN 5-88131-125-6.
Vol.2. 488 p. ISBN 5-88131-126-4.

Zaleskii, V. V., Kallistratova, R. F. *Комментарий к Федеральному закону «О некоммерческих организациях».* [Commentary to the Federal Law "On Non-Commercial Organisations"]. 2d. rev. ed. M.: Iurait, 1999. 260 p. 3000 ptd. ISBN 5-85294-064-X.

Zamotaev, A. A. *Местное самоуправление: основные понятия и термины.* [Local Self-Government: Basic Concepts and Terms]. M.: Munitsipalnaia Vlast, 1999. 396 p. 2000 ptd. ISBN 5-93158-001-8.

Заработная плата: Комментарий к КЗоТ. [Wages: Commentary to the Code of Laws on Labour]. Comp. A. V. Verkhovtsev. 2nd. rev. ed. M.: INFRA-M, 1999. 144 p. 18000 ptd. ISBN 5-86225-917-1.

Защита прав человека и соблюдение законности органами внутренних дел: Материалы международной научно-практической конференции (10 декабря 1998 г.). [Defence of Human Rights and Compliance with the Legality of Internal Affairs Agencies: Materials from an International Scientific-Practical Conference (10 December 1998)]. Eds. L.Sh. Berekashvili, V. P. Ignatov. M.: Shchyt-M, 1999. 207 p. 5000 ptd. ISBN 5-93004-046-X.

Защита прав потребителей: Разъяснения по применению закона Российской Федерации «О защите прав потребителей». [Defence of Consumers' Rights: Explanations on the Application of the Russian Federation Law "On the Defence of Consumers' Rights]. M.: INFRA-M, 1999. 26 p. 3000 ptd. ISBN 5-86225-745-4.

Защита прав потребителей: Сборник законодательных и нормативных актов Российской Федерации. [Defence of Consumers' Rights: Collection of Legislative and Normative Acts of the Russian Federation]. M.: Novaia Volna, 1999. 128 p. 5000 ptd. ISBN 5-7864-0074-3.

Защита прав ребёнка. [Defence of Children's Rights]. M.: Ros. blagotvorit. fond "Niet alkogolizmu i narkomanii" ("NAN"), 1999. 120

p. 1500 ptd. ISBN 5-88516-035-X.

Земельное право: Учебник для вузов. [Land Law: Textbook for Institutes of Higher Education]. Ed. S. A. Bogoliubov. M.: NORMA-INFRA-M, 1999. 388 p. 30000 ptd. ISBN 5-89123-228-6, ISBN 5-86225-734-9.

Земельный кодекс. [Land Code]. M.: Izdanie g-na Tikhomirova M. Iu., 1999. 61 p. 3000 ptd. ISBN 5-89104-015-9.

Земельные споры: Сборник документов. [Land Disputes: Collection of Documents]. Ed. M. Iu. Tikhomirov. M.: Izd. g-na Tikhomirova M. Iu., 1999. 376 p. 30000 ptd. ISBN 5-89194-030-2.

Земля и право: Сборник нормативных актов. [Land and Law: Collection of Normative Acts]. Ed. V. Kh. Uliukaev. M.: Bylina, 1999. 511 p. 3000 ptd. ISBN 5-88528-247-1.

Zhapparov, Sh. *За закрытой дверью: Записки прокурора-журналиста.* [Behind Closed Doors: Notes of a Procurator-Journalist]. Orenburg: Kn. izd-vo, 1999. 188 p. 2000 ptd. ISBN 5-88788-061-9.

Zhilinskii, S. E. *Предпринимательское право (правовая основа предпринимательской деятельности): Учебник для вузов.* [Entrepreneurial Law (Legal Basis of Entrepreneurial Activity): Textbook for Institutes of Higher Education]. 2nd. rev. ed. M.: NORMA-INFRA-M, 1999. 661 p. 6000 ptd. ISBN 5-89123-354-1, ISBN 5-16-000028-3.

Жилищное законодательство России: Сборник нормативных документов с комментарий. [Housing Legislation of Russia: Collection of Normative Documents with Commentary]. Comp. D. V. Primakov. M.: Biznes-Inform, 1999. 351 p. 4000 ptd. ISBN 5-89563-001-4.

Жилищный кодекс. [Housing Code]. M.: Izdanie g-na Tikhomirova M. Iu., 1999. 77 p. 3000 ptd. ISBN 5-89194-015-9.

Жилищный кодекс РСФСР: Официальный текст по состоянию на 1 февраля 1999 г. [RSFSR Housing Code: Official Text as of 1

February 1999]. Intro. P. V. Krasheninnikov. M.: NORMA-INFRA-M, 1999. 77 p. 4000 ptd. ISBN 5-89123-336-3.

Жилищный кодекс РСФСР: По состоянию на 15 февраля 1999 г. Закон Российской Федерации «Об основах федеральной жилищной политики»: По состоянию на 15 февраля 1999 г. [RSFSR Housing Code: As of 15 February 1999. Law of Russian Federation "On the Fundamental Principles of Housing Policy": As of 15 February 1999]. M.: OLMA-Press, Novosibirsk: IUKEA, 1999. 112 p. 11000 ptd. ISBN 5-224-00276-1, ISBN 5-86750-100-0.

Жилищный кодекс РСФСР: С изменениями и дополнениями на 15 февраля 1999 г. [RSFSR Housing Code: With Changes and Additions for 15 February 1999]. M.: Prospekt, 1999. 72 p. 7000 ptd. ISBN 5-7896-0076-X.

Жилищный кодекс РСФСР: С изменениями и дополнениями на 1 июня 1999 г. [RSFSR Housing Code: With Changes and Additions for 1 June 1999]. M.: Prospekt, 1999. 72 p. 10000 ptd. ISBN 5-8369-0050-7.

Жилищный кодекс РСФСР: С изменениями и дополнениями на 15 октября 1999. [RSFSR Housing Code: With Changes and Additions for 15 October 1999]. M.: Prospekt, Kodeks, 1999. 72 p. 10000 ptd. ISBN 5-8369-0050-7.

Жилищные споры: Сборник документов. [Housing Disputes: Collection of Documents]. Ed. M. Iu. Tikhomirov. M.: Izd. g-na Tikhomirova M. Iu., 1999. 152 p. 3000 ptd. ISBN 5-89194-034-5.

Ziber, U. *Организованная преступность Японии и Германии: Сравнительный анализ на основе работ Коиши Миядзавы.* [Organised Criminality in Japan and Germany: Comparative Analysis on the Basis of the Work of Koishi Miyadzava]. M.: Ros. iurid. izd. dom, 1999. 32 p. 1500 ptd. ISBN 5-88635-030-6.

Zinchenko, S. A., Shapsugov, D. Iu., Korkh, S. E. *Предпринимательство и статус его субъектов в современном российском праве.* [Entrepreneurship and the Status of Its Subjects in Contemporary Russian Law]. Rostov n/D.: SKAGS, 1999. 198 p.

1000 ptd. ISBN 5-89546-037-2.

Zlatopolskii, D. L. *Государственное право зарубежных стран: Восточной Европы и Азии: Учебник.* [State Law of Foreign Countries: Eastern Europe and Asia: Textbook]. M.: Zertsalo, 1999. 306 p. 10000 ptd. ISBN 5-8078-0050-8.

Zorin, V. Iu., Amanzholova, D. A., Kuleshov, S. V. *Национальный вопрос в Государственных Думах России.* [The National Question in the State Dumas of Russia]. M.: Rus. mir, 1999. 520 p. 3000 ptd. ISBN 5-85810-048-1.

Zvekov, V. P. *Международное частное право: Курс лекций: Для вузов.* [International Private Law: Course of Lectures: For Institutes of Higher Education]. M.: NORMA-INFRA-M, 1999. 686 p. 30000 ptd. ISBN 5-89123-264-3, ISBN 5-86225-974-0.

Zviagintsev, A. G., Orlov, Iu. G. *Российские прокуроры.* [Russian Procurators]. M.: Mol. gvardiia, 1999. 570 p. 5000 ptd. ISBN 5-235-02343-9.

Zviagintsev, L. M., Pliukhina, M. A., Reshetnikova, I. V. *Доказывание в судебной практике по гражданским делам: Учебно-практическое пособие.* [Proof in Judicial Practice in Civil Cases: Instructional Practical Manual]. M.: NORMA-INFRA-M, 1999. 283 p. 3000 ptd. ISBN 5-89123-377-0.